"In the third edition of *Stop Walking on Eggshells*, Paul Mason and Randi Kreger update their classic work on borderline personality disorder (BPD). This edition adds new research and information to their seminal work and raises the standard. This book is a must-read for anyone whose family has been affected by BPD."

> —**Daniel S. Lobel, PhD,** clinical psychologist in private practice in
> Katonah, NY; and author of *When Your Daughter Has BPD* and
> *When Your Mother Has Borderline Personality Disorder*

"This third edition is filled with the wisdom and tips that come from the authors' continuing work with people with BPD and their loved ones. I'm so glad they have added narcissistic personality disorder (NPD) in this edition, because the overlap of NPD and BPD is present in so many of the high-conflict individuals I see in relationships and conflicts that end up in court today. Family members, friends, professionals, and (frankly) everyone needs to read this book to understand and deal with much of the surprising and outrageous behavior we see in close relationships all around us now."

> —**Bill Eddy, LCSW, JD,** attorney, therapist, mediator, coauthor of
> *Splitting*, and author of *5 Types of People Who Can Ruin Your Life*

"This third edition of *Stop Walking on Eggshells* makes a very important contribution to better understanding the complexities of working with individuals displaying behaviors consistent with both BPD and NPD. The authors recognize that multiple factors and other diagnoses may also be operational and need to be taken into account. The advice and recommendations are practical, well explained, and give hope to clinicians and families, as well as those struggling with these perplexing disorders."

> —**Debra Resnick, PsyD,** clinical psychologist in private practice in the
> Philadelphia, PA, area who has been teaching and practicing d̶i̶a̶l
> behavior therapy (DBT) for approxima⸱ ̶

"An important resource for clients who are being emotionally abused. It identifies two types of BPD—conventional and unconventional. While conventional BPDs typically exhibit overt behavior such as self-harm and suicidal ideation, unconventional BPDs don't believe they have any problems. They project their pain onto others and refuse to take responsibility for their harmful actions. As an expert in emotional abuse, I have identified this behavior as emotionally abusive."

—**Beverly Engel, LMFT**, internationally recognized expert in emotional and sexual abuse, and best-selling author of *The Emotionally Abused Woman* and *The Emotionally Abusive Relationship*

"*Stop Walking on Eggshells* is the quintessential book for families to understand BPD. The cases and examples are compassionate, accurate, enlightening, and starkly realistic—providing a true sense of how people with BPD think and feel, as well as how family members experience their behaviors. It includes comprehensive strategies, techniques, and responses for the most difficult situations, and provides the newest information about causes and help for BPD."

—**Margalis Fjelstad, LMFT**, author of *Stop Caretaking the Borderline or Narcissist* and *Healing from a Narcissistic Relationship*, and coauthor of *Raising Resilient Children with a Borderline or Narcissistic Parent*

"Very impressive! This third edition of *Stop Walking on Eggshells* is a compendium of practical advice. Written in a friendly style, it's like reading a letter from someone who really cares about you. New chapters, such as the chapter on BPD in children and teenagers, further enhance the book, discussing a previously ignored issue. I strongly recommend this five-star book."

—**Christine Adamec**, coauthor of *When Your Adult Child Breaks Your Heart*

"For the last twenty years, *Stop Walking on Eggshells* has been my 'gold-standard' recommendation for learning how to live with, love, and care for people who struggle with BPD. Now, Mason and Kreger have improved and updated this masterpiece to include how to cope with narcissistic personalities as well. If you feel like you're walking on eggshells around people in your life, then read this new edition."

—**Jeffrey C. Wood, PsyD**, psychologist, coauthor of *The Dialectical Behavior Therapy Skills Workbook*, and author of *The Cognitive Behavioral Therapy Workbook for Personality Disorders*

stop
walking on
eggshells

THIRD EDITION

Taking Your Life Back
When Someone You Care About Has
Borderline Personality Disorder

PAUL T. MASON, MS
RANDI KREGER

New Harbinger Publications, Inc.

Publisher's Note

NEW HARBINGER PUBLICATIONS is a registered trademark of New Harbinger Publications, Inc.

New Harbinger Publications is an employee-owned company.

Distributed in Canada by Raincoast Books

Copyright © 2020 by Paul T. Mason & Randi Kreger
New Harbinger Publications, Inc.
5720 Shattuck Avenue
Oakland, CA 94609
www.newharbinger.com

All Rights Reserved

Acquired by Catharine Sutker; Cover design by Amy Shoup

Library of Congress Cataloging-in-Publication Data

Names: Mason, Paul T., author. | Kreger, Randi, author.
Title: Stop walking on eggshells : taking your life back when someone you care about has borderline personality disorder / Paul T. Mason and Randi Kreger.
Description: 3rd edition. | Oakland : New Harbinger Publications, 2020. | Includes bibliographical references.
Identifiers: LCCN 2020026609 (print) | LCCN 2020026610 (ebook) | ISBN 9781684036899 (trade paperback) | ISBN 9781684036905 (pdf) | ISBN 9781684036912 (epub)
Subjects: LCSH: Borderline personality disorder--Popular works. | Borderline personality disorder--Patients--Family relationships.
Classification: LCC RC569.5.B67 M365 2020 (print) | LCC RC569.5.B67 (ebook) | DDC 616.85/852--dc23
LC record available at https://lccn.loc.gov/2020026609
LC ebook record available at https://lccn.loc.gov/2020026610

Printed in the United States of America

25   24

10   9   8   7   6

Fasten your seatbelts. It's going to be a bumpy night.

—Bette Davis, *All About Eve*

No matter how confused, self-doubting, or ambivalent we are about what's happening in our interactions with other people, we can never entirely silence the inner voice that always tells us the truth. We may not like the sound of the truth, and we often let it murmur just outside our consciousness, not stopping long enough to listen. But when we pay attention to it, it leads us toward wisdom, health, and clarity. That voice is the guardian of our integrity.

—Susan Forward, PhD

This book is for the children, young and old, whose lives have been affected by borderline personality disorder. And to our teachers: the hundreds of people who told us their stories, shared their tears, and offered us their insight. You made this book possible.

Contents

PART 3
Resolving Special Issues

Acknowledgments

First and foremost, I would like to thank the two men in my life who made this book possible: my husband, Robert Burko, and my good friend and literary agent, Scott Edelstein.

Scott was more than my agent: he was my mentor, my coach, my emergency hotline, my chief cheerleader, my number-one believer. When I doubted this book would ever get published, he assured me that it would. When I felt like quitting because the sacrifices were too great, he reminded me of the people whose lives I had changed. His sense of humor and unwavering support sustained me and helped me believe in myself. Without him, there would be no third edition.

Three clinicians have helped me greatly, mostly with the research involving chapter 3, on narcissism. I thank them from the bottom of my heart. They are:

- Wendy T. Behary, author of *Disarming the Narcissist: Surviving and Thriving with the Self-Absorbed* (disarmingthenarcissist.com). She is the founder and clinical director of the Cognitive Therapy Center of New Jersey, which specializes in working with people with NPD.

- Bill Eddy, a lawyer, therapist, and mediator. He is the co-founder and Training Director of the High Conflict Institute in San Diego, California (highconflictinstitute.com). He is the coauthor of *Splitting: Protecting Yourself While Divorcing Someone with Borderline or Narcissistic Disorder* and the author of many other books. Moreover, he's the sweetest lawyer I have ever known, and he cares deeply about adults and children embroiled in high-conflict issues.

- Elinor Greenberg, PhD, psychologist and author of the book *Borderline, Narcissistic, and Schizoid Adaptations: The Pursuit of Love, Adoration, and*

Safety. She has a blog about narcissism at psychologytoday.com. She also specializes in working with narcissistic clients.

Thank you, Wendy, Bill, and Elinor. I couldn't have done it without you.

I would also like to thank Margalis Fjelstad, the savvy author of *Stop Caretaking the Borderline or Narcissist: How to End the Drama and Get on With Your Life* and *Healing from the Narcissistic Relationship: A Caretaker's Guide to Recovery, Empowerment and Transformation*. She and I both write for family members who have a relative with traits of both borderline and narcissistic disorder. We're a very small club. In many ways, she has been a mentor to me and given freely of her knowledge. Thank you, Margalis.

I would like to acknowledge Rick Remitz and Fahar Faizaan for their dedication in establishing the borderline personality disorder nonprofit organization, The Black Sheep Project, and for giving me a once in a lifetime chance to build it from the bottom up. Thank you for letting me be the BPD consultant on your new movie. May it earn millions of dollars at the box office.

I would also like to thank author Christine Adamec, who was instrumental in helping me write chapter 10, Waiting for the Next Shoe to Drop: Your Borderline Child. As a coauthor of *Stop Walking on Eggshells for Parents: How to Help Your Child with Borderline Personality Disorder Without Sacrificing Your Family or Yourself*, she was the perfect guide.

Dozens of clinicians, experts, and BPD advocates from all over the globe contributed their insights to this book. Other people I interviewed include Joseph T. Bergs, MD; Lori Beth Bisbey, PhD; Barbara Blanton, MSN; James Claiborn, PhD; Kenneth A. Dachman, PhD; Jane G. Dresser, RN; Bruce Fischer, PhD; Marybelle Fisher, PhD; John M. Grohol, PsyD; John Gunderson, MD; Perry Hoffman, PhD; Janet R. Johnston, PhD; Otto Kernberg, MD; Jerold J. Kreisman, MD; Marsha M. Linehan, PhD; Richard A. Moskovitz, MD; Thomas Meacham, MD; Susan B. Morse, PhD; Cory F. Newman, PhD; Andrew T. Pickens, MD; Margaret Pofahl, ACSW; Joseph Santoro, PhD; Larry J. Siever, MD; and Howard I. Weinberg, PhD (Rest in peace, Perry Hoffman. You are deeply missed by everyone in the BPD community.)

Many books not related to BPD were also influential in my thinking. Chief among them was *The Dance of Anger*, by Harriet Goldhor Lerner, PhD. Its fundamental concepts are interwoven into every page of this book. When I first read it many years ago, it changed my life. I feel honored to be able to pass along Lerner's wisdom, and I am indebted to her for her inspiration. Books by

Susan Forward, PhD, also influenced this work, chiefly *Emotional Blackmail* (1997) and *Toxic Parents* (1989). I highly recommend all three books.

Finally, I would like to thank my publisher, New Harbinger Publications; my mother, Janet Kreger, for supporting my writing efforts since grade school; and Edith Cracchiolo, my guardian angel throughout this project.

—R. K.

Many people have encouraged me and supported me in the writing of this book. I wish to thank them all, and am especially grateful to the following:

- Monica, my wife of thirty-one years, whose love and unconditional faith and belief in me throughout this project, and everything we've done together over the years, mean everything to me. And to my children, Zachary, Jacob, and Hannah, who, in their own unique ways, consistently remind me of the important things in life.

- My graduate school mentor, Kathleen Rusch, PhD, who nurtured and supported my earliest interests in borderline personality disorder. In the main, without her coaching and confidence, this book would not have been possible.

I would like to similarly acknowledge all the clinicians and advocates who contributed their insights, experiences, and expertise to this. While there are far too many to list here, I continue to be inspired by the work they do every day in service to people with BPD and their families.

Finally, I would like to thank my coauthor, Randi Kreger, and our literary agent, Scott Edelstein, who approached me with the idea to write the first edition of this book in 1996. Never did we dream that, nearly twenty-five years later, we'd be working on a third edition.

—P. M.

Introduction to the Third Edition

More than one million copies in fifteen languages—that's how many people have purchased copies of *Stop Walking on Eggshells* since New Harbinger published its first edition in 1998. Back then, most people were just getting started with cell phones and the internet.

At first, this book was turned down by many publishers because "No one knows what borderline personality disorder means." The two of us had to fight for every scrap of information we could find.

Today, there is actually a sitcom in which one of the main characters has the disorder (not that it's an *accurate* depiction). But the name BPD is out there—and, today, more people know what it means than ever before. The internet is teeming with information from clinicians, people with the disorder, and family members.

And a lot of it is due to the success of this book. Back in 1996, we intended to write the best guide to BPD for families. But the book turned out to be the basic go-to guide about BPD for anyone and everyone. We went viral before "going viral" was a thing. Once people heard a description of borderline behavior, they immediately recognized someone they knew, and bought the book. Many became advocates for the cause of helping families and protecting kids. They told us that being able to put a name on their loved one's behaviors changed their lives.

Here's a preview of what you're going to see that's new in this revised and updated Third Edition:

Updated information on the most recent BPD research, as well as new strategies and surprising recent discoveries about the disorder.

A focus on men as much as women: Recent research has determined that half the people with BPD are male. So there is a section in this book on men with BPD, and on how the disorder appears differently in men and women. There is also a special section, included in Appendix D, for men who find themselves on the receiving end of domestic violence.

Information on narcissistic personality disorder (NPD): We've added a chapter on narcissistic personality disorder because a new study has shown that about four out of every ten people with BPD also have NPD. Most of these people with BPD are of the unconventional type, who deny that they have the disorder and resist treatment. Randi's experience in interviewing hundreds of folks with BPD, and the people who care about them, confirms this conclusion.

An updated and greatly expanded chapter for the parents of kids who have BPD: This chapter provides a wealth of guidance, ideas, and information—as well as empathy, understanding, and inspiration.

An all-new, updated resources section: This includes books, websites, organizations, and a great many other sources of assistance, information, and hope.

Detailed information on conventional vs. unconventional BPD: Over the past twenty-two years, as a journalist interviewing thousands of people, Randi documented two different types of BPD. People with one form of the disorder often act 180 degrees differently from people with the other, even though both groups experience the same borderline traits internally. There will be times in this book when we speak of only one type or the other. When we do, we will note it in the text.

The first group, the *conventional* type, is people who have been diagnosed with BPD, and who can usually be found within the mental health system. They are in pain, seek treatment, and identify as having BPD. They meet the conventional depiction in the scientific literature and are eligible to be included in research studies, because they almost always harm themselves and feel suicidal.

The second, much larger group believes that they have no problems. They project all their pain onto others and never accept any accountability for their actions. They have an aggressive opposition to receiving therapy; they insist that the problem lies with everyone else's insensitivity or fragility; they usually function at a high level; they deny their pain by projecting it onto close loved ones; and they make those loved ones into their targets of blame. We call this form of BPD *unconventional* because the people who have it do not feel suicidal and do not harm themselves, making them ineligible as research subjects. The people in this second, unconventional group are rarely formally diagnosed as having BPD. Paradoxically, despite the name *unconventional*, they are much more common than the conventional, formally diagnosed folks.

In chapter 2, we'll discuss these two forms of BPD in detail.

About Us

A few years after the first edition of this book was published, Randi wrote *The Stop Walking on Eggshells Workbook: Practical Strategies for Living with Someone Who Has Borderline Personality Disorder*. In 2008, she also wrote another major book on BPD, *The Essential Family Guide to Borderline Personality Disorder: New Tools and Techniques to Stop Walking on Eggshells*.

Her advocacy efforts for families include holding workshops in Japan, serving as a BPD expert for a major motion picture, and blogging on BPD and NPD for four years on psychologytoday.com. She also appeared in a documentary discussing BPD and has given presentations about BPD nationwide and in Japan, including for the National Education Alliance for Borderline Personality Disorder.

In 2019, she began managing an online group that focuses on BPD education and support, called Moving Forward (movingforward@groups.io and https://groups.io/g/movingforward/join). It replaces her Welcome to Oz group. Her current projects include writing several books: one for parents and grandparents on preventing and healing BPD/NPD child abuse, and another about new tools to move forward when someone you care about has BPD/NPD. She is also working on a new edition of her book co-written with Christine Adamec and Daniel S. Lobel, *Stop Walking on Eggshells for Parents: How to Help Your Child with Borderline Personality Disorder Without Sacrificing Your Family or Yourself*. To be notified when those are available, join her mailing list at her website, stopwalkingoneggshells.com.

Paul Mason, MS, FACHE, serves as the vice president of Ascension Medical Group in Wisconsin. In this role, Paul provides management, leadership, and operational support for more than 200 clinicians and their medical practices. Paul is board certified in healthcare management and is a fellow of the American College of Healthcare Executives.

Both of us welcome you to this revised and updated Third Edition. We're glad you're here. In the pages to come, you'll find a wealth of useful tools, current information, and, above all, sanity and hope.

PART 1

understanding
BPD behavior

Does Someone You Care About Have Borderline or Narcissistic Personality Disorder?

After fifteen years of marriage, I still couldn't figure out what I was doing wrong. I researched in libraries, talked to doctors, spoke to counselors, read articles, and chatted with friends. I spent fifteen years wondering, worrying, and believing too much of what she was telling me about myself. I doubted myself and hurt so much without knowing why. Then one day, I finally found the answers on stopwalkingoneggshells.com. I started crying with relief. Although I can't get my significant other to admit she needs help, at least I finally understand what's going on. It's not my fault. Now I know the truth.

—Sophie

Is This Book for You?

You picked up this book because you're always tense in a relationship; you never know what to expect from a loved one; and being around them feels like walking on eggshells. Even when the relationship is going well, you are anxiously waiting for things to take a painful turn.

- Is the relationship always focused on your loved one's needs and wants, never on yours? Have you begun to lose track of your own needs and wants?

- Does your loved one make unreasonable demands, and keep insisting on them, to the point where you feel that saying "no" is not worth the pain?

- Have you tried to explain your point of view a million times and never gotten through? Are they so unwilling to understand you that you wonder if they're even capable of it?

- Does your loved one never show a trace of empathy for what you go through?

- Do they act normal in front of other people, but insult you, call you names, and otherwise treat you very badly when the two of you are alone?

- When you fight, is winning and being right more important to them than your feelings—or than the issue being discussed?

- Do they talk in confusing circles, or twist what you say and use your own words against you?

- Do they blame and criticize you obsessively?

- Does what they say often make no logical sense?

- Is it clear that they've lost all perspective on who you actually are?

- Are you the focus of their intense, violent, or irrational rages that grow way out of proportion to what instigated them?

- Do you feel manipulated and lied to, as if they'll say anything to get what they want?

- Do they need to always be in control?

- Do they have meltdowns when things don't go as planned, or they don't get their way?

- Do you feel like you're dealing with someone whose emotional maturity is like a toddler's—even if they are very educated or have a high position at work?

- Do you feel exhausted, confused, spread too thin, overwhelmed, depressed, hopeless, frustrated, or completely misunderstood?

If you answered yes to many of these questions, we have good news for you: you're not going crazy. It's not your fault. And you're not alone. You may be having these experiences because someone close to you has traits associated with borderline personality disorder (BPD), narcissistic personality disorder (NPD), or both.

In the pages that follow, we'll share some true stories of people who discovered that someone they cared about had one or both disorders. As with all examples in this book, these are drawn from the thousands and thousands of stories that have been shared online over the course of twenty-two years. (Details have been changed to conceal identities and protect people's privacy.)

Jon's Story of Being Married to a Woman with BPD and NPD

Being married to Gina is heaven one minute, hell the next. Her moods change by the second.

Even when I do exactly as she asks, she gets mad at me. One day she ordered me to take the kids somewhere because she wanted time alone. But as we were leaving, she threw the keys at my head and accused me of hating her so much I couldn't stand to be in the house with her. When the kids and I got back from the movie, she acted like nothing had happened. She wondered why I was still upset and told me that I have problems letting go of my anger.

It wasn't always like this. Before Gina and I got married, we had a whirlwind, fantasy courtship. She idolized me—said I was perfect for her in so many ways. The sex was incredible. I wrote her love poems and bought her expensive gifts. We got engaged after four months, and a year later we were married and on a ten-thousand-dollar dream honeymoon.

But right after the wedding she began taking meaningless little things and turning them into mountains of criticism, interrogation, and pain. She accused me of wanting other women constantly and would point out imaginary examples to substantiate her claims. She became threatened by my friends and began cutting them down. She said bad things about my business, my past, my values, my pride—anything connected to me.

Still, every so often the old Gina comes back—the one who loved me and thought I was the greatest guy in the universe. She's still the smartest, funniest, and sexiest woman I know, and I'm still very much in love. I wish I could get her the help she desperately needs so she can be this person all the time.

Mary's Story of Parenting a Child with BPD

We knew something was wrong with our adopted son, Richard, when he was eighteen months old. He was cranky, cried a lot, and would scream for three hours straight. At age two, he began having several tantrums a day—some lasting for hours. Our doctor simply said, "Boys will be boys."

When Rich was seven, we found a note in his room saying he was going to kill himself when he turned eight. His elementary school teacher referred us to a local psychiatrist, who told us Rich needed more structure and consistency. We tried positive reinforcement, tough love, and even diet modification. But nothing worked.

By the time Rich was in junior high, he was lying, stealing, skipping school, and raging out of control. The police became involved when he attempted suicide, started cutting himself, and threatened to kill us. He would dial the child abuse hotline each time we disciplined him by sending him to his room. Our son manipulated his teachers, his family, and even the police.

He could be very sharp and charm people with his wit, good looks, and sense of humor. Every counselor was convinced that his behavior was our fault. By the time they saw through his deception, he would refuse to go back. And each new therapist never took the time to read through his chart, which by now was several inches thick.

Finally, after threatening a teacher at school, he wound up in a short-term treatment center. At various times we were told that he had attention deficit disorder or suffered from post-traumatic stress disorder from some unknown trauma. One psychiatrist said he was suffering from "depression with psychotic disorder." Lots of people told us he was just a bad kid.

After four hospitalizations, our insurance company told us they would no longer pay. The hospital said he was too sick to come home. And the local psychiatrists were advising us to go to court and have ourselves declared unfit parents.

Somehow, we found a state-subsidized inpatient hospital, where he received his first BPD diagnosis. They put him on various meds, but said that there was little hope of him getting better.

Rich did manage to graduate from high school and start college, which ultimately was a disaster. His maturity level now is about age eighteen, although he's twenty-three. Reaching adulthood has helped some, but he still fears abandonment, can't sustain a long-term relationship, and has quit four jobs in two years. His friends come and go because he can be overbearing, obnoxious, manipulative, and opinionated. So he depends on us for money and emotional support. We're all he has left.

Kendra's Story of Having a Mother with BPD and NPD

I was never interested in girly things, but my mother dressed me up like a little princess and paraded me off to her friends. When we were alone, she would criticize me relentlessly for getting the clothes dirty, not acting right in front of her friends, or not being interested in being the best-dressed and most popular girl in school. That was always her dream, not mine.

My "nada" tapes play in my head, which are all the bad things she said to me that repeat continuously. They seem impossible to erase: The times after my parents divorced and she said I was destroying the family. The meals where she would complain about my manners and tell me they were so bad I wouldn't have any friends.

I am forty-two, yet my mother still feels compelled to tell me what is wrong with my life, my house, and my family—whatever. I'm actually a well-known and much-admired software developer, one of the first women in my industry. But her friends and associates don't know what that means, so it's useless to her. Our relationship is mainly over the telephone, and when the phone rings, my heart sinks. I make sure I am never alone with her. Never.

Ally's Story of Having a Sister with BPD

My sister, Sarah, felt deep hurt, anguish, and trauma that created emotional glass shards I spent most of my childhood tiptoeing around. Even though I was younger, my mother taught me to appease Sarah and keep her happy, which is like keeping a volcano from erupting. So many nights of little sleep, chaos, and being called awful names. I questioned my sense of reality. I was always on edge, trying to keep the peace. This has profoundly affected how I connect with others today.

I was always committed to relating with Sarah to show her how much I loved her. But lately my emotional and physical safety have been threatened. My sense of self was completely torn down, my struggles and vulnerabilities were used against me, I was hit, and some possessions were broken. I had to make the hardest decision of my life: to cut off contact.

I miss the good times. When things were good, they were really good. But I don't miss the terrible abuse or the feeling of losing myself. When I feel really sad, I remind myself that going "no contact" is one of the most loving actions I can take. I will always love Sarah. I hope one day I'll fully accept that she can't show me love and care in the same way.

Now that you've read these experiences and peeked inside the lives of others who love a highly challenging person, it will be clear whether this book is for you, and whether one or more of the stories you just read remind you of a loved one.

Before we go on, though, please know that your safety and well-being are our main concerns. So take a moment to see if you need help immediately.

Signs That You Need Help Right Now

If any of the following situations applies to you, set down this book and get help immediately. Later, once you are safe, you can come back to it for information, clarity, and inner resolution.

Seek immediate personal or professional support if your loved one does (or has already done) any of the following:

- Threatens violence or physical action; or puts a violent hand on you, even if it doesn't hurt too bad; or destroys objects; or makes you feel physically unsafe in any way.

- Takes, or threatens to take, the children from you.

- Makes, or threatens to make, false accusations of child abuse against you.

- Lies to a police officer about something you didn't do to get you arrested or in legal trouble.

- Breaks the law.

- Expects you to take part in an illegal action.

- Puts you or your family in harm's way.

- Steals money from you, or puts you or your family at financial risk.

- Routinely threatens divorce.* (If they straightforwardly tell you that they no longer wish to be with you, do not hang on. Begin planning now for a divorce or separation. And do not be surprised if they blame you for instigating the breakup.)

If you are feeling trapped and helpless, seek therapy right away. Therapy can also help if you are currently coping in unhealthy ways, such as drinking, taking mind-altering drugs, eating too much, or isolating yourself.

Getting help promptly is especially important in any of these situations:

- You have considered (or are considering) killing or harming yourself.

- You are in a deep depression.

- Friends have expressed concerns about your mental or emotional state.

Here are some good places to start:

- National Domestic Violence Hotline: 1-800-799-7233

- Suicide Prevention Line: 1-800-273-8255

- Child Abuse Hotline: 1-800-422-4453

- Therapist Search: psychologytoday.com/us/therapists/

Once you are safe, keep in mind that you are not going crazy, and—despite what your loved one may insist—you are not the cause of all the problems. More likely, the truth is that they have a personality disorder.

What Is a Personality Disorder?

When relating one on one, people like Gina, Rich, Kendra's mother, Sarah, and millions of others seem to have individual quirks, triggers, and time-bombs as part of their dysfunctional personalities. But these personalities (as you will see) are dysfunctional in the exact same ways, regardless of the

---

* In this case, please read *Splitting: Protecting Yourself When Divorcing a Borderline or Narcissist*. Then prepare for them to divorce you. Keep in mind that it typically takes months to put together a case with the proper documentation. If you wait for your partner to make the first move toward divorce, by the time you act they may already have removed important documents, personal items such as photographs, etc.

person's heritage, upbringing, or level of professional success. They all have what's called a *personality disorder.*

The Mayo Clinic describes a personality disorder as a type of mental disorder in which someone has a rigid and unhealthy pattern of thinking, functioning, and behaving. A person with a personality disorder looks at the world in a distinctly different way than you do—a way that causes significant problems and limitations in their relationships, their social activities, and their work or studies.

So, what exactly is the difference between an odd, forceful, or conflicting personality and a personality disorder? There's no perfect way to distinguish this, but someone very likely has a personality disorder if they are continuously disruptive, toxic, or out of line. Everybody—except perhaps the person with the disorder—recognizes that something's wrong. (One exception is if the person behaves quite normally in public and acts out only in private, typically with someone they're close to. This is not uncommon for people with BPD.)

Mental health professionals often need to determine when long-term sadness becomes clinical depression; or when mental illness might cause a very thin person to imagine they're fat; or when an odd or eccentric style actually reflects a personality disorder. To help them do this, they turn to the *Diagnostic and Statistical Manual of Mental Disorders* (DSM), which has been published regularly and revised by the American Psychiatric Association since 1952. The *DSM* lists different mental conditions, defines them, and lists criteria necessary to establish a diagnosis.

As of this writing, in 2020, the *DSM* is in its fifth edition, known as the *DSM-5.* The *DSM-5* is by no means flawless or uncontroversial, since mental illness is often more difficult to detect, quantify, and treat than physical illness. But the *DSM-5* is used or relied upon by mental health professionals as well as the federal government and insurance companies, to evaluate someone's mental condition.

The *DSM-5* lists ten personality disorders and groups them into three groups, or "clusters," based on shared key features. The A and C groups describe things like eccentric thinking and behavior (such as paranoid-personality disorder) and anxious, fearful thinking and behavior (such as extreme avoidance), both of which are outside the scope of this book. Our concern here is the B group, which is characterized by overly emotional, dramatic, erratic behavior. The Cluster B group describes the following disorders, which we'll summarize and put into accessible language below[**]:

- **Borderline Personality Disorder (BPD):** People show wild mood swings; see other people in black and white terms; act impulsively; are highly (and easily) triggered by real or imagined abandonment; and seem to either hate people or love them. These kinds of behaviors lead to intense and unmanageable relationships.

- **Narcissistic Personality Disorder (NPD):** People are highly self-centered, and generally hide a fragile sense of self-worth behind a façade of being superior. They believe they deserve special treatment, so they find people who are willing to fuel this sense of entitlement. Then they belittle, manipulate, and insult these other people.

- **Antisocial Personality Disorder (APD):** People prey on others with no regard for what is right or wrong. They violate other people's rights; exhibit criminal behavior; and may be consistently irresponsible. They show no guilt or remorse. They have no empathy. They routinely lie, and may use charm and wit to manipulate others for their personal gain. (These are the people we colloquially call *sociopaths*.[***])

- **Histrionic Personality Disorder (HPD):** The word *histrionic* means "dramatic" or "theatrical." People with HPD depend upon the approval of others because they don't have a true self-worth. Someone with HPD has an overwhelming desire for attention, which they often get by behaving in an overly dramatic, lively, flirtatious, and/or enthusiastic way.

We hope that your understanding of your messy situation with your loved one is now beginning to get clearer. Learning about personality disorders can

---

[**] For more clinical descriptions, you can go to your local library and read the *DSM-5* for yourself.

[***] It is possible to have more than one Cluster B personality disorder at once. Many professionals use the term *malignant narcissism* to describe a combination of NPD and APD. However, this classification and term are not formally recognized as a diagnosis in the *DSM-5*.

be a powerful, transformational experience for people caught up in the unpredictable whirlwind of relationships with folks who have these disorders.

Before we dive deeper, however, we need to give you some warnings.

Don't Reveal Your Diagnostic Suspicions to Your Loved One

As you read this book, you may be eager to talk about what you're learning with the person you believe has the disorder. This is understandable. The fantasy goes like this: a light bulb will go on in the person's head, they will be grateful to you, and they will rush into therapy to conquer their demons.

Unfortunately, the reality usually differs. Your loved one is quite likely to respond with rage, denial, a torrent of criticism, and accusations that *you* are the one with the disorder.

Other scenarios are possible, too. A person with BPD traits may feel such shame and despair that they attempt to hurt or kill themselves. Or they may use the information to deny responsibility for their behavior, as in, "I can't help what I do; I've got BPD."

It's true that—as you'll discover in chapter 2—some people with the *conventional* form of BPD *do* look for treatment, and are in such great emotional pain (and, perhaps, have harmed or tried to kill themselves) that they are open to getting a diagnosis. But it's best to not tell them that you think they may have the disorder. Instead, show them hopeful, non-stigmatizing material on the disorder and let them decide for themselves if they meet the criteria.

If, as is more likely, your loved one has the *unconventional* form of BPD, they may insist that everyone else is the problem. They will have no interest in therapy, and they will be verbally and emotionally abusive. There is a 99 percent chance that they will DARVO: *deny, attack, reverse,* claim *victimhood,* and make you into the *offender.*

The DARVO script typically goes something like this: "No, I don't have a personality disorder (*deny*), you mental case (*attack*). You're the one with problems (*reverse*)! I can't believe you could think of me this way (*victim*). If anyone has a personality disorder, it's you (*offender*)."

Remember that you and your loved one come from two different places. You are thinking in terms of explaining their behavior and getting help for them. They are more likely to hear that you are trying to win an argument by calling them insane and telling them that everything about them is wrong.

So, do not share your diagnostic suspicions with your loved one unless *they* have asked you to help them look for answers about how they feel and what they do.

Clarifying the Traits You Witness

In chapters 2 and 3, we will cover both BPD and NPD in depth. But first, to help you better understand exactly whom you're dealing with, please take the quiz below. It will help you to see more clearly how these two disorders look in everyday life, and it will guide you in how you approach the information in this book. It will also help you know whether it's more likely that your loved one has BPD, NPD, or both. (Remember, it's possible to have more than one personality disorder at once.)

This quiz is not a diagnostic tool. It is based on a simple list of common, real-world ways in which spouses, siblings, parents, children, and friends describe their difficult loved ones.

Is Your Loved One Borderline, Narcissistic, or Both? And How Concerned Should You Be About Them?

Which of the following statements describe your loved one? Note each statement that describes something your loved one often does.

_____ 1. *They are more concerned with how things might look to others than with how they actually are.*

_____ 2. **Their emotions can change in the blink of an eye. But once those emotions have changed to something highly charged, it's hard for the person to come back down again.**

_____ 3. *They never ask me about how my day went. It's always about them and what's going on with them. I am supposed to listen and pay attention to their problems, but to deal with my own problems by myself.*

_____ 4. **They can fly into sudden, soul-shattering rages, often over something seemingly trivial—and sometimes for no reason at all that I can see. These rages leave me feeling devastated.**

_____ 5. **Whenever I get really close to them and we're having a great time, soon afterward they sabotage it all. I get really excited because we're so close, and then they ruin it.**

_____ 6. _They feel entitled, like they should get the best of everything, and that they should always come first._

_____ 7. _They seem to think that the rules are for other people to follow—but for them to ignore._

_____ 8. **They get very upset at me when they feel I am abandoning them, even if I've simply come home late or can't be available for a phone call when they want me to be.**

_____ 9. **They constantly text or call me to find out my whereabouts.**

_____ 10. **They need me to tell them, over and over, that I love them—but then they don't believe me when I do.**

_____ 11. _They don't have a very deep emotional life. I have tried digging, and there doesn't seem to be much there. They have so many defenses._

_____ 12. **To them, I'm either the best or the worst—never in between. And when they feel one way, they can't remember ever feeling the other way.**

_____ 13. _Sometimes they yell horrible things at me that make me feel small. In response, I sometimes cry, but it doesn't make much difference to them._

_____ 14. **They talk about how horrible they feel, especially about themselves. I can see they're in a lot of pain.**

_____ 15. **Sometimes they cut themselves, or hurt themselves in some other physical way.**

_____ 16. **They've told me that sometimes they feel like they want to die.**

_____ 17. _The kids love it when my loved one is in a good mood. But the minute the kids start acting like kids, my loved one is impatient for me to take them off their hands. If the kids won't leave them alone, they'll shout at them. I have heard them say terrible things to each of the kids._

_____ 18. **They can't see the difference between what's in their own best interests and what's in the kids' best interests. When they were** feeling lonely, they kept all the kids home for school. When they're mad at me, they say things like, "You don't love me—or the children."

_____ 19. *They take advantage of me and others. They ask me to do all kinds of things for them, and they do very little to nothing in return. And they don't seem to understand why that's not okay.*

_____ 20. **They can't function on their own, really, even though they're an adult. They quit jobs when they're given a task they dislike, and they get involved with dangerous or abusive romantic partners.**

_____ 21. **They don't let children be as independent as they should be because they rely on them for social support.**

_____ 22. **I'm worried for my grandchildren. My child isn't really capable of keeping them safe. I want to call social services, but if I do, they will never speak to me again, and I could lose my precious grandchildren.**

_____ 23. *They're incredibly passive-aggressive.*

_____ 24. *They say they will clean the living room, or find their own place to rent, but then they don't. Then they will talk about how they couldn't because they are a victim of some sort or another. They are never accountable for anything.*

_____ 25. **They're incredibly impulsive. They act without thinking things through, and then they get into trouble.**

_____ 26. *When I have a crisis, not only are they unsupportive, but they're so self-absorbed and unempathetic that all they talk about is how it affects them.*

_____ 27. **They just took off and left one day. Everything was fine, and then they were gone. Now they're telling everyone I abused them. It's all over social media. WTF? What happened?**

_____ 28. *I can't tell them any good news about my life, like a promotion, because they just get jealous and put down my accomplishment.*

_____ 29. **I never know what mood they're going to be in when I come home. It could be anything at all, from happy to furious to depressed. It really stresses me out.**

_____ 30. *They envy others and think others envy them.*

Understanding These Statements

- All the statements in **bold** are traits of borderline personality disorder.

- All the statements in *italics* are traits of narcissistic personality disorder.

- Remember that your loved one may have either or both disorders.

- Add the total number of statements in **bold** that you checked. The more of these you checked, the more likely it is that your loved one has BPD.

- Add the total number of statements in *italics* that you checked. The more of these you checked, the more likely it is that your loved one has NPD.

- Add the total number of *all statements* that you checked. If this total is 12 or higher, you are right to be concerned—and you would be wise to spend a good deal of time with this book. If your total is 16 or more, you should be *very* concerned.

The High-Conflict Personality (HCP)

People with BPD, NPD, and certain other personality disorders also share certain broader behavior patterns. These people are known as *high-conflict personalities*, or *HCPs*. This is a term originated by therapist, author, and mediator Bill Eddy.

Eddy says that high-conflict people have a pattern of behavior that habitually increases conflict rather than reduces or resolves it. This usually happens over and over again, in many different situations, with many different people. The particulars of the situation are not what cause or increase the conflict. The real cause is how the HCP processes relationships and conflicts.

Here are the common attributes of HCPs:

Internal Fragility

Most HCPs are shame-based, insecure, and troubled by feelings of worthlessness. For HCPs, admitting that they made a mistake is intolerable and unthinkable. Even admitting that they *could* make a mistake is intolerable. That admission would be catastrophic for their self-image, so they refuse to take any responsibility.

An HCP can't admit that their opinion is flawed, or say "I'm sorry." If they did, they would feel insignificant, inferior, and shameful—and they would imagine that this insignificance, inferiority, and shame would be vividly on display for everyone to see. So they will defend themselves in any way they know how. These defenses, which hurt other people so much, are their *survival skills*, which they perceive as necessary to ward off what, to them, is a psychological death. The best way for them to ensure their psychological survival is to be in control of their environment and the people in it at all times. That's why it's their way or the highway, and compromise and flexibility seem impossible.

Projection, Criticism, and Blame

When a person projects, they cannot accept a quality that exists in themselves. Instead, they see it in—and project it upon—another person. Essentially, they blame someone else for having the same faults they refuse to see in themselves.

HCPs project their own perceived badness and unworthiness onto others. This projection is a defense mechanism that allows them to feel better about themselves, in a manner similar to rationalization and denial.

All-or-Nothing Thinking

HCPs tend to split people and situations into black-and-white extremes. Either they love you and you're their soulmate and savior, or they hate you and you're trying to destroy their life.

HCPs tend to put people on pedestals, admire them, flush them with compliments, and promise to be their soulmate, bestie, or perfect partner— then make an abrupt turn and continually find fault, sometimes leaving or discarding those very same people.

For HCPs, there often cannot be any shades of gray. This is called *splitting*. You may recognize this all-or-nothing, black-and-white thinking when you hear an HCP say things like, "You *always* do this," and "You *never* do that."

Unmanaged Emotions

Even in everyday exchanges, HCPs can become very emotional about their points of view, often catching everyone else by surprise with their intense fear, anger, yelling, or disrespect. Their emotions are often way out of proportion to the situation or the issue being discussed. Yet HCPs are often clueless about the devastating and exhausting emotional impact they can have on others.

HCPs often seem unable to control their own emotions, and may later regret how they expressed them. But they may also defend what they did as totally appropriate—and insist that you should, too.

There are also some HCPs who don't lose control of their emotions, but use emotional manipulation to hurt others. They trigger upset feelings in others in ways that are not obvious, sometimes while they outwardly seem very calm. So, for example, you might feel betrayed when you discover a lie they told to make themselves look better or to put themselves at an advantage. Or you may be shocked when they twist your own words and turn them against you. Or you may feel small when they position themselves as your intellectual superior. Or they may belittle you for a concern you expressed, or hurt you with a mean verbal jab, which they may then insist was just a joke.

Extreme Behaviors

People with BPD can exhibit a wide range of extreme behaviors, including:

- over-emotional reactions (such as suddenly throwing objects, or saying the meanest possible thing to a loved one)

- overtly trying to control others

- hiding others' personal items

- physically preventing someone from leaving a conversation

- threatening retribution when someone doesn't agree

- becoming violent

You'll read many examples of these and other extreme behaviors in the next two chapters.

Always keep in mind that, while something you say or do may *trigger* an HCP's extreme behavior, you never *cause* it. Instead, your words and actions bring up the person's profound internal pain, which in turn generates their extreme behavior.

Don't Get Stuck on a Diagnosis

It's easy to imagine that things will improve once your loved one receives a diagnosis of BPD (or NPD, or both). In practice, however, this is rarely the case. In fact, it's more likely than not that your loved one will refuse to see a clinician or pursue a diagnosis.

For now, your goal should be to temper your expectations for the person you care about. If they do have a personality disorder, you can't expect them to act like a healthy, well-adjusted person. That sets them up for failure—and it sets you up for disappointment.

Our goal is to give you the confidence, tools, and information you need to make your relationship with your loved one—and yourself—as strong and as positive as possible.

That said, if, when you come to the end of this book, you decide that you want to have little or no contact with this person in the future, that's okay, too. You have the right to decide whether a relationship is working for you or not.

Know There Is Hope

BPD and NPD are probably the two most misunderstood psychiatric diagnoses. And the biggest misperception is that people with these disorders never get any better. It's true that some of them don't. But some do.

In reality, if your loved one is willing to go to treatment and work hard at it, they may improve. Medications can help reduce any depression, moodiness, and impulsivity associated with their disorder. We have met people who were formerly diagnosed with BPD, NPD, or both—and who have recovered, who feel good about themselves, and who give and receive love joyfully.

Even if the person you love refuses help and treatment, there's still hope. Although you can't change them, you can change yourself. By examining your own behavior and modifying *your* actions, you can get off the emotional roller coaster and reclaim your life.

As you read this book, remember that the knowledge you gain will help you see what is actually happening during interactions with your highly challenging loved one. Just being able to observe with understanding will strengthen you.

In the following pages, we will provide you with plenty of tools, perspectives, and ways to take control of your own life—whether your loved one changes or not. So read on, knowing that later chapters will teach you more about what you can do...*for you.*

CHAPTER 2

What Is Borderline Personality Disorder?

As you read this chapter, keep in mind that the behaviors you witness in the person you love are usually unconscious. They are designed to shield the person from intense emotional pain—*not to hurt you.* This knowledge will help you to separate the person from their disorder.

It's common to struggle to understand borderline thoughts, feelings, and behaviors, because we assume that people with BPD think and feel the way we do. But they simply don't. Nevertheless, it can be an understandable mistake, because sometimes people with BPD seem completely normal.

To truly understand borderline behavior, however, you have to leave your reality and journey into borderline territory. And the better you understand this territory, the more possibilities open up for your relationship.

Essentially, people with BPD look to others to manage their feelings for them. Someone with BPD wants others to provide them with things they find difficult to supply for themselves, such as self-love, stable moods, and a sense of identity. Most of all, they are searching for a nurturing caregiver whose never-ending love and compassion will fill the black hole of emptiness and despair inside them.

Rachel Reiland, author of *Get Me Out of Here: My Recovery from Borderline Personality Disorder,* had BPD for many years, but has fully recovered. In an email, she describes the conflicting feelings that used to underlie her behavior:

I always had this insatiable hunger for something I couldn't define, except to call it the bottomless pit of need. Something that made me scared to get close to anybody for fear they'd discover I was rotten and disturbed. So I diversified. I had lots of friends and didn't get too close to any of them.

If I let my guard down and one friend found out how weird I was—well, I had fifty-nine others.

But now a romantic relationship has kicked in. The stakes are high with one person meaning so much. This is different—the guy needs me, too. So maybe it's safe here. Be with me every day and every night. Look at me, listen to me. I'm here. Oh, this is incredible! Finally, the one person who can take all of this need!

Hey…wait a minute! He says he wants to watch TV in peace. What the hell do I do now? I am frustrated…Damn it. I hate this guy! I let my guard down—doesn't he know how hard it was for me to do that? How dare he rather watch TV? Or be out with his friends? How dare he find out how disturbed I am? I'm furious and embarrassed as hell. He's seen the bottomless pit of need.

I lash out. Let him have it. I rage. I scream until I collapse in exhaustion. And then I wake up and I see how much I've hurt him. And I despise myself. I'm scared to death because I know he's gonna walk. I'm so vulnerable. I'm not tough at all. Please don't leave. I need you! How can I show you?

I cry, I beg, I tell him what an incredible man he is, how patient he is. You should hate me! I'd be better off dead. You'd be better off without me! Oh, please, let me make it up to you. Let's make incredible love anywhere, anytime!

Whew! He's back. Thank God I didn't blow it permanently. He cares…

When I realize that I've caused irrevocable damage, when the cycle has repeated itself so often I'm convinced that I've irrevocably blown it—whether or not he has reached this conclusion—I cut the cord and find somebody else. And go through the whole damned thing again.

Folks with BPD are most vulnerable with the people closest to them: parents, spouses, children, and siblings. These people have the most power to hurt them by abandoning or rejecting them. And the mere thought of someone leaving them causes them so much pain that, in order to avoid that scenario, they may leave a relationship before the other person leaves them.

When they're not being triggered, or when they're with people they're not close to, people with the unconventional form of BPD may often act quite normal. Most of the time, they don't look or sound like they have a disorder.

And some people with the conventional type of BPD—especially those in therapy—can have an excellent intellectual understanding of BPD. They may even have researched the topic thoroughly. When people with conventional BPD are not overcome by intense pain, they may understand that their feelings don't always reflect reality. They may be very, very sorry for the ways in which they have hurt others. But this intellectual understanding doesn't prevent them from becoming triggered and emotional all over again a few hours or minutes later.

In the chart below, we've grouped the traits of BPD into thoughts, feelings, and actions. In the rest of the chapter, we'll unpack these in more detail, so you can begin your exploration of what they mean for you and your relationship. In each individual, of course, these traits may vary in intensity, with some being serious problems and others being less severe.

COMMON BPD THOUGHTS, FEELINGS, AND ACTIONS

THOUGHTS	Impaired perception and reasoning
	Splitting—i.e., seeing things solely in black-or-white terms (no grays)
	Shifting back and forth between black and white; when in one mode, having no memory of ever being in the other
	Putting particular people on pedestals—then knocking them off
	When under stress, dissociating, running on autopilot, or being "out of it"
	Lack of a clear sense of identity
FEELINGS	Highly sensitive to potential signs of abandonment or rejection
	Equally afraid of engulfment
	Dark moods that are poorly regulated, very intense, and slow to recover from
	Highly and quickly changeable emotions
	Desiring closeness, yet feeling smothered in its presence
	Feeling a dark hole of emptiness inside
	Intense, seemingly unmanageable emotional pain
	Sudden, uncontrollable rage

ACTIONS	Impulsiveness, which can sometimes be extreme
	Failure to think through the potential consequences of an action
	Suicide or self-harm (for people with conventional BPD)
	Compulsive behavior involving sex, substance abuse, eating, spending, etc.
	Reckless driving
	Unleashing torrents of criticism and blame on others
	Uncontrollable raging
	Impulsive aggression, sometimes involving physical fights, especially among men with BPD
	An inability to express any anger at all (among some people with conventional BPD)

For someone with BPD, this 1-2-3 punch of thoughts, feelings, and actions results in a pattern of unstable, intense, roller-coaster relationships. It also commonly results in the people around them becoming hypervigilant, as if land mines had been planted around them, constantly hoping that they don't say or do something that will light the person's very short fuse.

Let's look more closely at some of these traits. As you read, note which ones remind you of your loved one.

Splitting

People with BPD view others through extremes of idealization and devaluation—as either the wicked witch or their fairy godmother, a saint or a demon. When you seem to be meeting their needs, they cast you in the role of superhero. But when they think that you've failed them, or they want to be independent, you become the villain.

Because people with BPD have a hard time integrating a person's good and bad traits, their current opinion of someone is often based on their last interaction with them. It's as if they lack a long-term memory.

If you have a partner with BPD, when you first got together, they may have thought you were the most magnificent person on Earth. This feels great to almost everyone, but it is like nectar to folks who grew up in families where they didn't feel important, or loved for themselves, or allowed to feel and express their emotions.

But what goes up must come down. Your partner with BPD is looking for a 24/7 white knight and a life that is happy ever after. When you continue living your own life—which involves a job, friends, and your family—the person with BPD may become jealous, and start demanding that you give up large chunks of your life. At that point, you get batted off the pedestal and turned into a villain.

While you can't prevent this entirely, when your loved one wants to put you on a pedestal, don't believe you belong there, because it's actually a trap—and it will be a rough ride down. Remind your loved one that you are not a perfect, ideal person. And when they split you in the opposite way, remind yourself that their anger and accusations are not actually about you.

There's another key aspect to this splitting: people with BPD also split *themselves*, often into victim or hero—or into someone capable or someone incompetent.

People with BPD commonly base their sense of self-worth on their latest achievement—or the lack of one. They judge themselves as harshly as they judge others—so, at times, whatever they do is never good enough. At other times, they see themselves as helpless victims of other people—even when their "victimhood" is partly or entirely the result of their own actions.

Fear of Abandonment

Imagine the terror you would feel if you were a child lost and alone in the middle of New York's Times Square. Your mom was there a second ago, holding your hand—then, suddenly, the crowd swept her away. You look around frantically, trying to find her, but can't see her anywhere.

This is how people with BPD feel nearly all the time: isolated, anxious, and terrified at the thought of being alone. To someone with BPD, meeting a caring, supportive person is like finding a friendly face in a crowd of strangers. They are sure that this person can keep them from feeling so lost. When that person decides to stay, the person with BPD often idolizes them.

But then this idolized human being does something that the person with BPD interprets—correctly or incorrectly—as a signal that they're about to leave. Then the person with BPD panics, typically bursting into rage, or begging them to stay—or possibly both.

It can take very little to trigger this fear of abandonment. One woman with BPD refused to let her boyfriend leave their apartment to do their laundry, because the thought of him leaving their home terrified her. Often this terror can overwhelm someone with BPD, causing them to lash out in ways that make no sense. For example, one man told his wife that his physician had diagnosed him with a potentially fatal illness. His wife, who had BPD, was so afraid of losing him that she raged at him for visiting his doctor.

Let's listen to some other stories of this fear, told by folks who have been affected by BPD:

Tess, Who Has BPD

When I feel abandoned, I feel a combination of isolation, terror, and alienation. I panic. I feel betrayed and used. I think I'm going to die. One night I called my boyfriend, and he said he would call me back because he was watching TV. So I did my ironing to pass the time. He didn't call. I waited. He didn't call. This terrible feeling of being abandoned came over me again. It hurt so bad because the day before, I had started to believe that he really loved me. By the time the phone rang at 10 PM, I had decided to break up with him—get rid of him before he could get rid of me. He had still been watching the movie. I felt so ridiculous, but the pain, the fear, and the poker in my gut were very real.

Beth, Whose Husband Has BPD

The harder I try to placate my borderline husband, the fiercer his reaction becomes. The moment I give up and start to walk away, he turns into a clinging vine. It's like that old burlesque routine of the clown trying to pick up his hat. Every time he bends down to grab it, he accidentally kicks it further away. Finally, he gives up in disgust. And as he walks away, the wind blows his hat after him.

Amina, Whose Wife Has BPD

If I'm five minutes late coming home from work, my wife will call to find out where I am. She pages me constantly. I can't go out by myself with friends anymore because she reacts so strongly—she'll even page me while I'm watching a movie. It's so stressful that I've stopped going out with friends unless she feels like coming along.

Fear of Engulfment

Paradoxically, people with BPD also typically have a deep fear of being smothered by someone close to them. They are afraid that this other person will invade their inner space and diminish whatever sense of self they *do* have. They sometimes fear that they will be taken over.

If this sounds familiar, know that you're not actually invading or diminishing your loved one. But that doesn't stop their fear.

You may have experienced this as a frequent push-pull. You have a great time with your loved one in the evening; then, the first thing the next morning, they start an argument, or complain bitterly because the time you spent cuddling in bed made them get up late. Or, they insist on breaking up with you, then desperately want to get back together a few days later—and this pattern repeats itself, over and over. This creates disappointment, confusion, and havoc.

Dissociation

For people with BPD, their volatile emotions and/or the situations and challenges in their lives may be so painful that they feel a need to escape them altogether. So they dissociate, to varying degrees. The more stressful the situation, the more likely they are to dissociate.

Have you ever arrived home from work without remembering how you got there? You've traveled the route so many times that your brain lets your eyes and reflexes do the driving. This "out of it" feeling is a mild, common, and entirely healthy type of dissociation. People who severely dissociate, however, feel unreal, strange, numb, or detached. They may or may not remember exactly what happened while they were "gone."*

In extreme cases, people with BPD may even lose all contact with reality for a brief period of time. If your loved one reports memories of shared situations quite differently from you, it's probably because of their dissociation, not your memory being faulty.

---

* One form of extreme dissociation is what used to be called *multiple personality disorder,* and is now called *dissociative identity disorder* in the *DSM-5.*

Rage and Mood Swings

If you are close to someone with BPD, you are probably very familiar with their Jekyll-and-Hyde mood changes and their temper tantrums.

People with BPD feel *all* emotions intensely, not just anger. But borderline rage is especially notable because it can be intense and unpredictable, and because it is usually utterly unaffected by logical argument. It is like a torrential flash flood, a sudden earthquake, or a bolt of lightning on a sunny day. And it can disappear as quickly as it appears—or it can persist for hours or days.

Some people with the conventional type of BPD have the opposite problem: they feel unable to express their anger at all. Marsha M. Linehan, PhD, writes that people with BPD who under-express anger "fear they will lose control if they express even the slightest anger, and at other times they fear that targets of even minor anger expression will retaliate."

People with either form of BPD must endure frequent dark, intense, and unstable moods. These typically include anxiety, acute hopelessness, despair, depression, and deep unhappiness. There are some prescription medications that can help reduce the number or severity of these dark episodes. But for your loved to be prescribed such a medication, they first need to seek treatment for their disorder.

The brain of someone with borderline personality disorder is biochemically different from most people's. In a person with BPD, both their brain structures *and* their brain chemistry regularly turn their emotional centers on to full strength. Imagine a big, muscled bully pounding the logical centers of your brain into submission. That's what it's like for people with BPD. And, long after most people would have cooled down, the bully is still throwing punches—and your loved one is still upset.

That said, don't let yourself be raged upon or physically hurt—even if you're bigger and stronger than the person with BPD. Later in this book, we'll teach you how to walk away from borderline rages, and how to set limits around them.

When your loved one begins to rage, quickly remove children from the area. And don't rage back; that will make things worse. And remember: you don't need anyone's permission to get to safety. Call the police if you need to.

Don't be surprised if, after you do walk away, your loved one immediately comes after you, and makes all sorts of promises to get you back in the room—after which they may resume raging or making their point. For people with BPD, there is never a middle ground between these two extremes.

Here are some real-life stories of borderline raging and mood swings:

Jeremy, Who Has BPD

When I can't control my surroundings, I become nervous and angry. It gets much worse when I am under stress. When triggered, I can go from perfectly calm to full-blown, white-hot rage within a fraction of a second. I think that my temper comes from the abuse I suffered when I was a child. At some point, I decided that I didn't have to take my parents' abuse anymore. Raging back became a matter of survival. So now, it's hard for me to feel concerned about the other person's feelings—in fact, I want them to hurt because they've hurt me. I know this sounds bad, but that's the way I feel when I'm in the middle of an outburst. I'm just trying to survive the best way I know how.

Richard, Who Is Married to Someone with BPD

After two years of abuse, I told my borderline wife Laurie that maybe we should separate for a while. She started screaming at me, saying I just wanted to sleep around. She said really ugly things about how I couldn't make her happy. I was so devastated that I just stood there with my mouth hanging open. Then she picked up a plate and threw it at me.

Dina, Who Is Married to Someone with BPD

Living with my husband is heaven one minute and hell the next. I call his personalities Jovial Jekyll and Horrible Hyde. I walk on eggshells, trying to please someone who blows up just because I spoke too soon, too quickly, in the wrong tone, or with the wrong facial expressions.

Emptiness

People with BPD continually feel a dark hole of emptiness inside them. This symptom is hard to explain if you haven't experienced it.

So try this. Close your eyes. Imagine you're about to move to an unfamiliar city where you don't know anyone, and where everyone speaks a different language. You're going by yourself because you have no family. Now, take away all of your spiritual or religious beliefs.

Then ponder what makes your life meaningful. Now pretend you can't do or have any of those meaningful things anymore. From now on, you'll be living without meaning.

That's how people with BPD feel, more or less all the time. This is why they may grab onto you like you're a life raft on the *Titanic*. Being alone leaves them without a sense of who they are—or causes them to feel like they do not exist. They have faith that you will fill that deep, empty hole for them.

But, of course, you can't. No one can do that. One man with BPD said it was like trying to fill the Grand Canyon using an eyedropper.

This emptiness is behind the chaos that people with BPD routinely cause. Your loved one gets so angry because you cannot fill that hole. And they believe that the reason you can't is because you aren't trying hard enough. You didn't spend every moment with them. You didn't fulfill their every need. You tried to have a life of your own.

People with BPD usually don't know how to express this emptiness. Instead, they may:

- Act like different people, depending on whom they are with

- Depend on others around them for cues about how to behave, what to think, and how to be

- Feel panicked and bored when alone

- Create chaos

The holy grail of the life of someone with BPD is to find that caring, compassionate person who will magically fill their empty insides, take care of them and their needs, and never leave them feeling alone again. But the central irony is that the disorder causes them to do things that push other people away. As a result, they live with emptiness, fear, panic, and rage twenty-four hours a day.

Here is one person's story of this emptiness and a lack of a clear sense of self:

Salia, Who Has BPD

I have a chameleon-like ability to take on the coloring of the individual I am with. But the act is done more to fool me than to fool them. For the time being, I have become who I'd like to be. I am not some kind of a Machiavellian manipulator with nothing better to do than ruin lives. The process isn't even really conscious. It's been going on for so long now that I don't even know who I really am. I feel unreal—like a phony. If I had any true control over it, I would simply revert back to "myself" whenever I felt threatened. But I don't know who that is.

Pain Management Behaviors

In order to deal with the overwhelming pain they feel, folks with BPD typically act impulsively, even recklessly.

Everyone has urges they would love to indulge if they could: eat every chocolate in the box, buy a great new sweater in every color, or drink one last glass of champagne to toast the New Year. But most people are aware of the long-term consequences—weight gain, a massive credit card bill, or a nasty hangover. People with BPD don't always have that awareness. And even when they do, they usually aren't able to control their impulses. As one woman with BPD explains, "When my two-year-old wants something, she wants it now. When I am shopping, I can't tell myself no, so I buy it, even though I'm in debt."

All of us are familiar with this sequence: you have a thought, which leads to a feeling, which leads to an action. You *think* you're going to get fired, and you *feel* scared that you might lose your home as a result, so you *take action* and send out your resume to potential employers.**

In people with BPD, the same sequence of thought to feeling to action takes place—but the initial thought is often unjustified or irrational. It is frequently also painful, which in turn leads to an impulsive reaction.

So, for example, Orin's boss didn't smile at him in the hall or take the time to chat with him. Orin's rejection antennae go up. He thinks about how hard he's worked for the past two years, and how his boss doesn't appreciate him. He gets very angry as he ponders this.

The next time Orin passes his boss in the hall, he finds himself asking with a raised voice, "Hey! Is there a reason you're not talking to me anymore? Did I do something wrong? Because in my last evaluation you rated me as outstanding." But, in fact, nothing was wrong. His boss had simply been in deep thought, and in a hurry.

Substance abuse is a common form of pain management for people with BPD, especially men. These folks are likely to:

- abuse more than one drug (e.g., cocaine and alcohol)

** There is an entire type of therapy called *cognitive behavioral therapy*, or CBT, which is built around improving people's lives by first changing their thoughts, which changes their moods, which then affects their actions.

- be depressed

- have frequent harmful accidents

- attempt suicide, perhaps more than once

- have even less impulse control than folks with BPD who don't abuse drugs or alcohol

Unfortunately, when someone with BPD abuses drugs, alcohol, or both, it can be difficult to determine which of their actions are related to BPD and which ones stem from their substance abuse.

Additional Borderline Traits

People with BPD have other commonly observed attributes that are not part of the formal DSM definition. These include:

A Strong Sense That Their Feelings Equal Facts

To an extent, we all use our emotions to determine what we believe. Advertisers and politicians know this; that's why they create TV ads that tug at our heartstrings and make their competitors look terrible.

But people with BPD—and, as you will see in the next chapter, folks with NPD—take every one of their emotions to be 100 percent true and accurate. They act based on their emotional reality all the time. Logic has nothing to do with it.

If you've ever tried to logically argue your loved one out of their feelings, you know it's a hopeless endeavor. That's why we don't recommend it. You'll find several effective alternatives later in this book.

Pervasive Feelings of Shame

John Bradshaw's book *Healing the Shame That Binds You* is not specifically about borderline personality disorder. Yet his explanation of toxic shame, and the feelings and behaviors it engenders, epitomizes how people with BPD feel:

> *Toxic shame is experienced as the all-pervasive sense that I am flawed and defective as a human being. It is no longer an emotion that signals our limits; it is a state of being, a core identity. Toxic shame gives you a sense of worthlessness, the feeling of being isolated, empty, and alone in*

a complete sense. Exposure to oneself lies at the heart of toxic shame. A shame-based person will guard against exposing his inner self to others, but more significantly, he will guard against exposing himself to himself.

Bradshaw sees shame as the root cause of rage, extreme criticism and blame, inappropriate caretaking, codependency, addictive behavior, excessive people pleasing, and eating disorders.

People with the conventional form of BPD tend to become consumed by their shame. Folks with the unconventional form tend to deny—both to others and to themselves—that they have any such shame.

Impulsive Aggression

People with BPD may, perhaps suddenly, make threats, break things, and speak in a loud and angry tone. Some may become violent. Here is how one woman with BPD describes this trait:

Sometimes I criticize my fiancé's every move, telling him that if he loved me, he wouldn't do that. When I belittle and blame him, I feel that I might be abandoned or embarrassed or that he is somehow not showing me love. I feel fearful. I am so upset that I yell and scream and knock over objects. My decision making is poor. Just yesterday I threw my engagement ring in the garbage during my rage at him. When I find things are fine, I feel very reassured and embarrassed and swear to myself I won't ever feel that way again. But I always do.

Undefined Boundaries

People with BPD have difficulty setting and maintaining personal limits. As one man with BPD explains:

I was brought up thinking that the perfect intimate relationship had no boundaries. Boundaries only meant a rift between people. Boundaries meant I had to be alone, separate, have an identity. I didn't feel good enough to have a separate identity. I needed either total enmeshment or total isolation.

Control Issues

People with BPD often need to feel in control of other people, because they feel so out of control with themselves. In addition, because they feel vulnerable and afraid, they try to make their world more predictable and manageable by controlling it as much as possible.

Vulnerability opens us up to being shamed. To someone with BPD, controlling others is a way to ensure that no one can ever shame them. In practice, however, people with BPD often attempt to control others by putting them in no-win situations, creating chaos, or accusing others of trying to control them.

Conversely, some people with BPD may cope with feeling out of control by *giving up* all of their own power and choosing a lifestyle where all choices are made for them. This might involve joining the military or a cult. Or they may align themselves with abusive people who control them through fear or coercion.

Lack of Object Constancy

When we're lonely, most of us can soothe ourselves by remembering the love that others have for us. This can be very comforting, even if these people are far away—sometimes even if they're no longer living. This ability to hold others close, even in their physical absence, is called *object constancy*.

Many people with BPD find it difficult to evoke an image of a loved one to soothe them when they feel upset or anxious. To someone with BPD, if that person is not physically present, they don't exist on an emotional level. That's why your loved one may call, text, or email you frequently—just to make sure you're still there and still care about them.

Situational Competence

Some people with BPD, especially those with the unconventional form of the disorder, can be quite competent, self-confident, and in control of themselves in some situations. Many are high achievers and perform very well at work or in school. Many are very intelligent, creative, and artistic.

It can be very confusing when your loved one acts so self-assured in one situation and then falls apart for seemingly no reason in another. This *situational competence* is a hallmark of BPD.

Lack of Trust in Others

Folks with BPD can't trust others because they believe, on a fundamental level, that they don't deserve to be loved or cared about. This is why, no matter how many times you reassure them, they can't accept your reassurance. Meanwhile, the black hole inside them never gets filled.

Lying, Embellishing, and Misrepresenting

As we've explained, people with BPD often experience and remember situations through a highly emotional lens, and are convinced that their feelings equal facts. So they may tell their own emotional truth, which may have little or no relationship to the actual truth.

In other cases, people with BPD embellish the truth, and then, over time, further embellish it and/or start to believe it themselves.

Folks with BPD may also tell lies for the same reason the rest of us sometimes do: to make themselves look better, to dodge a negative consequence, or to avoid admitting to making a mistake. (Remember, to someone with BPD, making a mistake means *being* a mistake.)

Self-Absorption

While 16 to 39 percent (depending on the estimate) of people with BPD also have narcissistic personality disorder, many folks with only BPD can also act self-absorbed at times. They may frequently bring the focus of attention back to themselves. Two common ways they may do this are complaining vigorously of an illness (which may be real, exaggerated, or imaginary) or acting inappropriately in public.

Testing Your Love

Since people with BPD can't accept that you really care about them—or don't understand why you or anyone would—they may routinely test your love by acting out in a way that will displease, anger, or harm you. Then they take note of what you do in response. According to the highly emotional logic of BPD, if they do something terrible to you, and you accept it without complaining or becoming upset, that shows that you care about them. But if you respond in the way that most people would, by expressing your anger or displeasure, that means that you don't really have positive feelings for them.

For example, you and your loved one agree to meet for lunch at noon at Jane's Café. You get there at 11:56; they show up at 1:02, over an hour late. Their logic goes like this: if you genuinely love them, you should forgive them for their lateness, and be willing to put aside all your own desires and concentrate solely on fulfilling their needs. Adolescents and adult children with BPD are especially likely to do these "love tests," because they know that their parents will probably put up with these tests out of fear, obligation, and guilt.

But if you are given these "love tests," you lose either way. If you fail the test by becoming irritated or angry, firmly holding a personal boundary, or holding the person with BPD accountable, they may feel that you have confirmed your lack of love for them. You will also have confirmed their own unworthiness to be loved by anyone. But if you pass the test by tolerating their unfair action, they may simply escalate their behavior next time—for example, by showing up for your next scheduled lunch *two* hours late. Then, when you finally blow up in anger, you become the bad guy, and they become the victim.

You may be wondering, "What kind of test is this? No matter what happens, we both fail!" You're right. It doesn't make any sense to someone without BPD. But it makes perfect sense in the borderline world.

Projecting Their Own Unwanted Traits on Others

Because they lack a clear sense of who they are, and because they feel empty and inherently defective, people with BPD (especially those with the unconventional form of the disorder) often deny their own unpleasant traits, behaviors, or feelings. Then they attribute these traits to someone else—typically their partner, or someone else who cares deeply for them.

Therapist Elyce M. Benham explains that projection is like gazing at yourself in a hand-held mirror. If you think you look ugly, you simply turn the mirror around. Voilà! Now the homely face in the mirror belongs to somebody else.

Sometimes this projection is an exaggeration of something that has a basis in reality. For example, your loved one may accuse you of hating them when actually you just feel irritated at them. Or they may tell you that you're rudely ignoring them, when in fact you've just been temporarily distracted by a centipede scurrying up your pant leg.

However, the projection may also come entirely from your loved one's imagination. They may accuse you of flirting with a salesclerk when you were just asking for directions to the shoe department.

Either way, your loved one's unconscious hope is that, by projecting this unpleasant stuff onto you, they will feel better about themselves. And they *do* feel better, for a few minutes, or even a few hours. But soon enough, the pain comes back. So they have to play the projection game again and again.

Remember, this projection might not only be unjustified; it might make no logical sense at all. As one woman with BPD explained, "I hate myself so much I can barely see straight. When I am drowning in hate, it floods over everyone and everything, and I feel so justified for feeling such loathing toward everyone—mostly my husband. He seems so utterly disgusting, so pitifully stupid."

Viewing the World in a Childlike Way

At times, your loved one's view of the world can seem very childlike. In fact, all of the patterns of thinking, feeling, and acting that we've discussed— splitting, fears of abandonment and engulfment, identity issues, demands for control, projection, the manipulation of others, and a lack of empathy—all correspond to particular developmental stages in normal children. Many experts say that, in terms of emotional development, people with BPD are two years old.

In his model of psychodevelopment, Erik Erikson says that the first stage a newborn human being goes through involves learning what and whom to trust and what and whom to mistrust. The second stage, which occurs between eighteen months to three years, is about autonomy vs. shame and doubt. During this second stage, children learn self-control and desire more independence. People with BPD are still struggling with some of the normal tasks of these two initial stages.

One woman with BPD put it this way: "I definitely feel like a child! People say to me, 'Grow up.' They accuse me of being a crybaby and having temper tantrums. Do they think I want to act this way? Do they think it's fun to have your emotions rule you? Do they really believe I can mature twenty years in minutes? You wouldn't ask that from a real two-year-old, so don't ask that from me, either."

Bipolar Disorder Vs. Borderline Personality Disorder

Bipolar disorder and *borderline personality disorder* are two mental illnesses that can cause significant pain and suffering in someone's life. Despite being commonly talked about together, they are two distinct disorders with different diagnostic criteria and significantly different treatments. Bipolar disorder is a mood disorder, while BPD is a personality disorder.

People with bipolar disorder sometimes appear to be depressed, and they experience lengthy and profound episodes of depression (much like people with major depression). They feel sad, lose interest in activities, feel worthless, and have difficulty with concentration and focus. A person with bipolar disorder also experiences episodes of mania, which is characterized by impulsive behavior, an elevated mood, heightened energy without the need to sleep, and racing and/or grandiose thoughts.

It's true that people with borderline personality disorder typically have unstable moods and depression. But BPD is not defined by changes in mood. Also, the mood shifts in people with BPD are related to the things going on in their life, while the cycles of mania and depression in bipolar disorder do not depend on external events.

Another difference is that bipolar cycles are slow, often measured in months or even years, while borderline mood shifts can occur in a split second. Furthermore, bipolar disorder involves only mania and depression. In contrast, with BPD, *all* emotions go up and down. Anger, jealously, happiness, and other emotions are felt very intensely.

Because the mood swings in BPD are relational and situational, clinicians used to believe that the disorder is not as serious or disabling as depression or bipolar disorder. We now know otherwise, of course. We also know that BPD is more common than bipolar disorder and schizophrenia combined.

The treatments for BPD and bipolar disorder are very different. People with bipolar disorder usually require medication to get better. But there is no medication that treats the core of BPD. Rather, three classes of medication (antidepressants, mood stabilizers, and small doses of antipsychotic medications) are used to treat certain symptoms of BPD, such as impulsivity and mood swings.

The Borderline Family

When there is an addict in a family, it is common for the entire family system to eventually organize itself, in a deeply unhealthy way, around the addict and their addiction. In similar fashion, when a family includes someone with BPD, eventually everything that family does may revolve around the person with BPD and their thoughts, feelings, actions, and demands. In the process, the legitimate needs of other children and adults may get sacrificed. Family members may lose a bit more of their self-awareness and boundaries each day, until they don't who they are anymore.

At the center of this family system is the person with BPD, who is desperate for attention and emotional relief. They believe that someone else holds the key to their happiness, because they can't be happy alone. They need someone else to *make* them happy. They can't soothe themselves, calm themselves down, or deal with anxiety, anger, or other feelings without someone else there to take the blame, comfort them, or make everything all better. In this quest to feel better, they may manipulate everyone else in the family.

Here is how one woman with BPD (who has since recovered from the disorder) described how she dealt with other family members:

> *Often I realize my motivations only after the incident is over. Once, I was so upset that my husband was ignoring me at Christmas that, right in front of him, I began destroying all the gifts he had just given me. My husband stopped me as I was about to rip apart the gift I loved most: a book of love poetry. When I saw the book, it dawned on me that I never would have ruined it. I was more interested in seeing my husband try to stop me. If I had been living alone, the whole episode would never have happened. So why did I do it? The answer was ugly and harsh, shameful and disgusting. Manipulation. I felt deeply ashamed.*

Although [people with BPD] can be apparently manipulative, they don't think about the behavior as such. They're trying to meet their needs in the only way they know how. Somebody has to relieve their anger or anxiety or distress or sense of impending annihilation right now. They are trying to elicit a response to soothe them, to help them feel better.

—Larry J. Siever, MD

Borderline Personality Disorder in Men

According to a 2008 study—and our experience—half of the people with BPD are male, and half are female. The commonly held view that most people with the disorder are women is simply incorrect.

From an early age, many men are taught not to have (or not to express) emotions other than anger. As a result, most men with BPD aren't equipped to deal with the intensity of their emotions, their mood swings, or the long time it takes them to calm down. Many don't have friends they can talk to about any of this. And the great majority of men with BPD don't seek treatment. Is it any wonder, then, that BPD rage is often more explosive in men than in women?

This rage often results in men with BPD having encounters with law enforcement—and sometimes in their going to jail. Unfortunately, men with BPD are often misdiagnosed—or not diagnosed at all, but simply dismissed as abusers, murderers, violent offenders, perps, or creeps. When a woman who has just been abandoned for another woman kills her ex-partner and then herself, clinicians often think, *She probably had BPD*. But when a man does the same thing, clinicians tend to forget the suicide. They call the crime domestic violence, brand the man a murderer, and leave it at that.

Studies have demonstrated a clear gender bias in BPD diagnoses. When clinicians were given information about a sample patient named Chris, and were told that Chris was female, they were significantly more likely to diagnose her with BPD than when the same patient, with the same name and the identical history, was identified as male.

Differences Between Men and Women with BPD

The following attributes are more common in men with BPD than in women with the disorder:

- Substance abuse

- Unstable relationships

- A combination of BPD and narcissistic personality disorder

- A combination of BPD and antisocial personality disorder (i.e., sociopathy)

- Impulsivity

- Aggression (even after controlling for differing levels of the trait by gender)

These attributes are more common in women with BPD than in men with the disorder:

- A history of being in therapy

- Eating disorders

- Anxiety disorders

- PTSD

- A major mood disorder, such as depression or bipolar disorder

- Taking medication for a mental disorder

Real-World Types of BPD

People with BPD vary a great deal, but there is no consensus among researchers as to how to classify them into different categories. For helping family members, I group people with BPD into two general types with a gray area in the middle. First, the **conventional type** of borderline individual usually self-harms and may be suicidal. They welcome treatment. They may have a tough time keeping a job and often have a co-occurring disorder like an eating disorder or bipolar.

People with the other type, which I call the **unconventional type**, deny their pain and project it onto targets of blame, the people closest to them. Although they also feel shame, fear and low self-worth, they bury it deep and criticize and blame everyone else for their problems. They are never accountable, can keep a job like anyone else, almost never seek help, and do not self-harm or attempt suicide. Most of the readers of this book will have a family member of the unconventional type.

TWO TYPES OF BORDERLINE PERSONALITY DISORDER

	Conventional Type	*Unconventional Type*
How people with BPD deal with emotional pain	*Acting in:* Destructive toward self	*Acting out:* Destructive toward others
Willingness to obtain help	Yes	No
Co-occuring mental health issues	Bipolar, eating disorders	Narcissistic personality disorder
Functioning (ability to be independent)	Low ability	High ability
Impact on family members	Caretaking their BPD relative	Dealing with abuse

CHAPTER 3

Making Sense of the Narcissist

Narcissists are forced to define themselves based on the expectations, likes, and dislikes of others. Rather than relying on an internal sense of being good enough, narcissists are stuck seeking approval and reassurance. Without constant infusions of praise or flattery, their [sense of superiority and entitlement] becomes weak and unstable. The house built over the bottomless pit starts to creak and the floor begins to feel dangerously thin.

—Mark Ettensohn, *Unmasking Narcissism: A Guide to Understanding the Narcissist in Your Life*

You may be asking yourself, "Why is there a chapter on narcissistic personality disorder in a book on BPD?" Good question.

You'll recall from earlier in this book that clinicians used to define the traits of BPD by looking at the people in the mental health system who had been diagnosed with the disorder. This turned out to be misleading, because the overwhelming majority of these folks have the conventional form of BPD.

In 2008, a team of researchers discovered that the people with BPD in hospitals and clinics were by no means a representative sample of all people with BPD. In fact, they are only a small minority.[*]

Instead of evaluating people inside the mental health system, the researchers behind this study went out into the community and conducted face-to-face interviews with 35,000 people. Among many other findings, they discovered that about 5.9 percent of people have BPD—not 2 percent, as was claimed in the DSM since the 1990s. Where did these extra people with BPD come from? They were the people with unconventional BPD. Almost all had not been formally diagnosed, and almost all were not in the mental health system. Most were men. And for every person with conventional BPD, there were about two with the unconventional form.

The researchers also discovered that nearly 40 percent of the people who have BPD *also* have narcissistic personality disorder. Put another way, if your loved one has BPD and is not currently in treatment for it, there is roughly a 40 percent chance that they have NPD as well. (If your loved one is male, that percentage is slightly higher, because about 65 percent of people who have NPD are male.)

So it's important that we take a closer look at NPD. We'll start by examining NPD as a whole. Then we'll look more closely at specific traits, in the same way as we did with BPD in chapter 2.

Healthy Vs. Unhealthy Narcissism

We all need some narcissistic traits in order to keep getting up after the world knocks us down again and again. Think of the politician who loses a big race, only to run again two years later, or the actress whose latest movie was a bomb, so she makes her own indie film. Healthy narcissism helps us through difficult times and helps make us more resilient.

Narcissistic personality disorder crosses the line from healthy function to dysfunction. Someone with NPD inhabits a different reality from most people. In this alternate reality, they were born to be a metaphorical king or queen, and they give little or no thought to the lives of the peasants who work the land, keep their belly filled, and warm their bed at night.

---

[*] For an overview of this study, go to https://www.ncbi.nlm.nih.gov/pubmed/1842 6259; to read the full study, visit https://www.ncbi.nlm.nih.gov/pmc/articles/PMC26 76679/. These important results closely parallel the focus group research that Randi has done over the past 22 years.

Essential NPD Concepts and Terms

False Self (sometimes called *The Mask*): Like folks with BPD, most people with NPD cover up their feelings of inadequacy, worthlessness, and shame by projecting these unwanted traits onto others. But people with NPD also go a step further. They need to be much more than *not* inadequate, bad, or worthless. *They need to be better than everyone else.* To do this, they construct a False Self. This is like a Superman mask that covers up everything shameful about them. But after someone with NPD puts on the mask, over time (and to varying degrees) they forget it's a mask. They believe in, and buy in to, their own False Self. But this False Self is like Tinkerbell: once people stop believing in the False Self, it can metaphorically get sick and die.

This is why someone with NPD can *never* make a mistake, never admit to making one, never be held accountable for anything, and never admit that you (or anyone else) can ever do anything better than they can. This False Self is one reason why it's so hard to get someone with NPD to go to treatment—or, for that matter, to change in any way. If you felt that you had to choose between believing that you're a superhero and feeling that you're worthless—and that you need to closely examine your own pain— which would you choose?

Narcissistic Supply: In the same way that an automobile runs on gas, and all human beings run on food and water, people with NPD run on what is called *narcissistic supply*. Because narcissists are unable to provide themselves with self-esteem, they require a regular supply of esteem from others. This ongoing narcissistic supply is essential to keeping their False Selves inflated and strong.

Examples of narcissistic supply include admiration, praise, attention, being envied, having an impressive title, owning expensive things, special treatment, adulation, being feared, approval, affirmation, respect, applause, celebrity status, sexual conquest, awards, and any other means of being viewed as special or the top dog.

Narcissistic Injury: When, for any reason, the narcissistic supply stops flowing, or the person with NPD is blamed or criticized for something, the result is a *narcissistic injury*. The relevant event, action, inaction, utterance, or thought threatens to expose them by blowing up the mask of their False Self. This narcissistic injury triggers their feelings of deep vulnerability, shame, and inadequacy.

Common narcissistic injuries include losing a partner, a job, or a dispute in court. Even losing an argument, or making an ordinary and readily forgivable mistake, can be a source of narcissistic injury for someone with NPD. Divorce can be a major narcissistic injury, which is why so many narcissists act like bullies in court, taking revenge on their soon-to-be ex-spouses, and putting their children into the middle of the dispute.

Narcissistic Rage: Narcissistic rage and borderline rage are similar. Unlike normal anger, this rage is usually unreasonable, out of proportion to the precipitating event, and intensely aggressive (or passive-aggressive). Reactions include intense outbursts of anger, simmering resentment, the silent treatment, and/or cutting sarcasm. The more humiliated or embarrassed the person with NPD feels, the more extreme their rage is likely to be.

Now let's look at the ways in which folks with NPD tend to think, feel, and act.

COMMON NPD THOUGHTS, FEELINGS, AND ACTIONS

THOUGHTS	They believe they are superior, entitled, special, and above the law.
	They fantasize about a perfect world in which they are even more superior and entitled.
FEELINGS	They can't put themselves in anyone else's shoes. They can't empathize with anyone but themselves.
	They need admiration from morning until night, because the moment that admiration goes away, the underlying shame and sense of worthlessness threaten to seep in from the edges.
ACTIONS	They routinely use other people as pawns to get what they want.
	They simply don't care whether they hurt others—and have no interest in helping them.
	They act arrogantly toward "lesser life forms" such as you and everyone else.

Let's zoom in for a closer look at some of these traits. As you did in chapter 2, take note of which ones, if any, remind you of your loved one.

A Strong Sense of Superiority and Entitlement

Narcissists are full of self-importance. They are absolutely convinced that they are superior to others, and so should be entitled to have anything and everything they want. They want two scoops of ice cream when others have one—and they want to make sure that no one else gets two. They want a red Ferrari—and, when they drive it, they know that the rules of the road only apply to the unspecial people, not to them. They only want to involve themselves with other superior people, and with the clubs, organizations, and institutions that cater to them.

To shore up their sense of superiority, people with NPD often lie about or exaggerate who they are, what they have done or achieved, what positions they have held, and what accolades they have received.

A narcissist's sense of entitlement is not the same as healthy self-esteem (sometimes called *self-worth* or *self-regard*). A person's healthy self-esteem honors who they are and fosters a belief that they deserve good (but not necessarily special) things in life. We build our sense of self-esteem through accomplishments that are the result of our hard work, effort, and dedication.

In contrast, someone with NPD has a sense of entitlement that has nothing to do with work, effort, or accomplishment. They are like a toddler who never learned that they are not the center of the world. This is why, like a small child, they become enraged when their immediate demands aren't met. If other people don't hop to fulfill their needs, they need to exact retribution. People with NPD often act in an arrogant, haughty way, especially to people they consider "beneath" them, like restaurant servers and retail clerks.

Here are three stories that highlight the superiority that folks with NPD feel:

Sam, Who Was Married to Someone with NPD

My ex Sarah believed herself to be above everyone in Chicago after living in the suburb of Skokie. When I met her, she told me she had been the creative director at a big advertising agency, her children had attended Ivy League universities, and she had jet-stetted with celebrities. She said she was superior in her breeding, background, and culture.

After a few months, I found out she had been only an assistant production intern and had heavily used cocaine and amphetamines. Before she met me, she had been a stay-at-home mom for 15 years...

Katie, Whose Former Boyfriend Had NPD

When he was feeling good about himself, then he would act as if I wasn't good enough and that he needed to move on. He would say things like, "I don't know if you are what I want. I guess I'll never know. I think I want more and I know there are a lot of other girls that express their interest in me. Maybe I should be dating them."...I would say, "That's fine; if that is how you feel, I will walk away." But when I would say that, then he would turn around and say, "No, I don't want to lose you." It was all a game. When I stopped playing I became "evil."

Robbie, Whose Former Girlfriend Had NPD

She only wanted to associate with people she deemed "spiritual" and more "conscious" than most people. Her friends had "higher-up" jobs that she could benefit from, like attending cool parties, gatherings, workshops, poetry readings, etc.

A Lack of Empathy

People with NPD can't put themselves in your—or anyone's—shoes. They can't imagine how you would feel about anything—even the death of someone you loved. This lack of empathy is a central hallmark of NPD in the same way that a fear of abandonment is central to BPD. Do not expect someone with NPD to listen to, commiserate with, or emotionally support you, whether in a crisis or in an ordinary conversation.

This lack of empathy feels deeply foreign to most of us. After all, even many animals show evidence of empathy. But it is a standard part of the NPD package. You may not realize just how deep it goes until you really need the support of your loved one—if, for example, your close relative dies, or you get seriously ill—and they complain that your tragedy is diminishing *their* life.

This lack of empathy also means that someone with NPD has no capacity for intimacy. This is a hard message to take in, we know. But we encourage you to become honest about what's *not* beneath your loved one's veneer of superiority. There is no potentially loving, caring person inside, waiting to be released.

Here is what some people have said about a lack of empathy in their loved ones with NPD:

Ruth, Whose Sister Had NPD

I could spend an hour detailing how I felt hurt and she would sit there, cold as ice. When it was her turn to speak, she tore down every word that came out of my mouth until I had to apologize for expressing how I felt. I ignored this red flag and made excuses to myself and others.

Randy, Whose Former Boyfriend Had NPD

My partner would...tell me I'm wrong for feeling the way I did, and if I didn't like it there was something wrong with me.

Narcissists do not consider the pain they inflict on others; nor do they give any credence to others' perceptions. They simply do not care about thoughts and feelings that conflict with their own. Do not expect them to listen to, validate, understand, or support you.

—Les Parker, PhD

This is not to say that someone with NPD can't give you a showy gift on the right occasion. They may even be able to mimic the things people typically say when they are empathizing. But it's all for show; it's not real.

An Ongoing Need for Admiration and Attention

If someone with NPD doesn't get enough admiration and attention, they feel like they will wither away, like a vase of flowers in a hot closet. Often they respond to this lack of narcissistic supply by lashing out at others.

Here are two stories of this common NPD behavior:

Tom, Whose Former Girlfriend Had NPD

My ex-girlfriend constantly needed to be acknowledged, adored, and admired. She would get mad at me if I didn't call her each morning on my way to work and on the way home (we didn't live together), yet she would also get upset because she said it felt like pressure for me to call her. She said, "I don't want to have to answer, but I want you to call and at least leave a message because I need to know that I matter." The same thing occurred with her wanting me to text her all the time. If I didn't respond to her texts within a few minutes, she would text again and say, "Did you get my text?"

Nedimah, Whose Father Had NPD

At my wedding, my father refused to speak to me because there wasn't enough attention paid to him as father of the bride. Then he enlisted the rest of the family to participate in his woundedness. When I got back from my honeymoon, my brother accused me of telling the photographer not to take pictures of my half-siblings. Of course, I'd done no such thing; I had plenty of pictures of them. But my father had told everyone that this was what I'd done.

Compulsive Fantasizing

People with NPD routinely indulge in fantasies of unlimited success, power, brilliance, beauty, or ideal love. This is partly how they fend off inner emptiness, feel special and in control, and avoid feelings of defectiveness and insignificance.

We all fantasize, of course—but most of us can easily discern fantasy from reality. Folks with NPD often walk—or cross—the line between magical thinking and reality. And once they cross it, they may present their fantasy as reality to others, *gaslighting* them. (Gaslighting is a form of emotional abuse that is seen in many abusive relationships. It involves manipulating a person by forcing them to question their own thoughts and memories, and the events occurring around them. A victim of gaslighting can be pushed so far that they question their own sanity. The term *gaslighting* comes from a 1938 play and films released in 1940 and 1944, called *Gas Light*.)

Here is how one woman described this behavior:

Yuko, Whose Husband Had NPD

Before my husband went into therapy, he frequently based our plans on fantasy scenarios of sudden wealth (winning the Lotto) rather than on a realistic in-the-here-and-now plan. In terms of our relationship, he had built up a happy-ever-after scenario that had no basis in reality. He had himself so convinced of the happy-ever-after scenario that he wasn't even able to hear me when I expressed the need for the trust/honesty issues between us to be addressed.

Narcissists are actors playing a part. They are expert liars, and, even worse, they believe their own lies. Practiced in dishonesty, they can't tell the difference between their own version of truth and a falsehood. They may take the past and rearrange it to make themselves look good. They rarely if ever admit fault, and they never say they're sorry.

—Rokelle Lerner, author of *The Object of My Affection Is in My Reflection: Coping with Narcissists*

Exploiting Others

Folks with NPD routinely take advantage of others. A person with NPD will readily stiff a house painter, tree trimmer, piano tuner, or other small business owner who doesn't have the resources to take them to court. They might date someone else just to make their partner jealous. And they might park in a space reserved for the handicapped to save themselves a few steps.

They also don't appreciate what others do for them. In fact, if you are generous, or have a caretaking personality, they may treat you the worst.

Here are some examples of this exploitation:

Annika, Whose Former Boyfriend Had NPD

My boyfriend James broke into my house while I was at work. When I got home, the house was ransacked. I immediately called him about the mess; he said yes, it was him, and if I had a problem with it then I should call the police.

LeJohn, Whose Wife Has NPD

Although our family doesn't have a lot of money, my wife Sheila bought herself expensive silk dresses and pearl earrings. She had unnecessary plastic surgery that was not covered by insurance. When I dared to question it, she lied about canceling the surgery.

Abbie, Whose Husband Has NPD

My husband Dan tried to convince me that he shouldn't have to warm up dinner himself when he gets home late, so I shouldn't go out at night with the kids.

Low Emotional Development

You'll recall from chapter 2 that, in terms of emotional development, folks with BPD are stuck at Erik Erikson's second stage, which involves autonomy vs. shame and doubt, and which occurs sometime between 18 months and three years. People with NPD are stuck at a somewhat later stage, which Erikson describes as industry vs. inferiority, and which normally occurs in children ages 6-11.

At this stage, kids learn to develop a sense of proficiency, morality, and confidence. However, children who have not fully developed through the earlier stages—i.e., they have not developed trust, initiative, and an ability to learn autonomously—will grow to doubt their ability to be successful. If they are not supported by caring adults at this stage, they may develop low self-esteem, culminating in a strong sense of inferiority.

This is also the age when children learn how to express their feelings and control their urges without direct supervision. They should be able to comprehend the consequences of their actions, understand their feelings, show empathy, and offer help when they see someone in distress. These are precisely the things that adults with NPD struggle with.

Except for rage, folks with NPD have shallow emotional lives because so much must remain hidden, both from themselves and from others. This shallowness makes them hard to get to know, because there doesn't seem to be much of a real person beneath the façade. This is the opposite of most people with BPD, who feel and express a very wide range of emotions.

People who have both BPD and NPD can exhibit *both* sets of traits. Think of a layer cake. Each layer of icing might be BPD, while each layer of cake is NPD. In other words, the traits exist side by side, but do not blend together. When two traits are in opposition—for example, people with BPD have intense emotions and those with NPD have shallow ones—one disorder usually predominates, and that tends to determine which traits most often present themselves. That said, each individual's personality is unique.

Fear of Public Exposure

To someone with NPD, public exposure of their hidden shame is terrifying and intolerable. So they do two things: they lie, withdraw, misdirect, and make wild accusations of others in order to avoid this exposure, and they project their shame onto others.

The Two Types of NPD

Narcissistic personality disorder takes two fairly distinct forms: *grandiose narcissism* and *vulnerable* (or *covert*) *narcissism*. Let's examine each one.

The Grandiose Narcissist

A grandiose narcissist comes across as highly confident and self-assured. They *know* for an absolute fact that they're superior. They will seek revenge upon, or go into a rage against, anyone who gives them *any* negative feedback or fails to treat them with respect. They care little about relationships and a great deal about power and control. Despite their deep, hidden shame, they often act shamelessly.

Think of the CEO who gets rid of thousands of employees, vetoes raises for most of the others, insists that these decisions increase shareholder value, takes credit for saving the company millions of dollars, and then demands a huge raise for themself. Think of the politician who spends six figures on redecorating their office, uses government funds for private trips, and accepts campaign contributions in exchange for tailoring legislation to benefit the donors' industry.

When faced with a narcissistic injury, a grandiose narcissist will insist that they are utterly blameless and perfect—and then launch a vicious, no-holds-barred counterattack. They will try to straight-on annihilate anyone or anything they perceive as a potential threat.

> *The key with grandiosity (seeing yourself as more important than other people) is to respond instead of react. When you respond, you give yourself space to take in what is happening and choose the best way to proceed. Narcissists are incapable of responding in a thoughtful and balanced manner when they are feeling insecure. That's because such feelings threaten to destabilize their false self. Your task is to do what the narcissist cannot.*

> *Take a chance and step into your own vulnerability. Allow yourself to feel the bad feelings that the narcissist's grandiose behavior is triggering in you. If you are able to hold these feelings and not react to them, you'll be able to see that they really belong to the narcissist. The narcissist has given you their bad feelings of not being good, important, or lovable. By giving you these bad feelings, the narcissist is communicating something that he could never explicitly say. Once you've seen this, you can make a choice of how to respond.*
>
> —Mark Ettensohn, *Unmasking Narcissism*

The Vulnerable Narcissist

A vulnerable narcissist differs from a grandiose narcissist in three significant ways:

1. A vulnerable narcissist is typically less obvious about their narcissism. Rather than declare themselves "perfect" or "the best," they may simply radiate self-confidence and competence. If you point out that their shoe is untied, they are more likely to bend down and tie it than angrily accuse you of trying to make them look stupid. Their narcissism may become apparent only over time.

2. Unlike a grandiose narcissist, who will respond to criticism and failure by simply lashing out, a vulnerable narcissist may have a genuine emotional reaction. When faced with a narcissistic injury, they may feel humiliated, degraded, or empty. They may withdraw socially and weave a narrative about how they have been victimized, again and again. They can become seriously depressed by criticism or failure.

3. Vulnerable narcissists are often passive-aggressive. They may enthusiastically agree to something you propose, then do exactly the opposite once your back is turned. They may make and break promises, procrastinate, act sullen, or be very stubborn.

We don't yet know what causes either type of NPD, although it appears that both genetic and environmental causes are involved. As in people with BPD, folks with NPD appear to have differences in important areas of the brain. With BPD, we see differences in the part of the brain involving emotions. With NPD, the differences are in the part involving empathy.

Treating NPD

Most—but not all—people with NPD will never get better. They will stay exactly the same way for the rest of their lives, no matter what anyone else says or does.

That said, some folks with NPD do recover or improve. At least one form of treatment has proven effective for some people with the disorder. Wendy Behary is a top expert in the field, the author of the book *Disarming the Narcissist*, and a specialist in schema therapy, a therapy developed specifically for people with NPD. Behary maintains that only a carefully structured therapy such as schema therapy can poke a hole in the defenses of someone with NPD.

Behary also strongly believes that for a person with NPD to enter therapy, there must be a very serious and very painful consequence for not going. For example, they must know that if they don't go, their partner will leave them, or their parents will disown them, or they will lose their job. (Furthermore, that consequence *must* be implemented if the person with NPD chooses to not go to therapy.)

Also, going to therapy and doing the work it requires are two different things. Many people with NPD try to charm and/or humiliate therapists, or convince them that the problems lie with other people. Because therapists are fallible human beings, sometimes the folks with NPD succeed. For therapy to be successful, the person with NPD must also be willing to take off their mask in front of the therapist—which might mean becoming temporarily overwhelmed with feelings of worthlessness, shame, emptiness, and loneliness.

In addition, the therapist must be extremely skilled, very confident, and sharp enough not to succumb to a narcissist's attempts to woo, charm, or humiliate them. Lastly, your loved one will need to remain in therapy, and do hard work, for years. Undoing the patterns of a lifetime requires serious effort.

Where BPD and NPD Converge—and How They Differ

Because many people with BDP also have NPD, it can be difficult to disentangle the two, especially when someone has the unconventional form of BPD. This disentangling is often part of a therapist's job.

That said, we've provided two checklists that can help you make a tentative determination about whether your loved one has NPD, unconventional BPD, both NPD and unconventional BPD, both NPD and conventional BPD, or neither. The first checklist looks at similarities, the second at differences.

Similarities Between People with Unconventional BPD and Those with NPD

- Both rely on other people to manage functions that most of us are able to manage ourselves. (People with BPD look to others to manage their moods; people with NPD want others to prop up their low self-esteem.)

- Both live in alternate realities in which feelings create facts.

- Both project their "badness" onto other people, who become their target of blame.

- Both blame everybody but themselves. Neither will admit that they were wrong or made a mistake.

- Neither will take responsibility for their words and actions.

- Both can be critical and judgmental—and both have to be right at all times.

- Both may carry grudges, see themselves as victims, and expect loved ones to throw them a pity party.

- Both are unwilling to listen to what they don't want to hear.

- Both may become exceedingly jealous over little or nothing.

- Both feel a great deal of shame, which they cover over with layers of self-deception.

- Both often lie.

- Both try to control other people and their environment in order to feel safe. People with BPD use that control to maintain their emotional stability; people with NPD use it to prop up their self-esteem.

- Both are exquisitely sensitive to stimuli that can trigger hot-button issues, and lots of drama.

- Both need plenty of attention.

- Both are so busy getting their own needs met that they have little energy left for others.

- Both have stunted emotional development. People with BPD are at about age two; people with NPD are at about age six.

- Both are still struggling with issues that most people master in childhood.

- Both are impervious to logic when they are triggered.

- Both can be emotionally and verbally abusive.

- Both have unstable or impaired relationships, which involve criticism and blame, and which often end with forcing the other person to leave.

- Both may use manipulative or coercive techniques such as gaslighting, the silent treatment, emotional blackmail, unreasonable expectations, and magical thinking.

- Both see things in black or white, with no shades of gray.

Most Significant Differences Between People with BPD (Either Conventional or Unconventional) and Those with NPD

Borderline Personality Disorder	Narcissistic Personality Disorder
The person's major issue is a fear of abandonment	The person's major issue is feeding their ego through narcissistic supply
Their emotions are very variable and very intense	Their emotions are shallow, except for rage
Fear of both abandonment and engulfment	A pervasive sense of grandiosity
Suicidal thoughts; self-harm	A sense that they are entitled to the best of everything, and that they do not have to follow the rules that others do
Outwardly exhibits feelings of abandonment, woundedness, and vulnerability	A tendency to exploit others
Dissociation	An exaggerated sense of importance
An unstable sense of self	A strong sense of superiority
Chronic feelings of emptiness	No empathy for others
May have a genuine interest in other people	Does not try to get to know others, except to exploit, impress, or manipulate them

CHAPTER 4

Living in a Pressure Cooker: How BPD Behavior Affects You

Living with someone who has BPD is like living in a pressure cooker with thin walls and a faulty safety valve.

Living with someone who has BPD is like living in a perpetual oxymoron. It's a seemingly endless host of contradictions.

I feel like I've been through the spin cycle on a washing machine. The world is whirling around, and I have no idea which way is up, down, or sideways.

—From the Welcome to Oz family member
support community at www.BPDCentral.com

Filled with self-loathing, people with BPD may:

- accuse others of hating them

- become so critical and easily enraged that people eventually want to leave them

- blame others and put themselves in the role of victim

BPD is not infectious. It is not like the measles. But people who are exposed to these behaviors can unwittingly become an integral part of the dynamics. Friends, partners, and family members usually take these behaviors personally and feel trapped in a toxic cycle of guilt, self-blame, depression, rage, denial, isolation, and confusion. They try to cope in ways that do not work long-term or that even make the situation worse.

Meanwhile, your loved one's unhealthy behaviors are reinforced because you accept responsibility for the feelings and actions that belong to them.

In this chapter, we'll discuss some common ways you may react to BPD behavior. Then we will provide you with questions to help you determine how BPD behavior might affect you personally.

Meanwhile, your loved one's unhealthy behaviors are reinforced because you accept responsibility for the feelings and actions that belong to them.

Common Thinking About BPD

These beliefs do not reflect the thinking of everyone who has a person with BPD in their life. You must judge what is pertinent in your circumstances.

Beliefs and Facts

BELIEF: I am responsible for all the problems in this relationship.

FACT: Each person is responsible for 50 percent of the relationship.

BELIEF: The actions of the person with BPD are all about me.

FACT: The person with BPD's actions result from a complex disorder caused by a combination of biology and environment.

BELIEF: It's my responsibility to solve this person's problems, and if I don't do it, no one else will.

FACT: By trying to take charge of the person with BPD's life, you may be giving them the message that they can't take care of themselves. You're also avoiding the opportunity to change the relationship by focusing on yourself.

BELIEF: If I can convince the person with BPD that I am right, these problems will disappear.

FACT: BPD is a serious disorder that profoundly affects the way people think, feel, and behave. You can't talk someone out of it no matter how persuasive you are.

BELIEF: If I can prove that their accusations are false, they will trust me again.

FACT: Lack of trust is a hallmark of BPD. It has nothing to do with your behavior; it has to do with the way people with BPD view the world.

BELIEF: If you really love someone, you should take their physical or emotional abuse.

FACT: If you love yourself, you won't let people abuse you.

BELIEF: This person can't help having BPD, so I should not hold them accountable for their behavior.

FACT: It's true that your loved one didn't ask to have BPD. But with help, they can learn to control their behavior toward others.

BELIEF: Setting personal limits hurts the person with BPD.

FACT: Setting personal limits is essential for *all* relationships—especially those in which one or both people have BPD.

BELIEF: When I try to do something to help my situation and it doesn't work, I shouldn't give up until it does work.

FACT: You can learn from what hasn't worked and try something new.

BELIEF: No matter what my loved one with BPD does, I should offer them my love, understanding, support, and unconditional acceptance.

FACT: There is a big difference between loving, supporting, and accepting the person and loving, supporting, and accepting their behavior. In fact, if you support and accept unhealthy behavior, you may be encouraging it to continue and perpetuating your own suffering.

Grief Over Borderline Behavior

Many people who are being devalued by someone with BPD cherish clear and powerful memories of the times when their loved one thought they could do no wrong. Some family members say they feel like the person who loved them has died and that someone they do not know has taken over their loved one's body.

One person we interviewed said, "If I had cancer, at least I would die just once. This emotional abuse ensures that I die many, many times and that I will always live on the edge."

Elisabeth Kübler-Ross, author of *Death: The Final Stage of Growth* (1975), outlined five stages of grief, which are appropriate for people who care about someone with BPD. We have adapted these stages to directly address BPD issues.

Denial

People who love someone with BPD tend to make excuses for their loved one's behavior or refuse to believe that their behavior is unusual. The more isolated they are, the greater the chances they will be in denial. This is because without outside input, it's easy to lose your sense of perspective about what is normal. People with BPD can be skillful at convincing others that their behavior is someone else's fault. This can keep you in a continual state of denial.

Anger

Some people respond to angry attacks from their loved one with BPD by fighting back. This is like adding gasoline to a fire.

Others maintain that anger is an inappropriate response to borderline behavior. Some say, "You wouldn't get mad at someone for having diabetes—why would you be angry when they have BPD?"

Feelings don't have IQs. They just are. Sadness, anger, guilt, confusion, hostility, annoyance, frustration—all are normal and to be expected by people faced with borderline behavior. This is true no matter what your relationship is to the person with BPD. This doesn't mean that you should respond to your loved one with

People with BPD can be skillful at convincing others that their behavior is someone else's fault. This can keep you in a continual state of denial.

anger. But it does mean that you need a safe place to vent your emotions and feel accepted, not judged.

Bargaining

This stage is characterized by concessions meant to bring back the "normal" behavior of the person you love. The thinking goes, "If I do what this person wants, I will get what I need in this relationship." We all make compromises in relationships. But the sacrifices that people make to satisfy the people with BPD they care about can be very costly. And the concessions may never be enough. Before long, more proof of love is needed and another bargain must be struck.

Depression

Depression sets in when you realize the true cost of the bargains you've made: loss of friends, family, self-respect, and hobbies. The person with BPD hasn't changed. But you have.

> You need a safe place to vent your emotions and feel accepted, not judged.

Sarah

For three years he told me the problem was me—that my shortcomings ruined everything. And I believed him. I turned my back on some of my good friends because he didn't like them. I rushed home after work because he said he needed me. Then we had a big fight, and now I'm lonely and depressed because I don't have anybody else to turn to.

Dreams die very hard. The child of a borderline parent may spend decades trying to win that parent's love and approval. When nothing seems good enough, it may take years for them to mourn the loss of unconditional parental love they never really had.

Fran

I spent many years grieving for my borderline son when I realized the dreams I had for him might never come true. I began mourning in earnest when my son's therapist asked me what I would do if my son needed to live in a residential facility for the rest of his life. I just started sobbing. The therapist explained that the child I thought I had had died, along with the future I had pictured for him. But when I was done grieving, I would have a new child, and I would have new aspirations for him.

Acceptance

Acceptance comes when you integrate the "good" and "bad" aspects of the person you care about and realize that they are not one or the other, but both. In this stage, many people who love someone with BPD have learned to accept responsibility for their own choices and hold other people accountable for their choices as well. Each can then make their own decisions about the relationship with a clearer understanding of themselves and the person with BPD.

Common Responses to Borderline Behavior

Borderline behavior causes many reactions in loved ones. Some of the more common responses are addressed here.

Bewilderment

Phil

At first everything looks and sounds normal. Then, unexpectedly, strange twists and reversals of reality occur; off-kilter shifts in the time-space continuum hurl me onto the floor as my wife suddenly roars at me for something I can't begin to understand. Suddenly, I realize I've crossed into the Borderline Zone!

Phil is baffled because of a reaction called "impulsive aggression," a core feature of borderline personality disorder. According to *The Essential Family Guide to Borderline Personality Disorder* (2008), by Randi Kreger, coauthor of this book, impulsive aggression is an impulsive, hostile, even violent reaction, triggered by immediate threats of rejection or abandonment paired with frustration. The source of these feelings may be obvious or triggered by something unseen (as it probably was in Phil's case).

Acceptance comes when you integrate the "good" and "bad" aspects of the person you care about and realize that they are not one or the other, but both.

Kreger's colloquial term for impulsive aggression is "border-lion," because it's like a ferocious beast that is spontaneously uncaged when someone with BPD's emotions are so strong and overwhelming they can no longer be contained. The border-lion's "claws" can be turned outward (raging, abusive language, actual physical violence) or inward (self-harm, suicide attempt) (Kreger 2008).

Loss of Self-Esteem

Beverly Engel, in *The Emotionally Abused Woman* (1990), describes the effect of emotional abuse on self-esteem:

> Emotional abuse cuts to the very core of a person, creating scars that may be longer-lasting than physical ones. With emotional abuse, the insults, insinuations, criticism, and accusations slowly eat away at the victim's self-esteem until she is incapable of judging the situation realistically. She has become so beaten down emotionally that she blames herself for the abuse. Emotional abuse victims can become so convinced that they are worthless that they believe that no one else could want them. They stay in abusive situations because they believe they have nowhere else to go. Their ultimate fear is being all alone.

Feeling Trapped and Helpless

The person with BPD's behaviors cause a great deal of anguish, but leaving seems impossible or improbable. You may believe that you are trapped in the relationship because you either feel overly responsible for the safety of your loved one or you feel overly guilty for perhaps "causing" them to feel and behave the way they do. Threats of suicide or harm to others can paralyze people who love someone with BPD and make you feel as if leaving the relationship is too risky.

Withdrawal

You may leave the situation, either emotionally or physically. This could include working long hours, remaining silent for fear of saying something wrong, or terminating the relationship. This may result in the person with BPD feeling abandoned and acting out more intensely. You may leave children alone with your loved one for longer periods of time. If your loved one with BPD acts abusively toward the children, you may not be there to protect them.

Guilt and Shame

Over time, accusations can have a brainwashing effect. You may come to believe that you are the source of all the problems. This is extremely damaging when it happens to children, who look up to their parents and who do not have the capacity to question an adult with BPD's accusations or assumptions.

Parents of people with BPD are also vulnerable to this. They believe that they have been horrible parents when they simply made the same mistakes most parents make. Some parents we interviewed berate themselves endlessly, trying to figure out what they did to cause their children's disorder. When they can't, they conclude that the problem must be biological. But that doesn't take them off the hook either, since they then feel responsible for the child's biological heritage.

"Emotional abuse cuts to the very core of a person, creating scars that may be longer-lasting than physical ones."

Adopting Unhealthy Habits

Excessive drinking, overeating, substance abuse, and other unhealthy habits are typical ways many people, not just people who love someone with BPD, try to cope with stress. Initially, the habits soothe anxiety and stress. As these coping strategies become more habitual and ingrained, they only compound the situation.

Isolation

The unpredictable behavior and moodiness of people with BPD can make friendships difficult. That's because:

- Making excuses or covering up for your loved one's behavior can be so emotionally exhausting that some people find it's not worth the effort to sustain friendships.

- Many people who love someone with BPD say that friends often suggest solutions that are simplistic or unacceptable, which leaves them feeling misunderstood.

- Some say they lose friendships because their friends don't believe them or grow tired of hearing about their struggles.

Frequently, those who love someone with BPD become isolated because their loved one insists that they cut off ties with others. Too often, they comply. Once a person who cares about someone with BPD becomes more isolated, several things can happen:

- They may become more emotionally dependent on their loved one.

- Because they are out of touch with the real world, the outrageousness of BPD behavior may seem normal once there is nothing to compare it to.

- Friends can no longer observe the relationship and talk about unhealthy components of the relationship.

With things bottled up inside, people who love someone with BPD are left to deal with their problems on their own.

Hypervigilance and Physical Illnesses

It is very stressful to be around someone who may berate you at any moment with no visible provocation. In an attempt to gain some control over what appear to be unpredictable behaviors, people who care about someone with BPD often find themselves "on alert." Being on alert requires a heightened sense of arousal both physically and psychologically that, over time, can wear down the body's natural defenses against stress, leading to headaches, ulcers, high blood pressure, and other illnesses.

Adoption of BPD-like Thoughts and Feelings

Caring for someone with BPD often means seeing things in black and white or only looking for all-or-nothing solutions to problems. Moodiness is also extremely common when you care about someone who has BPD—you're often in a good mood when your loved one is up and a bad mood when they're down.

> Being on alert requires a heightened sense of arousal both physically and psychologically that, over time, can wear down the body's natural defenses against stress.

> In a way, the person with BPD takes you with them on a roller-coaster ride. As distressing as this is, it's an opportunity to glimpse what it's like to have BPD.

Codependence

You might perform valiant and heroic acts of kindness, no matter what the price to yourself. In an effort to help the person they love, many people who care about someone with BPD:

- swallow their anger

- ignore their own needs

- accept behavior that most people would find intolerable

- forgive the same transgressions again and again

This is a common trap—especially if the person you love who has BPD had an unhappy childhood and you are trying to make up for it.

Many people who love someone with BPD assume that by subordinating their own needs for the sake of their loved one (or to avoid a fight), they are helping. While these motives are commendable, this actually enables, or reinforces, inappropriate behavior. People with BPD learn that their actions will have few negative consequences; therefore, they have little motivation to change.

Continuing to put up with BPD behavior rarely makes the person with BPD happy. And even if you endure their behavior, your loved one may become isolated because other people won't stand for it. How long will you be able to keep this up? One family member who smoothed things over for years in order to make up for his borderline wife's terrible childhood said, "I was concentrating on not abandoning her, no matter what she did. One day, I realized that, instead, I had abandoned myself."

> Continuing to put up with BPD behavior rarely makes the person with BPD happy.

Dean

I felt like such a failure in this relationship. I thought that if I could just persuade my wife to get the help she needed, everything would be all right. Despite the abuse, I felt like I couldn't leave. How could I abandon someone who'd already suffered so many misfortunes? I thought that if I just tried harder, I could make up for all the abuse she suffered when she was a kid.

This was confirmed to me once when I did try to leave. I'll never forget the look on her face as she told me with big sad eyes that she was happy I came back. "Why are you glad?" I asked. She responded, "Because who else is going to make my life better?" I decided to see a counselor. One day he said to me, "Aren't you being a bit pompous? Who do you think you are, God? You're not God. You are not responsible. And you can't fix this person. Your job is to accept that fact. Live with it. And make the decisions you have to make to live your life."

"You're not God. You are not responsible. And you can't fix this person. Your job is to accept that fact."

Effects on the Relationship

Borderline behaviors such as verbal abuse, perceived manipulation, and defense mechanisms can shatter trust and intimacy. They make the relationship unsafe, because you can no longer feel confident that your deep feelings and innermost thoughts will be treated with love, concern, and care.

Susan Forward and Donna Frazier, in *Emotional Blackmail* (1997), explain that targets of emotional blackmail may become guarded about certain subjects and stop sharing major parts of their lives, such as embarrassing things they've done, frightening or insecure feelings, hopes for the future, and anything that shows they're changing and evolving.

What's left when we must consistently walk on eggshells with someone is superficial small talk, strained silences, and lots of tension. When safety and intimacy are gone from a relationship, we get used to acting. We pretend that we're happy when we're not. We say that everything is fine when it isn't. What used to be a graceful dance of caring and closeness becomes a masked ball in which the people involved are hiding more and more of their true selves.

Targets of emotional blackmail may become very guarded about certain subjects and stop sharing major parts of their lives.

Is This Normal?

It can be very hard to determine what kind of behavior is normal and what isn't. The following questions may help. The more "yes" answers you give, the more we recommend that you take a hard look at how the behavior of the person with BPD in your life might be affecting you.

___ Do people in healthy, happy relationships tell you that they don't understand why you are still putting up with their behavior?

___ Do you try to avoid contact with these people?

___ Do you feel the need to cover up some of their behavior?

___ Have you betrayed other people or told lies to protect your loved one or your relationship with them?

___ Are you becoming isolated?

___ Does the thought of spending time with your loved one give you unpleasant physical sensations?

___ Do you have other possibly stress-related ailments?

___ Has your loved one ever expressed their anger at you by attempting to cause you legal, social, or financial difficulties?

___ Has this happened more than once?

___ Are you becoming clinically depressed? Signs of depression include:

- becoming less interested in normal activities

- taking less pleasure in life

- gaining or losing weight

- having sleep difficulties

- having feelings of worthlessness

- feeling tired all the time

- having trouble concentrating

___   Have you considered suicide? Do you think that friends and
loved ones would be better off without you? (If yes, seek help
immediately.)

___   Have you acted in ways that go against your fundamental
values and beliefs as a result of your relationship with the
person with BPD? Are you no longer able to take a stand for
what you believe in?

___   Are you concerned about the effects of this person's behavior
on children?

___   Have you ever interceded to prevent abuse from occurring?

___   Have you or your loved one ever put each other in physical danger
or in a situation where physical danger was possible or likely?

___   Are you making decisions out of fear, obligation, and guilt?

___   Does your relationship seem to be more about power and control
than kindness and caring?

In part 2 we will give you some steps for getting off the emotional roller
coaster and taking charge of your life.

PART 2

taking back
control of your life

Now that you understand more about the disorder and how it affects you, the next step is to learn specific strategies to successfully manage your life and avoid getting swept up in the chaos all around you. While you can't change the disorder itself or make your family member seek therapy, you do have the power to fundamentally change the relationship.

In the first edition of this book, we described a variety of techniques for effecting change in no particular order. In this edition, we will take you to the next level by using the framework laid out in coauthor Randi Kreger's 2008 book *The Essential Family Guide to Borderline Personality Disorder: New Tools and Techniques to Stop Walking on Eggshells*.

While there is some overlap in the tools themselves, *The Essential Family Guide* prioritizes them to create a step-by-step system that will enable you to organize your thinking, learn specific skills, and focus on what you need to do instead of becoming overwhelmed.

The tools are:

Tool 1: Take good care of yourself: obtaining support and finding community, detaching with love, getting a handle on your emotions, improving self-esteem, mindfulness, laughter, and wellness.

Tool 2: Uncover what keeps you feeling stuck: owning your choices; helping others without rescuing; and handling fear, obligation, and guilt.

Tool 3: Communicate to be heard: putting safety first, handling rage, active listening, nonverbal communication, defusing anger and criticism, validation, and empathetic acknowledging.

Tool 4: Set limits with love: boundary issues, "sponging" and "mirroring," preparing for discussions, persisting for change, and the DEAR (Describe, Express, Assert, and Reinforce) technique.

Tool 5: Reinforce the right behaviors: the effects of intermittent reinforcement.

Keep in mind that the following is not a comprehensive look at the system, which is outlined in the second half of *The Essential Family Guide to Borderline Personality Disorder*. This is just a look at those elements in the revised edition of this book. But it's a great start to get you on track to successfully manage your life and the relationship.

Keep in mind that BPD is a complex disorder and those with it are predictably unpredictable. Customize these strategies for your particular situation. Ideally, find a therapist who can help you personalize and integrate these techniques so they become part of your life.

CHAPTER 5

Making Changes Within Yourself

No one can make you feel inferior without your consent.

—Eleanor Roosevelt

You Can't Make Your Loved One Seek Treatment

Here is the good news: You have a right to all of your opinions, thoughts, and feelings. Good or bad, right or wrong, they make you who you are. And here is the bad news: Everyone else has a right to their opinions, thoughts, and feelings, too. You may not agree with everyone else, and they may not agree with you. But that is okay. It is not your job to convince everyone to see things your way.

It can be frustrating and heartbreaking to watch people you love act in ways that hurt themselves and others. But no matter what you do, you can't control others' behavior. Moreover, it's not your job—unless, of course, the person with BPD in your life is your minor child. Even then, you can only influence the child's behavior—not control it. Your job is:

- to know who you are

- to act according to your own values and beliefs

- to communicate what you need and want to the people in your life

You can always encourage people to do what you want through subtle or blatant rewards and punishments. But it is still their decision how to act.

Reasons for Your Loved One's Denial

It may be obvious to you that the person in your life with BPD needs help. But it may not be obvious to them. For people with BPD, admitting that anything about them is less than perfect, let alone acknowledging that they may have a personality disorder, can send them into a spiral of shame and self-doubt.

Imagine feeling empty, virtually without a self. Now think about admitting that what little self you can recognize has something wrong with it. To many people with BPD, this is like ceasing to exist—a terrifying feeling for anyone.

To avoid this, people with BPD may employ a powerful and common defense mechanism: denial. They may maintain that nothing is wrong with them, despite clear evidence to the contrary. They would rather lose things very important to them—jobs, friends, and family—than lose themselves. (Once you understand this, you will truly appreciate the courage of people with BPD who do seek help.)

Think about something you accomplished that seemed insurmountable. Getting a college degree, perhaps, or losing thirty pounds. Try to remember how your intense desire to achieve this goal made it possible. Now, imagine that your intense need was to avoid this goal. How likely is it that someone else can make you get that degree or lose that weight?

People with BPD may seek to avoid confronting problems other people want them to face. They may ask for help or try to alter their behavior—but not on your schedule. If they change, it will be in their own time and in their own way. In fact, it could be detrimental to force others to admit to having problems before they are ready.

Linda (BP)

Denying our problems is a coping mechanism that helps us borderlines keep the pain and fear under control. The larger the fear, the larger the denial. Please don't try to rip away the denial from borderlines who aren't ready to face the blackness inside. It may be all that's keeping them alive.

So a person with BPD has destroyed a relationship? They move on to the next one and the next one after that and so on and so forth. A person with BPD loses a job over their behavior? They blame the boss and move on to the next one and then the next. They lose custody of their children? It's the damned court system. The fear of change and the fear of the unknown are quite compelling. Thus, denial can be extremely powerful. And in the case of someone with BPD, the fears are so vast, so encompassing, and so overwhelming that denial can be absolute.

When Will Your Loved One Seek Help?

What motivates people with BPD to seek help? In general, people alter their behavior when they believe that the benefits of doing so outweigh the obstacles to change.

The specific catalysts for change, however, vary greatly. For some people, the unbearable emotional turmoil of living with BPD is worse than the fear of change. For others, it is realizing how their behavior is affecting their children. Some face their demons after losing someone important to them because of their behavior.

Rachel Reiland (author of *Get Me Out of Here,* **a memoir about her recovery from BPD).**

As a former borderline, I believe there does have to be some kind of shock or jolt that serves as a catalyst for change. At various times in my life, I was forced into therapy. I didn't have a sincere desire to change; I didn't want to lose something. And that just isn't enough.

My own shock was the look in my four-year-old son's eyes when I lost it and began smacking him until his thighs and face were red. He hadn't done anything wrong. I was beating him for being a kid when I didn't feel like being a mother. And when he initially started bawling, it made me angrier. I hit him harder.

> People alter their behavior when they believe that the benefits of doing so outweigh the obstacles to change.

Ultimately, he stopped crying. And in his eyes, opened wide in terror, I saw the reflections of my own eyes from years ago—reflections I had spent a lifetime running away from.

I couldn't blame what I had done on a husband who wasn't making enough money. I couldn't blame it on a power-hungry boss, bitchy neighbors, or any of the scores of people I was convinced had it in for me. Looking in my son's helpless and horrified eyes, I could see it was me. And I knew that I could no longer live with the person I had become.

You Can't Make Your Family Member Seek Help

According to *The Essential Family Guide to Borderline Personality Disorder: New Tools and Techniques to Stop Walking on Eggshells,* by coauthor Randi Kreger, techniques like crying, pointing out the person's flaws, logic, reasoning, and begging and pleading are counterproductive to motivating someone with BPD to seek therapy. Most of the time, all that results is fault finding and counteraccusations (*You're* the one who needs help, not me!).

Even ultimatums are unhelpful. Apprehensive that their loved one might actually carry out their threat, your loved one may agree to see a therapist, perhaps with the partner or other family members. Therapy, however, goes nowhere. That's because even the best BPD clinicians can't help a patient who doesn't want to be helped.

Once the immediate threat dissipates, they find some reason to drop out of therapy. This is especially likely if the therapist is a good one, skilled at bringing the focus to the person with BPD's core issues instead of reinforcing their feelings of victimhood. However, if the therapist takes everything the person with BPD says at face value without probing further—and this is not uncommon—the therapist may inadvertently reinforce their twisted thinking, making things worse.

What You Can Do

There is nothing wrong with wanting to change the person with BPD in your life. You may be right: he might be a lot happier and your relationship might improve if he sought help for BPD. But in order for you to get off the emotional roller coaster, you will have to give up the fantasy that you can or should change someone else. When you let go of this belief, you will be able to claim the power that is truly yours: the power to change yourself.

Consider a lighthouse. It stands on the shore with its beckoning light, guiding ships safely into the harbor. The lighthouse can't uproot itself, wade out into the water, grab the ship by the stern, and say, "Listen, you fool! If you stay on this path, you may break up on the rocks!"

No, the ship has some responsibility for its own destiny. It can choose to be guided by the lighthouse. Or it can go its own way. The lighthouse is not responsible for the ship's decisions. All it can do is be the best lighthouse it knows how to be.

> For you to get off the emotional roller coaster, you will have to give up the fantasy that you can or should change someone else.

Stop Taking the Person with BPD's Actions Personally

People with BPD tend to see the world in black and white. And they tend to assume everyone else sees things the same way. In the face of this, people who have a consistent sense of their own self-worth have an easier time maintaining their sense of reality. No matter how the person with BPD in their life feels about them at any given moment, these people can be happy and secure in the knowledge that they're neither a goddess nor a demon. Most people, however, need some guidance in staying clear and focused when their loved one with BPD splits.

Alternate Interpretations

People who care about someone with BPD don't usually ask for help when their loved one sings their praises. But it's important to remember that the upside of splitting (idealization) also has its downside (devaluation). This doesn't mean that you should discount the good things your loved one is saying—by all means, enjoy them. But be careful about positive overstatements and exaggerations that are hard to live up to.

Also be cautious about declarations of love and commitment that come too soon, for they may be based on the person with BPD's image of you rather than the real you. It's important to keep your interpretation of things in mind, since the person with BPD's may often be too negative or too idealized.

Sometimes it's not the actual event but the person with BPD's interpretation of that event that prompts splitting. Consider an emergency department physician who treated a child who had been in a bad car accident. He tried to save the child's life, but she was already near death when the paramedics brought her in. Clearly, there is nothing he could have done. The doctor goes to the waiting room and tells the girl's parents that the child has died. The father does not take it well.

"You incompetent fool!" he shouts. "She wasn't badly hurt at all! You should have been able to save her. If our family doctor had been treating her, she would have survived. I'm going to report you to the authorities!"

> Sometimes it's not the actual event but the person with BPD's interpretation of that event that prompts splitting.

Most physicians would realize that the trauma and shock of his daughter's death could cause the father to lash out and blame them. They probably wouldn't take his words personally because they have comforted dozens of grieving relatives and they know this type of reaction is not uncommon. In other words, they would not take responsibility for the father's feelings. They would realize that his reaction had everything to do with the situation and little to do with them.

In this example, the incident that caused the father's response is external, obvious, and dramatic. With BPD, the cause of an argument is not necessarily the actual event but the person with BPD's interpretation of that event. As you probably know, you and the person with BPD may come to very different conclusions about what was said and done. Following are two such examples.

1. Robert says:

I have to work late. I'm really sorry, but I'm going to have to cancel our plans.

Kathryn hears:

I don't want to go out with you this evening because I don't love you anymore. I never want to see you again.

Kathryn says (in either an angry or tearful tone of voice):

How could you! You never loved me! I hate you!

2. Tom says:

I'm so proud of my daughter! Yesterday she hit a home run and won the game. Let's go to a movie tonight to celebrate.

Roxann hears:

I love my daughter more than you. She is talented, and you are not. From now on, I'm going to give all my love and attention to her and ignore you.

Roxann thinks:

He realizes that I'm flawed and defective. So now he's going to leave me. But no, I'm not flawed and defective. Nothing is wrong with me. So he's got to be the defective one.

Roxann says:

No, I don't want to go to a movie! Why don't you ask me what I want to do? You never think of me. You are so incredibly selfish and controlling!

We don't know why Roxann and Kathryn interpreted the men's comments in the ways they did. Perhaps they're afraid of being abandoned. Or perhaps BPD behavior like this is caused by faulty brain chemistry. Thus, although we can see what triggered the behavior—Tom's and Robert's comments—the cause may be unknown.

Triggers Vs. Causes of BPD Behavior

Understanding the difference between causes and triggers of borderline behavior is crucial to taking the behavior less personally. You can trigger borderline behavior quite easily as you go about your day. That doesn't mean, however, that you caused the behavior.

Imagine that you're having a bad day.

Your happy-go-lucky officemate walks in with a big grin on his face. "Wow, what a beautiful day it is today!" he exclaims. "Kind of makes you glad to be alive, doesn't it?"

"Not really," you snarl. "I'm trying to work. Can you keep it down?"

Your officemate triggered your rude retort. But he didn't cause it. If you care about someone

> You can trigger borderline behavior quite easily as you go about your day. That doesn't mean, however, that you caused the behavior.

with BPD, accept that sometimes they will act in ways that make no sense to you. This is something that people with BPD and the more obviously mentally ill have in common. Christine Adamec, author of *How to Live with a Mentally Ill Person* (1996), says:

> Once you begin to accept that a mentally ill person will sometimes behave irrationally, you alleviate some of your own internal stress and strain... [O]nce you do so you can begin to develop more effective coping mechanisms. No longer burdened by the "what-ifs" and "shoulds" in your mind, you can deal with the way things really are. And you seek out what works.

Seek Support and Validation

You may not know anyone else who cares about someone with BPD or has even heard of BPD. So you may have little or no support and no one to do "reality checks" with. For this reason, in 1995 coauthor Randi Kreger created a support community group at www.BPDCentral.com just for family members of someone with BPD called Welcome to Oz. People in the community share their stories and talk about having someone with BPD in their lives. For most of them, it is the first time they have connected with another person in the same situation.

If you care about someone with BPD, accept that sometimes they will act in ways that make no sense to you.

Many members of the group tell us that the list, more than anything else, has enabled them to depersonalize the behavior of the people with BPD in their lives. The stories are so similar—it really sinks in that the behavior is not about them. Many people find this to be a big relief.

Joining a local or internet support group can help you depersonalize the person's behavior. If that isn't possible, perhaps a friend or family member can lend a willing ear and will believe you. It's best to talk with someone who will not feel put in the middle between you and the person with BPD.

Don't Take BPD Behavior Personally

A woman who found out that her borderline husband had been having an affair asked us, "How can I not take it personally when my husband says he has been unfaithful and lying about it for the duration of our marriage? Am I supposed to feel good when he tells me he's going to leave me for her?" We explained that there is a big difference between working through your grief and not taking things personally.

Imagine if you were planning to have your wedding reception at the nicest hall in town, but two days before the wedding, lightning struck the hall and it burned to the ground. When you tried to find another site, you found that every other hall was booked. Naturally, you would be very upset and angry.

But you wouldn't feel personally attacked, as if the lightning bolt knew you and was deliberately trying to make your life miserable. You wouldn't blame yourself for things beyond your control. But that is precisely what many people do when faced with the actions of a person with BPD. They spend years assuming they're the source of the lightning when, in fact, they're only the lightning rod.

Keep a Sense of Humor

Many family members find that having a sense of humor helps.

Hank

It was October, and my wife and I were going to a Halloween party given by my friend, Buck. I was dressed as Charlie Brown, complete with striped shirt and stuffed beagle. She was Lucy. In one hand she carried a football and in the other a sign that said, "Psychiatric Advice, Five Cents." (Ironic, isn't it?)

Buck opened the door, and a terrible realization came over me: this was not a Halloween party! Everyone else had on sweaters and jeans. The three of us—me, my wife, and her friend—all realized my mistake at exactly the same time.

My wife immediately became very angry and started carrying on about how stupid I was. Ordinarily, I would react to her rages and verbal abuse with fear, anxiety, and confusion. This time I just couldn't stop laughing! While my wife raged, the two of us just cracked up. I thought about the episode the next time my wife lost it, and it made me feel better to realize I had a choice about how I was going to react.

Take Care of Yourself

The person in your life with BPD didn't ask to have the disorder. And you never asked for someone in your life to have BPD. But if you are a typical person who loves someone with BPD, you have taken on a huge chunk of the blame for the other person's problems, and you probably feel that you—and only you—can solve them.

Many people who love someone with BPD—especially those who have chosen their relationship—go through life trying to fix things for other people and rescue them. This gives them the illusion that they can change someone else. But it is just a fantasy that shifts responsibility away from the only person who has the power to change your loved one's life—them. You can:

- Spend twenty-four hours a day feeling your loved one's pain for them.

- Put your life on hold, waiting for them to come around to your way of thinking.

- Let your entire emotional life be dictated by the mood of the moment.

But none of that will help the person with BPD.

In our interview with Howard I. Weinberg, PhD, he said, "People with BPD need their friends and family members to be stable and clear—not to reject them and not to smother them. They need you to let them take care of themselves and to not do things for them that they can do for themselves. The best way to do this and help them is by working on yourself."

Patricia

For those of you who have decided to stay with your BPD family member, thank you, thank you! We so need your love and support. We need you to believe in us and encourage us in our recovery. But if you stay, seek therapy for yourself if necessary and make sure you don't lose yourself in the process. You can't lose your own identity. You must come first. Because if you lose it, then the person with BPD doesn't really have a supporter. They just have another person in their life with a lot of problems.

Detach with Love

Some family members practice detaching with love, a concept promoted by Al-Anon, an organization for people whose lives are affected by someone who abuses alcohol. Al-Anon developed a statement about personal limits that is also appropriate for people who care about someone with BPD, if you substitute "BPD behavior" for "alcoholism." The original reads, in part:

> In Al-Anon we learn individuals are not responsible for another person's disease or recovery from it.
>
> We let go of our obsession with another's behavior and begin to lead happier and more manageable lives, lives with dignity and rights.
>
> In Al-Anon we learn:
>
> - Not to suffer because of the actions or reactions of other people.
>
> - Not to allow ourselves to be used or abused by others in the interest of another's recovery.
>
> - Not to do for others what they could do for themselves.
>
> - Not to create a crisis.
>
> - Not to prevent a crisis if it is in the natural course of events.
>
> Detachment is neither kind nor unkind. It does not imply judgment or condemnation of the person or situation from which I am detaching. It is simply a means that allows us to separate ourselves from the adverse effects that another person's alcoholism [substitute "BPD behavior"] has upon our lives.
>
> Detachment helps families look at their situations realistically and objectively, thereby making intelligent decisions possible.

Take Your Life Back

Don't delay your own happiness. Grab it right now. There are many things you can do today to take your life back. Take some time off to reflect. It can remind both you and your loved one that you are two separate individuals. They will learn that they can live through a temporary separation and that you will still care about them when you return. Encouraging retreats actually builds the relationship.

> Do not try to be the person's therapist. That is not your role. If the person with BPD wants that kind of help, suggest that they see a mental health professional. If you no longer have contact with them, don't spend hours psychoanalyzing. It is not your job anymore—actually, it never was to begin with.

Memorize the three Cs and the three Gs:

- I didn't cause it.
- I can't control it.
- I can't cure it.
- Get off their back.
- Get out of the way.
- Get on with your own life.

Be good to yourself. Here are some ideas:

- Visit an art gallery.
- Buy an outrageously expensive chocolate truffle.
- Get a massage.
- Seek out friends and family.
- Volunteer or become politically involved.
- Realize that—illness or no illness—no one person can fulfill all of your needs.
- If you have let friendships falter, "unfalter" them.
- When you go out, do not spend all your time talking about the person with BPD.
- See a movie.
- Try a new food.
- Relax and enjoy yourself!

Have fun. The world will not stop if you take some time for yourself. In fact, you will be able to come back refreshed and with a broader perspective.

If you are eating or drinking too much or engaging in other unhealthy coping mechanisms, stop. Seek professional help if you need to. Maintain realistic expectations. Borderline behavior takes years to develop; it is ingrained. Don't expect miracles. Celebrate small steps in the right direction and appreciate the things you enjoy about the person with BPD.

Tanya

It helps to remind myself that I can't fix every-thing. I keep reminding myself that being in a situation where I feel helpless doesn't mean I'm a failure.

My therapist told me not to feel guilty about taking care of myself. It's going to take some time to really feel that that's okay. I know I have to deal with my own feelings. But sometimes I long to have my own life back for a little while.

> Celebrate small steps in the right direction and appreciate the things you enjoy about the person with BPD.

Bolster Your Identity and Self-Esteem

If the person in your life blames and criticizes you, your self-esteem may be in the gutter. If you had low self-esteem to begin with, the situation may be critical. Some people we spoke with—especially adult children of parents with BPD—let others take advantage of them because they felt they didn't deserve better. They stayed in abusive work situations or unknowingly sabotaged themselves as if to confirm their loved one's low estimation of their worth.

Many people with BPD are able to be supportive of their children and other people in their life. But some are not. If the person with BPD in your life is damaging your self-worth, take immediate steps to repair it. Don't depend on the person with BPD to affirm or validate your worth, because they may not be able to. It's not that they don't care about you—it's just that at this time, their own issues and needs may be getting in the way.

Chapter 6 discusses the issues of setting limits and responding to rage, blame, and criticism. Read it carefully and practice the communication techniques with a friend before using them in a real-life situation. You do not have to listen to anyone else tell you that you're an awful, terrible person. You have a choice.

Finally, seek therapy to deal with the stress of living with someone who has BPD. In a survey we conducted of people who love someone with BPD, seventy-five percent of the respondents said they had sought therapy themselves.

Take Responsibility for Your Own Behavior

You may feel like a crumpled newspaper in a tornado, buffeted about at the whim of the person in your life with BPD. But you have more control over the relationship than you probably think you do. You have power over your own actions. And you control your own reactions to troublesome BPD behavior. Once you understand yourself and the decisions you've made in the past, it is easier to make new decisions that may be healthier for you and the relationship in the long run.

In *Emotional Blackmail* (1997), Susan Forward and Donna Frazier discuss how even avoidance is an action taken:

> Every day, we teach people how to treat us by showing them what we will and won't accept, what we refuse to confront, and what we let slide. We may believe that we can make another person's troublesome behavior disappear if we don't make a fuss. But the message we send is, "It worked. Do it again."

Some people find this step of owning up to their own responsibility difficult because they hear the critical voice of their loved one in their head saying, "See, everything is your fault. I told you that something is wrong with you." To these people, taking this step almost seems like agreeing with their loved one's criticisms. If this describes you, silence those voices right now. We are not suggesting that you provoked or caused the person's behavior—rather, we are proposing that you may have unwittingly given your loved one permission to repeat behaviors that have worked in the past.

You do not have to listen to anyone else tell you that you're an awful, terrible person. You have a choice.

Consider How the Relationship Meets Your Needs

In our interview with Howard I. Weinberg, Ph.D., he said, "If you care about someone with BPD, remember that you did not choose them because you are sick. You chose this person because they were important to you."

You wouldn't be reading this book if the relationship was completely negative. You would just walk away. So something about the relationship is probably meeting your needs. These reasons may vary depending upon whether you are in a chosen relationship (friend, lover) or unchosen relationship (relative) with someone with BPD.

Many people stay in unhealthy relationships because the person with BPD is incredibly interesting, engaging, bright, charming, funny, witty, and alluring. One woman said that when she met her boyfriend, who has BPD, she felt like she was meeting a member of her own species for the first time.

Diane

I can understand why people who care about someone with BPD engage in discussion about the pathologies, the rages, and the rotten things people with BPD can do. A person with BPD has the capacity to destroy themselves and anyone close to them. It's healthy to vent this pain.

But sometimes, in the course of the books and the discussion and the clinical terminology, these reasons why you began the relationship become lost. You didn't fall in love with someone with BPD because you had some hankering to be destroyed. You did it because there were good qualities about the person. And they are just as characteristic of the person as the bad ones.

When the destructive bad qualities began to manifest themselves, you got through it by telling yourself that in the end, these good qualities supersede the bad ones. Well, maybe they will or maybe they won't. You're not a masochist; you're an optimist—which may or may not turn out to be warranted. It is hard to give up on that optimism and let go of a relationship that's so good otherwise.

Stop Making Excuses and Denying the Severity of the Situation

Remaining hopeful is essential. And it's true that everyone has good and bad qualities. But hope must be tempered with a realistic view of the situation and an assessment of the likelihood of change.

Kevin's girlfriend Judy was bright, talented, and very attractive. Best of all, she loved him. So Kevin overlooked behavior that would have been a wake-up call for others. For example, one day Judy showed up at

> You're not a masochist; you're an optimist.

his workplace and began screaming at him in front of his boss and coworkers. Several days later, he still couldn't figure out why she had been angry.

Judy also impulsively bought luxury items like crystal vases and designer clothing, even though she was on public assistance and lived with Kevin and her nine-year-old son in a roach-infested apartment. She would leave her son alone at home to go shopping.

Each time Judy and Kevin had a disagreement, she would throw him out of the apartment and destroy some of his possessions. This became so routine that he began leaving his treasured belongings with his parents. When Kevin's friends tried to convince him that Judy's behavior wasn't normal, Kevin would shrug his shoulders and say, "Oh well, nobody's perfect. Every relationship has problems."

> Denial of problems only enables and reinforces the negative behaviors.

Kevin is using denial as a way of keeping the relationship going and coping with painful feelings of his own. At this point, Kevin is likely to do anything to avoid conflict in the relationship. However, his denial of problems only enables and reinforces the negative behaviors of Judy. Kevin will need the support and perspective of his friends to begin to address these problems and address why he allows Judy to treat him so poorly. Kevin will also need to address why his relationship with Judy is so important that he allows her to treat him badly.

Understand the Effects of Intermittent Reinforcement

Let's say that you have a rat in a box with a lever. You teach the rat to press the lever. Every fifth time he presses the lever, he is rewarded with some food. The rat quickly learns to press the lever five times so he can claim his reward. But if you stop giving the rat food, he will quickly abandon the exercise.

Now let's say that you intermittently reinforce the rat with food; that is, you vary the reward schedule. Sometimes you reward the rat after two lever presses. Sometimes you wait until the fifteenth press. You alternate the reinforcement so he never knows when to expect the food. Then, once more, you take away all the food pellets. But the rat keeps pressing the lever. He presses it twenty times; no food. He presses some more. He thinks, "Perhaps the human is waiting for the ninety-ninth press this time."

When a behavior is intermittently reinforced, extinguishing the behavior takes a lot longer once the reward has been removed. Intermittent reinforcement can work both ways. You are intermittently reinforced when your loved one is in a good mood. You can't predict when it will occur next—but you know it could be soon. The person you care about with BPD can also be intermittently reinforced when you occasionally cave in to their demands.

Molly says, "I am caught right now in Sondra's charming behavior. I am thinking, 'Ah! This is the person I used to know.' My logic tells me not to reconnect with her. But my emotions are telling me another thing."

> If you feel "addicted" to someone with BPD despite their harsh treatment of you, consider whether intermittent reinforcement is playing a part in the relationship.

Recognize the Exhilaration of the Roller-Coaster Ride

Many people say that when things are good, they're really good. The flattery, attention, and obsessiveness are exhilarating to the ego. To feel so important to someone can be exciting and empowering. The exhilaration can be recognized immediately, especially if you have not been in this position of being an "idol" before.

You may also begin to look for the exhilaration—to anticipate the flattery and attention. And, after a while, when the flattery begins to gradually fade, you will miss it and may even make attempts to get your loved one with BPD to idolize you again. The law of intermittent reinforcement applies here again, since your loved one may intermittently engage in obsessiveness and flattery throughout the relationship. This in turn reinforces your commitment to the relationship.

Jim

I found my wife's initial obsessiveness with me very flattering. I mean, I never thought I was worth that kind of attention. Other women didn't pay much attention to me. But she worshipped me. It's easier to feel good about myself when I'm around someone who idolizes me.

When a behavior is intermittently reinforced, extinguishing the behavior takes a lot longer once the reward has been removed.

But our relationship was like an addiction. I kept going back for more, in spite of myself, filled with self-contempt and even a sort of subtle shame: "I hate myself for loving you."

So began our roller-coaster relationship; living vicariously through the sublime, dizzying heights, I was shaken by the sudden, despairing drops, the switchbacks, the topsy-turvy illogical loops, the stunning stops, and later, the absence, the silence, the flatness at the end.

How to Get Unstuck

Do you feel unable to move because danger lies in every choice, but at the same time feel compelled to do something? Does your satisfaction with this relationship depend on the person with BPD making significant changes—even though it sure hasn't happened yet?

The Essential Family Guide to Borderline Personality Disorder: New Tools and Techniques to Stop Walking on Eggshells, by coauthor Randi Kreger, lists the six most common reasons why people who care about someone with BPD feel stuck and what to do about them:

Unhealthy bonds forged by emotional abuse: Controlling, intimidating, punishing, and isolating behaviors can lead to a lack of motivation, confusion, and difficulty making decisions—all of which can keep people stuck.

Feelings of fear. These can range from the practical (will the person with BPD be able to make it alone?) to fear of conflict and the unknown.

Obligation, roles, and duty. "How can I not visit my mother on her birthday?"

Guilt. This can drive family members (especially parents) to lose their sense of judgment and go to ridiculous lengths to "absolve" themselves.

Low self-esteem. People with low self-esteem often try to relieve their shame by being good. "Goodness" comes from sacrificing themselves and what they want out of life to make up for their perceived inadequacies.

The need to rescue. Rescuers start out with the best of intentions—they want to help. They will often do anything to keep the peace and avoid conflict, including taking the blame for things that are not their fault. Ultimately, they feel manipulated, angry, and frustrated.

To get unstuck, you must take a different approach. Stop focusing so much on your family member and take a close look at yourself. Work on becoming more of your own person.

Kreger writes, "Own your choices. Recognize that you decide how to respond to the people, actions, and events in your life. You have choices— not necessarily fun ones, but choices nonetheless. Banish phrases like, 'He made me…' or 'She forced me to…' from your vocabulary unless they refer to a legal document. Rather than say, 'I have to,' say, 'Right now, I choose to.' Then, open yourself up to new ideas. If what you've been doing hasn't worked, do something else."

Suggestions from *The Essential Family Guide* include:

- Become more authentic. Act in accordance with your own attitudes and beliefs.

- Learn from the past. Are these feelings familiar? Have you been in a similar situation?

- Help others without rescuing. Express confidence in your family member's ability to start finding solutions to their own problems. That helps build confidence.

- Allow people to be who they are instead of what you want them to be. Send healthy support messages like, "I'm here if you need me, but your choices—and the consequences—belong to you."

Make Decisions for Yourself

Acknowledging that you have the authority to make your own decisions is the first step toward making new choices and changing your life for the better.

Some people who love someone with BPD think they are helpless in their relationship when, in actuality, they are feeling scared. Fear and anxiety are not the same as being helpless. You might be fearful that your efforts toward limit setting and change will be met with rage and anger. Therefore, in an effort to avoid negative reactions from your loved one with BPD, you might describe yourself as feeling "helpless." Moreover, believing you are helpless may also serve the purpose of ridding yourself of any responsibility for making changes or for creating a better life for yourself. You may think that if you're "helpless" that means you're a "victim"—a person that others can't blame for their situation.

Fear and anxiety are not the same as being helpless.

You must understand that you do have the power to change your relationships and your life, but it is likely going to be frightening at first. The alternative is to live a fairly unhappy and unsatisfying life in which fear dictates your choices and relationships.

Believe You Don't Deserve to Be Treated Badly

Do you sometimes think that being in an emotionally abusive relationship is better than being in no relationship at all? It sometimes feels easier to be hurt than to be alone, but in the long run, abusive relationships can cause you to lose yourself, which is the ultimate loneliness. People with self-esteem problems are very vulnerable to blame and criticisms. They come to believe they deserve this treatment. They think that if they leave, no one else will want them. Even emotionally healthy people can begin to question their own self-worth.

Alex

I had to examine why I would spend years in abusive relationships. I had to overcome my fears and learn that I am worthy of being in relationships with people who are good to me—without putting me on a pedestal or tossing me into the gutter.

John

I realized that one of the major reasons I stayed in this relationship was that I unconsciously thought I deserved that pain and anguish. Now I'm working on this so I won't be attracted to women like that in the future.

Everyone has the right to healthy relationships. However, after months or years of enduring excessive criticism, blame, and borderline rage, most people who love someone with BPD begin to question whether they deserve to have a healthy relationship. Do you believe that you have the following rights?

> Abusive relationships can cause you to lose yourself, which is the ultimate loneliness.

- to feel respected as a person

- to get your physical and emotional needs met

- to be appreciated and not taken for granted

- to communicate effectively with your partner

- to have your privacy respected

- to not constantly fight for control

- to feel good about yourself and your relationship

- to trust, validate, and support each other

- to grow within and outside the relationship

- to have your own opinions and thoughts

- to either stay in or leave the relationship

As you may know, rights are neither respected nor acknowledged unless someone stands up for them. Are you ready to stand up for your rights?

Face Your Own Issues About Being Needed

Codependence expert Melody Beattie, in *Codependent No More* (1987), developed a list of questions for people who feel like they must rescue others. Paraphrased, they include:

- Do you feel responsible for other people's thoughts, actions, and feelings?

- When someone tells you about a problem they have, do you feel it is your duty to solve it?

- Do you swallow your anger in order to avoid conflict?

- Do you find getting more difficult than giving?

- Do you somehow seem to enjoy life more during interpersonal crises? Have you avoided choosing partners whose lives seem to go too smoothly because you become bored?

- Do people tell you that you are a saint for putting up with something or someone? Does part of you enjoy this?

- Is it more tempting to concentrate on the problems of others than to solve difficulties in your own life?

Focus on Your Own Issues

Some people find that trying to change someone else is easier than changing themselves and that focusing on the problems of others helps them avoid their own problems. You may want to ask yourself:

- Do you have a firm sense of who you are apart from the person with BPD?

- Are you where you want to be at this point in your life?

- Is there anything in your life that you are avoiding that you might have to take a look at if you were not concentrating on your relationship with someone who has BPD?

- How much time do you spend worrying about this relationship?

- What would you do with that time if life with this person was perfect?

Nina

Because my boyfriends were so obviously out of line, I overlooked my own behavior. So I learned that my responsibility was to admit when I screwed up immediately, to be honest and open—even in the face of BPD rages and blame. I realized that the problems I faced with BPD partners were magnified versions of the problems I had with myself.

I kept thinking it was just those crazy men in my life and that if only they would change, everything would be fine. It was a painful realization to wake up one day and notice that there were no medals handed out to willing sufferers like me!

Where to Go from Here

Ask yourself:

- How did I end up in this position?

- What have I learned about myself?

- What choices have I made in the past, and are they the best ones for me right now?

- What is keeping me from standing up for myself? What can I do about it?

- What am I responsible for in this relationship? What can I do about it?

Note that we are not blaming you for what has happened to you in the past or for the choices you've made. But only you—not your loved one, your therapist, or your friends—can resolve these issues. It's up to you. Many introspective folks who care about someone with BPD have found that what they discovered about themselves was invaluable.

Alex

This was the greatest gift of being around people with BPD. I got to see myself and how I interact with others. As painful as these relationships were, I needed them to become the person that I am today.

Marilyn

I have been able to move from being a person who lived her life unconsciously to a person who lives a conscious life. Someone said that the unexamined life is not worth living. I am happy to say that my life is very much worth living!

Russell

It helps to view situations as opportunities for growth and personal education. Rather than see every conflict and tribulation as a crisis of unresolvable proportions, I recognize that I am the one with the problem—I detest this person's behavior—and I'm open to learning more about myself. It becomes more about my choices than about my helplessness. And I can learn a lot from my choices.

In this chapter, we've explored ways to better cope with BPD behavior, simply by making changes within yourself: accepting that you can't make your loved one seek treatment, not taking their actions personally, taking care of yourself, and taking responsibility for your own behavior.

Next, we'll look at beginning to change the way you interact with the person with BPD in your life.

CHAPTER 6

Understanding Your Situation: Setting Boundaries and Honing Skills

Identify Triggers to Intense Emotional Reactions

When you or your loved one have an intense reaction to something, chances are good that one of your triggers or "hot buttons" has been pushed. Hot buttons or triggers are stored-up resentments, regrets, insecurities, anger, and fears that hurt when touched and cause automatic emotional responses. By identifying specific actions, words, or events that seem to trigger emotional reactions—either in you or in the person with BPD—these reactions may be easier to anticipate and manage.

Keeping Track

Many family members find that keeping a daily log of their loved one's patterns of behavior helps them understand and depersonalize the person's actions. Parents of borderline children, especially, find records useful in helping obtain proper diagnosis and treatment for their child.

Whether you simply observe your loved one or jot down notes about their moods and behaviors, your intent is not to make judgments, but to stop reacting to the behavior emotionally and start learning from it. If there appears to be little relationship between your actions and those of the person with BPD, you will see more clearly that the person's behavior is not about you.

If it looks like an external factor triggers the behavior, try to determine what factors might be involved, such as:

- the person's general mood

- the person's stress level and/or responsibilities

- the time of day

- the presence or absence of alcohol

- physical factors such as being hungry or tired

- the immediate environment

If you can find patterns in the person's behavior, it may become more predictable.

Portia

Sandy and I are parents of a possibly borderline child. We used a spreadsheet to graph our son's moods and behaviors. The scale varied from –10, for extreme despair, to +10, for extreme optimism. A zero indicated a neutral mood. Our son's therapist was blown away by our documentation, and it helped the therapist determine if our son had BPD or bipolar disorder.

Henry

I never kept a journal, but over a ten-year period, I realized that Barbara's moods occurred in six-week cycles. It went like this:

1. *Explosive, violent raging that lasted from ten minutes to several hours*

2. *Silence that lasted for two to five days*

3. *Friendly, cheerful, affectionate behavior that would last three or four days. (When things were going well, Barbara would apologize and even ask me to find out what might be causing her "crazy behavior.")*

4. *A long deterioration that lasted four to ten weeks. Barbara became increasingly more critical, condemning, and short-tempered. She would deny her earlier apologetic remarks. Finally, there would be an angry explosion and the cycle would repeat anew.*

Once I recognized the patterns, I knew what to expect. This made things feel more manageable for me.

Your Triggers

Many people we talked to for this book told us that the person with BPD in their life seemed to be aware of their triggers. When the person with BPD felt threatened, they consciously or unconsciously protected themselves from painful feelings in ways that pushed these buttons.

For example, one person who loves someone with BPD had very poor self-esteem. She had never dated much, and she and her husband had gotten married during high school. The marriage was very difficult because her husband was emotionally abusive. Whenever she spoke of leaving, however, he would tell her that no one else would have her and she would never be able to support herself because she was not smart or talented enough to get a good-paying job.

Some of the things that the person with BPD says or does may sting badly. Others may not bother you. Rather than just reacting, observe and examine your own responses. Is the criticism true, or does it have a grain of truth? Remember, you don't have to accept or reject the statement in its entirety. Look for splitting (black-and-white thinking), overgeneralizations ("you always" or "you never"), and illogical connections ("You didn't take me to the party because you hate me").

Certain hot buttons get pushed so many times that even the slightest touch becomes painful. Hot buttons for you may include:

- being unfairly accused by your loved one

> Rather than just reacting, observe and examine your own responses.

- having needs, feelings, and reactions discounted or denied by them

- being overly admired or adored by your loved one (because it may be a set-up for later devaluation and criticism)

- other situations and conditions that usually precede rages or acting-out behaviors (e.g., one woman started trembling whenever the phone rang because she was afraid it was her mother)

FOG—Fear, Obligation, Guilt

In *Emotional Blackmail*, Susan Forward and Donna Frazier (1997) write that traits that make people vulnerable to emotional blackmail include fear, obligation, and guilt—FOG for short. FOG obscures your choices and limits your options to those the blackmailer picks for you:

- **Fear:** You may fear losing something: love, money, approval, access to your children, or the relationship itself. You may be afraid of your own anger or of losing control of your emotions.

- **Obligation:** Says Forward, "Memory, as employed by the blackmailer, becomes the Obligation Channel, with nonstop replays of the blackmailer's generous behavior toward us. When our sense of obligation is stronger than our sense of self-respect and caring, people quickly learn how to take advantage."

- **Guilt:** When your normal activities trigger the person with BPD, they shift responsibility for their upset feelings onto you. They may accuse you not only of devious behavior but of acting in this way to deliberately hurt them. Instead of questioning their assumptions, you may respond by feeling guilty.

Coping Strategies

Just becoming aware of your triggers can make coping with borderline behavior easier. Other strategies include:

- **Working on yourself:** For example, the woman with poor self-esteem might see a therapist and explore why she thinks so poorly of herself. Or she might take some classes at the local college to improve her professional skills or train for a higher-paying position. This way, she will be in a better position to depersonalize and deflect her loved one's criticism—or leave the emotionally abusive relationship.

- **Performing reality checks with others:** If the person with BPD accuses you of being ungrateful or inept, or of having other negative qualities, ask friends if they believe there's any truth to what they are saying.

- **Minimizing your exposure to situations that trigger you:** You have the right to take care of yourself.

- **Minimizing any visible reaction:** If the person with BPD knows the button-pushing is having the desired effect—whether consciously or unconsciously—chances are that the behavior will be repeated.

- **Realizing you can't control what people choose to think:** You can't make everyone happy—least of all someone who is projecting their own unhappiness onto you. Stop taking responsibility for your loved one's inner world and start taking responsibility for your own.

Determine Your Personal Limits

Personal limits, or boundaries, tell you where you end and where others begin. Limits define who you are, what you believe, how you treat other people, and how you let them treat you. Like the shell of an egg, limits give you form and protect you. Like the rules of a game, they bring order to your life and help you make decisions that benefit you.

Healthy limits are somewhat flexible, like a soft piece of plastic. You can bend them, and they don't break. When your limits are overly flexible, however, violations and intrusions can occur. You may take on the feelings and responsibilities of others and lose sight of your own.

> You have the right to take care of yourself.

On the other hand, when your limits are too inflexible, people may view you as cold or distant. That's because inflexible limits can act as a defense—not only against others, but also from your own feelings. You may have a hard time feeling sadness, anger, or other negative emotions. Happiness and other positive emotions may also at times be beyond your grasp. You may feel disconnected from others and even from your own experiences.

In *Codependent No More* (1987), Melody Beattie says that setting limits is not an isolated process. She writes:

> Setting boundaries is about learning to take care of ourselves, no matter what happens, where we go, or who we're with. Boundaries are rooted in our beliefs about what we deserve and don't deserve.
>
> Boundaries originate from a deeper sense of our personal rights—especially the right we have to be ourselves. Boundaries emerge as we learn to value, trust, and listen to ourselves. Boundaries naturally flow from our conviction that what we want, need, like and dislike is important.

Personal limits are not about controlling or changing other people's behavior. In fact, they're not about other people at all. They're about you, and what you need to do to take care of yourself. For example, you may not be able to stop nosy in-laws from asking you again and again when you plan on starting a family. But you can control whether you answer their questions and how much time you spend with them.

Sometimes you may choose to overlook your personal limits. For example, imagine that your elderly father slips on an icy walkway and asks if he can live with you and your family until he recovers from his injuries. Because you love your dad, you say yes—even though you value your privacy. The key here is that you feel you have a choice. It's like the difference between giving someone a gift and being robbed.

Emotional Limits

Emotional limits are the invisible boundaries that separate your feelings from those of others. These boundaries not only mark off where your emotions end and someone else's begin but also help you protect yourself when you are feeling vulnerable and provide others with access to your emotions when you are feeling intimate and safe with them.

Sometimes you may choose to overlook your personal limits... The key is that you feel you have a choice.

People with healthy emotional limits understand and respect their own thoughts and feelings. In short, they respect themselves and their own uniqueness. Anne Katherine (1993) says, "The right to say 'no' strengthens emotional boundaries. So does the freedom to say 'yes,' respect for feelings, acceptance of differences, and permission for expression."

Healthy Examples

Here are some illustrations of how people act in ways that respect their own thoughts and feelings:

- Dan believes that his father has borderline personality disorder. His younger brother, Randy, disagrees. Dan hasn't seen his father in a year, while Randy has dinner with him once a week. Dan and Randy feel free to discuss their opinions about their father though they have differing viewpoints. And they both enjoy their brotherly relationship, realizing that it's separate from their relationships with their father.

- Roberta's lover Cathy hates it when Roberta goes out with friends. Cathy is always invited along, but she wants to stay home because she thinks that Roberta's friends are "a complete waste of time."

  "Please don't go," Cathy pleads one evening as Roberta gets dressed to go out. "I'm lonely without you," Cathy says tearfully. Roberta gently reminds Cathy that she told her about her plans a week ago and that Cathy had time to find things to do on her own or with one of her own friends. But Cathy just keeps on weeping. "You must not love me anymore," she says.

  Roberta replies, "It sounds like you feel that I am rejecting or abandoning you. That must be very painful. You can believe that and make yourself feel bad or you can try to work through why you doubt my love for you. Let's talk about it when I get back. I'll see you at around eleven o'clock."

The Benefits of Personal Limits

Limits can be difficult to set and keep, but doing so has some invaluable incentives.

Limits can help you deal with these behaviors so that you don't feel like a puppet on a string.

Limits Help You Define Who You Are

Limits and the struggle for identity are tightly intertwined. People with weak limits often have poorly developed senses of identity. People with weak or nonexistent limits can have difficulty distinguishing between their own beliefs and feelings and those belonging to others. They also tend to confuse their problems and responsibilities with those of others. Left with an uncertain identity, they often take on someone else's or identify solely with one familiar role (e.g., mother, executive, or even borderline).

People with well-developed limits:

- appropriately distinguish themselves from others

- identify and take responsibility for their own feelings, beliefs, and values

- see feelings, beliefs, and values as important parts of who they are

- have respect for other people's beliefs and feelings—even if they are different from their own

- understand that another person's values and beliefs are equally important in defining who they are

Limits Bring Order to Your Life

If you're always at the whim of someone else's desires, your life can spiral out of control. People with BPD tend to change the rules, act impulsively, and demand attention on their schedule, not that of others. Limits can help you deal with these behaviors so that you don't feel like a puppet on a string.

Limits can also help you clarify your relationships with others, and setting limits ahead of time may help you avoid future problems.

Limits Help You Feel Secure

People who don't have limits are always at the mercy of others. They feel helpless when others act upon them, and they take whatever others dish out. On the other hand, people with limits feel more in control of their lives because they realize they have a choice about the behavior they will tolerate. They take the power that is truly theirs to say no. This provides them with a sense of security and control.

For example, Jane and Ben have been dating for several months. Jane's having a hard time because Ben can't decide how he feels about her. When he loves her, she's elated. When he backs off and "just wants to be friends," she's depressed and confused.

One day he has something to tell her. "I've met someone else," he says. "But I don't know if she's the one. I want to date both of you until I know for sure."

Clear limits will enable Jane to stick up for herself and tell Ben what she wants out of the relationship. Because she has healthy limits, she knows that her needs are just as important as Ben's. Jane can tell Ben how his actions have affected her, and she can evaluate his proposed arrangement based on her own values and beliefs. Jane understands that she has many options. She knows one of them is telling Ben that although she cares for him, she needs to leave the relationship because it's not meeting her needs.

Limits Promote Intimacy, Not Enmeshment

The idea used to be that when two people got married, they became one. Today's brides and grooms are more likely to believe that one and one still make two. Many couples acknowledge this at their wedding by having someone read from Kahlil Gibran's *The Prophet* (1976). In the passage on marriage, Gibran urges couples to have spaces in their togetherness. "Stand together yet not too near together: for the pillars of the temple stand apart, and the oak tree and the cypress grow not in each other's shadow."

Gibran is describing healthy limits. The opposite, enmeshment, is comparable to the oak tree and the cypress growing so close together that their branches and roots become entwined. Soon, there's no room for either tree to grow; parts of each tree die, and neither reaches its full potential.

> Unlike compromise, which is a conscious give and take, enmeshment involves denying who you are or what you need, to please someone else.

In *Boundaries: Where You End and I Begin* (1993), Anne Katherine says:

Enmeshment happens when the individualities of each partner are sacrificed to the relationship. Falling in love is exciting and involving. But the truth is, it's a fairly enmeshed stage of the relationship. It is validating for someone to have thoughts and feelings identical to our own. It feels wonderful. Eventually, though, perceptions will differ. How this is handled is critical for the relationship.

Sometimes people become enmeshed because one partner intimidates the other into giving up their own opinions, perspectives, and preferences. In other cases a partner takes on someone else's view voluntarily because they're so eager to feel close to someone. Denying part of themselves is preferable to being alone—at least at first. But the problem with sacrificing parts of yourself to please someone else is that it doesn't work in the long run. It might take many years, but eventually you realize that while you may have gained a relationship, you've lost yourself. In order to share yourself, you need enough of a sense of your own individuality to have something to present to the other. Even if you have a good sense of who you are, intimacy takes time, openness, a nonjudgmental attitude, listening, and acceptance.

Boundary Issues

Some people are lucky enough to have had parents and other role models who taught them about personal rights and limits and why they are important. Unfortunately, many adults grew up with damaged, trampled, or non-existent boundaries. In many cases, parents routinely violated their children's boundaries and rights or forced them into inappropriate roles.

Different kinds of boundary violations cause different kinds of problems for children when they become adults:

- If parents or other caregivers encouraged children to be dependent, as adults those grown children may believe that they need someone else to make them whole.

- Children of distant or abandoning parents may have a hard time connecting emotionally to others.

- Controlling parents teach their children that others have no rights.

- Overinvolved parents can make it difficult for their children to develop their own identities.

Some people with BPD have experienced childhood sexual or physical abuse—the most horrific violations of personal limits. The abuse, humiliation, and shame can severely damage personal boundaries. Abused children feel confused about what to let others do to them physically, how to let others treat them emotionally, and how to interact with others in socially appropriate ways.

> Children who experience abuse also learn to deny pain and chaos or accept them as normal and proper.

Adults who were abused as children may protect themselves by building strong walls between themselves and others, or they may withdraw physically or emotionally, rarely sharing their emotions. Others do the opposite, becoming too open. They may involve themselves in sexual relationships with people who don't really care about them.

Children who experience abuse also learn to deny pain and chaos or accept them as normal and proper. They learn that their feelings were wrong or didn't matter. They learn to focus on immediate survival—on not getting abused—and miss out on important developmental stages. As a result, they have problems developing their own identities.

Kamala

My mother and father physically, sexually, and emotionally abused me. They never loved me or cared about how I felt, so I never had the opportunity to go through the natural process of individuation and separation.

When I became an adult, I walked out into the "real" world looking and sounding fine. But I had no concept of the "other" and no boundaries whatsoever. To my underdeveloped sense of self, people around me were extensions of me. I hated and abused myself, so I hated and abused them.

When I tried to have normal relationships, other people's boundaries were my worst enemy. People with boundaries could say "no." "No" was a certain death; I could feel it in the pit of my stomach. People saw me as demanding, unendingly chaotic, grabbing, controlling, manipulating others. But it was really the cry of an insatiable, terrorized, wounded little girl, still struggling to grow up and survive.

When people don't have healthy limits, they need defenses, which damage intimacy. These defenses can include:

- control

- withdrawal

- blaming

- rationalizing

- intellectualizing

- name calling

- perfectionism

- black-and-white thinking

- threats

- fighting about false issues

- excessive concern for the other

"These are all handy ways to avoid feelings and avoid communication," says Anne Katherine in an interview. "The healthy alternative is to state your true feelings."

People without BPD can have weak limits, too, of course. However, they may be expressed in a different way. Whereas the person with BPD may refuse to take responsibility for their own actions and feelings, you may tend to take too much responsibility for what others say and do. This tendency may come from childhood experiences. As children, some people who care about someone with BPD were expected to act as emotional or physical caretakers for their parents or others. Frequently, they learned to deny their own needs and take on responsibility for other people's feelings, thoughts, and problems.

"The healthy alternative is to state your true feelings."

John

I was eleven years old when my brother was born. A year later, my twin sisters came along. Money, which had always been tight, became a real problem. When I was in junior high, my job was to come home right after school to look after my siblings and get dinner started. One day, though, I watched the cross-country track team warming up. I wanted to be there, running with them.

But when I asked my parents if I could join, my mother cried and said, "We need you here to look after the kids, John. If I quit my job to watch them, we'll have to move to a cheaper apartment." My father got angry. "You're selfish! Can't you think of anyone else for a change?"

John's parents discouraged him from seeing his needs as separate from theirs. In order to maintain his parents' love, he had to deny his true feelings. And as an adult, he continued to deny his feelings because it felt familiar and safer. John also grew up learning that his feelings didn't count. So when he got into a relationship with a person with BPD as an adult, he had difficulty keeping his limits, which he was not practiced in doing.

Scripts from the Past

Some people with BPD frequently won't accept responsibility, and some non-borderlines accept too much. Unaware that they're replaying painful scripts from the past, the person with BPD tries to persuade their loved one to become the focus of their pain and rage. Often, they all-too-willingly oblige.

The "bargain" that you strike with your loved one with BPD may be rooted in deep, largely unconscious beliefs about what it takes to survive in this world. For the person with BPD, feeling separated from someone else can be frightening. It makes them feel rejected, abandoned, and alone. So, consciously or unconsciously, they may discourage independence or independent thinking in people close to them.

Kamala

Before I got better, if people didn't have any protection in place for themselves I would aim right at them. Who doesn't want a target that they can sink? But what I was doing, and what a lot of people with BPD do, is not a game or a way to get kicks. It's about survival. People who had healthy boundaries in place left me feeling too defective, too out of control, and too vulnerable.

In response, many loved ones avoid doing anything to provoke a negative reaction from the person with BPD—at least at first. They may worry that if they assert themselves, they'll lose the relationship and be unloved and alone. And the person with BPD, who is taking care of their own pain in the only way they know how, can be skillful at convincing you that you are being selfish, irresponsible, or uncaring. Over time, you may even lose sight of just how far you have gone to accommodate your loved one's skewed sense of reality.

Pushing the Envelope

Without limits, BPD behavior can get drastically out of control. Some loved ones of people with BPD interviewed for this book have: willingly not answered their own work phones because their wives were afraid of other women calling; tolerated multiple affairs, including extramarital liaisons that led to pregnancies and sexually transmitted diseases; or not expressed any needs at all, because to do so would lead to accusations of being "needy and controlling."

> When you set and observe personal limits, you are also benefiting the person in your life with BPD.

Other loved ones of those with BPD have given up rewarding activities and friendships because of criticism; lied to friends and family members about the behaviors of those with BPD; tolerated regular physical abuse; gone without sex for more than a decade; not left the house for long periods of time because those with BPD refused to be alone; or allowed those with BPD to be abusive to their children.

You may have let someone violate your personal limits in the past. But that doesn't give the person permission to do it again—not unless you hand it to them. First, though, you have to decide what your limits are.

How Limits Help Your Loved One

Setting limits can be frightening at first. So it's crucial to remember that you're not setting them just for your own good. When you set and observe personal limits, you are also benefiting the person in your life with BPD. In fact, when you let them violate your boundaries, or do not set any for them, you may be making the situation worse. Some people believe that setting aside all their needs will eventually "fix" the person they love. This is not true.

George

> By setting and observing limits, you are acting as a role model for the person with BPD and others in your home.

I really don't care about how Kim treats me. Yes, she's done things that have caused me a lot of pain. But thanks to all I've learned about BPD, I know her suffering is so much greater than mine. I like knowing that I'm making a difference in her life. Isn't that what life's about—helping other people?

George's motivation is commendable. But giving up his own needs will not benefit his wife—or himself—in the long run. If George accepts responsibility for Kim's feelings and behavior, then she won't have to. If she's not held accountable for what she does, she won't have to look at how her behavior affects herself and those around her. And until she is held accountable by others and by herself and decides to change, she won't get better. In fact, she could get worse.

How long will George be able to remain in this relationship with Kim? What is he willing to give up in the long term (friends? security? self-esteem?) to have a relationship with someone who causes him a great deal of pain? Is this the example he wants to set for their children?

If you set and observe reasonable limits, and if you learn how to take care of your own needs and live your own life, chances are much greater that you will be able to stay in a long-term relationship with your loved one—and the possibility increases that your relationship will ultimately be happy and successful. By setting and observing limits, you are acting as a role model for the person with BPD and others in your home. Firm, consistent limits on your part will help the person with BPD eventually create limits for himself or herself.

The Right to Set Limits

Often, people who love someone with BPD look outside themselves for confirmation that it is okay to set limits in a certain area. They wonder if they have a right to get angry when one of their limits is not observed.

Many people—not just those who care for someone with BPD—seem to divide their feelings into two groups: justified and unjustified. Let's say that your friend Sue is thirty minutes late for your lunch date. If Sue finally arrives without an explanation and doesn't even apologize, you might call your anger at her justified. But if Sue doesn't show up at all and you find out the next day that this was because she was in a car accident, you might decide that your earlier response was unjustified.

People also spend a great deal of time arguing about who is "right" in how they feel and what they want. When they argue, they endlessly debate whose desires are more "normal." Harriet Goldhor Lerner, in *The Dance of Anger* (1985), explains the fallacy of such thinking:

> Most of us secretly believe that we have the corner on the "truth," and that this would be a much better world if every one else believed and reacted exactly as we do. Married couples and family members are especially prone to behave as if there is one "reality"

that should be agreed upon by all.

But it is our job to state our thoughts and feelings clearly and to make responsible decisions that are congruent with our values and beliefs. It is not our job to make another person think and feel the way we do or the way we want them to. We have to give up the fantasy that we can change or control another person. It is only then that we can reclaim the power that is truly ours—the power to change our own selves and take a new and different action on our own behalf.

Let's go back to the example with Sue. You're angry that she was late and didn't phone or apologize. Her position is that you should have gone ahead and eaten without her, and that if you didn't, then you can only blame yourself for being angry.

It's useless to debate whether you "should" feel angry, because the fact is that you do. It's your job to tell Sue how you feel. It's Sue's job to tell you how she feels. You don't have to—nor should you—feel it necessary to convince Sue that your way of thinking is best. Instead, you simply need to protect yourself in the future now that you know Sue's attitude about tardiness.

"Am I selfish?"

Believing that your own needs are selfish is another common trap that people fall into. Barb, a thirty-two-year-old woman, says, "I'm not sure I can continue trying to please my mother. My every minute is consumed with thoughts of helping her, but every now and then I think, 'Forget it, I can't do any more.' Is this selfish of me?"

Setting and enforcing boundaries is not selfish. It is normal and necessary. Some people who love someone with BPD mistakenly label their behavior "selfish" when they are simply watching out for themselves.

Terrell

When I was a kid, "selfish" was an insult in my home. It was something only "bad" people indulged in. But I learned that it was only when I started taking care of myself that I was really able to care for others.

Guidelines for Setting Limits

In the *Essential Family Guide to Borderline Personality Disorder*, author Randi Kreger (2008) discusses the "Five C's" planning method in the chapter "Set Limits with Love." Following is a brief summary.

Clarify Your Limits

Patricia Evans, in *The Verbally Abusive Relationship: How to Recognize It and How to Respond* (1996), suggests that certain rights are fundamental to relationships, including:

- the right to emotional support, encouragement, and goodwill from the other

- the right to be heard by the other and to be responded to with courtesy and respect

- the right to have your own view even if the other has a different view

- the right to have your feelings and experiences acknowledged as real

- the right to a life free from excessive accusations, blame, criticism, and judgments

- the right to live free from emotional and physical abuse

Asking yourself questions can help you better understand your personal limits:

- What hurts?

- What feels good?

- What are you willing to give up for the relationship?

- What are the things that others do that leave you feeling angry and taken advantage of?

- Are you able to say no to requests without feeling guilty?

- How physically close can you allow others to get?

- At what distance do you begin to feel anxious or uncomfortable?

- Does the person with BPD respect your physical limits?

Don't expect to be able to sit down and answer these questions in one night—or even one month. Setting limits is a lifelong process.

Calculate the Costs

How does *not* having the boundary affect you? Kreger writes, "We are so busy living our day-to-day lives that we don't keep very good track of the things that gnaw at us… [W]e ignore [them] and hope [they] will go away" (Kreger 2008).

Setting limits is a lifelong process.

Come Up With Consequences

Keeping in mind what not having limits is costing you, think about what you will do when (not if!) your family member plows right through your limits. Make the consequences proportional to the limit.

Create a Consensus

Ideally, the whole family should act in a consistent manner.

Consider Possible Outcomes

Things will get worse before they get better as your family member makes countermoves and tests you to see if you're serious. So prepare for this. If things could become unsafe for either you or your family member, you may need help from a professional.

Defuse Anger and Criticism

Steve

I read a story about a Zen seeker who goes to the master and sits across the table at tea time. The Zen master holds a stick in his hand, and he says, "If you drink your tea, I will hit you with this stick. If you don't drink your tea, I will hit you with this stick." So what do you do? Well, I think I figured it out. Take away the stick.

The depersonalization and detachment techniques outlined in chapter 5 are ways of "taking away the stick." The defusing techniques in this chapter can have the same effect. Practice the skills in this chapter in everyday situations—at first, preferably, with a person who does not have BPD.

Don't worry if you get angry or flustered or if you forget these tools in the heat of a real situation. That's expected. Remember that you're accomplishing something that even trained professionals have difficulty with. Reward yourself for every small step forward.

Use a Noncombative Communication Style

The first step of good communicating is to become a good listener. When it is your turn to listen, really listen. Don't think about what you are going to say. Do not become defensive and tune the person out, even if they are accusing you of things you never did or said. You'll have the chance to address this later.

Pay attention to the person's words, body language, expressions, and tone of voice. This will help you validate the person's feelings. People with BPD are not always in touch with their own emotions, and by listening closely you may be able to hear beyond the words and detect the feelings that lie beneath the surface.

In *When Words Hurt: How to Keep Criticism from Undermining Your Self-Esteem* (1990), Mary Lynne Heldmann says:

> Listening takes concentration and mindfulness. You must focus only on the speaker and forget about what you want to say. Whether or not you ultimately decide that you agree with your critic's perceptions, listening gives you the opportunity to learn.

Heldmann believes that things that get in the way of listening include preoccupation with your own point, distracting thoughts, deciding that you already know what the other person is going to say, and twisting the speaker's message to fit your expectations. (For more information about mindfulness, see Appendix B.)

Ways to show you are listening include being silent, pausing before speaking, making eye contact (unless this is threatening), physically turning toward the person, uncrossing your arms, and nodding when appropriate.

Paraphrasing and Reflexive Listening

Make "I" Statements. When responding to your loved one, make "I" statements, not "you" statements. You can't read anyone else's mind. You may be wrong about the person's intentions and feelings. But you are an expert on yourself. You're on safe ground when you describe your own emotions and motivations and let others do the same.

Let's say that you and your coworker Shelby must both pitch in to answer the phones at work. But it seems like you're carrying more of the load. Shelby takes long lunches. Shelby leaves the office for hours at a time. And when he is there, Shelby asks you to take messages for him because "he's busy."

So you decide to have a little talk with Shelby. Following are examples of "you" statements, which all make assumptions about Shelby's state of mind:

- "You are selfish for pushing this off on me."

- "You take long lunches so you won't have to answer the phone."

- "You must think that you're the only one who's busy around here."

No one likes to be told what their intentions are—least of all someone with BPD. Plus, these kinds of statements invite criticism. What if you're wrong about why Shelby is taking long lunches? Even if you're right, what are the chances that Shelby will agree with your statements about his selfishness and overinflated ego? Remember that feeling invalidated is a key trigger for people with BPD. "I" statements will help avoid this trigger.

Following are sample "I" statements you could use with Shelby. Use a confident voice and physical manner. Do not stammer or act apologetic for having feelings and opinions.

- "I feel like I am answering the phone more often, and this is causing problems for me because I can't get all my work done. Can we sit down and talk about this?"

- "I am having a hard time getting all my work done because I'm answering the phone so often. My understanding is that this is a task we are supposed to split evenly. I'd like to set up a time to talk to you about this."

Generally, "I" statements make people less defensive and more open to exploring a solution to the problem. However, it's possible that the person with BPD will hear a "you" statement even when you're really making an "I" statement. But don't give up. Over time, the person with BPD may begin to hear what you're really saying.

Restate Key Points. It is also helpful when communicating with someone who has BPD to restate their feelings and main points to show that you are actively hearing the person. This does not mean that you have to agree with what the person is saying. People who work in customer service jobs are often taught that one of the best ways to defuse a customer's anger is to acknowledge that person's feelings. This doesn't mean that the company is admitting fault. It does mean, however, that the company cares that the customer is having a difficult time.

Heldmann suggests paraphrasing, or repeating, the key points of the speaker's statements to show that you want to understand what the person is saying. Develop your own style of doing this so it comes across naturally.

Hold the Interpretation. Be careful not to interpret what the other person is saying. That may only make the other person angry and defensive. Here's the difference between paraphrasing and interpreting:

Person with BPD:

"You never call me anymore. I always have to call you. I am really beginning to wonder if you still want to be my friend or if you're going to reject me like everyone else. I'm really hurting bad right now. You're acting just like my ex-boyfriend Rick did when he decided he couldn't cope with a girlfriend who has BPD. You both make me sick. I didn't ask to have this disorder, you know. I hope you both rot in hell."

Their Loved One (paraphrasing):

"It sounds like you're really upset because you feel like I haven't called you lately. From what you're saying, it seems like you're worried that I don't want to be friends anymore and that I'm behaving just like Rick did a few weeks ago."

Their Loved One (interpreting):

"It sounds like you're mixing me up with Rick and assuming that because he left you, I will too. You must still be hurt over that and taking things out on me [notice interpreting and "you" statement]."

Make Neutral Observations. Reflective listening is another helpful style of communicating where you give the speaker your impression of what they are feeling to show you are listening and that you care. Says Heldmann:

> We all have feelings, and there is no point in challenging someone else's feelings or telling the other person not to feel that way. Making a neutral observation about the other person's feelings is, however, a good way to invite someone to open up, to give him or her room. It isn't necessary to be "right" in your statement of what the other person is feeling. Merely making your honest observation is often enough to open the door (Heldmann 1990).

If the other person's feelings are obvious, you may phrase your observation as a statement, such as, "I can see that you're very angry" or "You seem very sad right now." If the feelings are subtle and unstated, it may be better to ask a question: "Are you feeling scared right now that I might want to back out of our marriage?" Avoid excessive probing, though—your goal is to help the other person express his or her feelings, not analyze them.

Heldmann says, "Reflective listening can be difficult if the speaker is criticizing you. But if you can stay calm and in control, the speaker will have let off some steam and will probably feel better. And by allowing him free expression of his feelings, you have communicated your openness" (Heldmann 1990).

BPD-Specific Communication Skills

Some of the following suggestions are adapted from Marsha Linehan's workbook, *Skills Training Manual for Treating Borderline Personality Disorder* (1993b).

- Stay focused on your message.
  While you are talking, the other person may attack or threaten you or try to change the subject. This could be happening for many reasons. For example, the person may be trying to divert you because you are touching on a sensitive area. Ignore the attempts to distract you. Just calmly continue making your point and come back to the other subject later if it is appropriate.

- Simplify.
  When you are communicating about a sensitive issue, or if the person with BPD seems upset, simplify your communication. You and your loved one may be feeling such strong emotions that there is little energy left for either of you to do much high-level thinking. Make each sentence short, simple, clear, and direct. Leave no room for misinterpretation.

- Give positive feedback, appropriate to the person and your relationship.
  One person with BPD says, "I try to focus on what is right about me, but most of the time the people in my life keep reminding me 'You're mentally ill; you're borderline.' I am working hard to see the possibilities and a future in which I can be happy and productive. This is not made easier by those who label me and refuse to recognize my individuality and potential to grow."

- Ask questions.
  Turn the problem over to the other person. Ask for alternative solutions. For example, try "What do you think we should do here?" or "I'm not able to say yes, and you seem to really want me to. How can we solve this problem?"

- Be aware of your own voice inflection and nonverbal communication.
  These may communicate as much as, or more than, the words you use. Speak calmly, clearly, and confidently.

When stating what you want or need, don't let your voice rise at the end as if you were asking a question. This is called "uptalk," and it undermines what you are saying.

Responding to Attacks and Manipulation

Sometimes the responses discussed in the previous section are not appropriate because the person with BPD is "snipping" at you rather than initiating an honest conversation about something you said or did that bothered them.

In these types of instances, you may feel attacked, manipulated, or undermined. Examples include:

- "Your sister was always prettier than you."

- "I'd be a better kid if you were a better parent."

- "I see you're going out with your friends again" (said in a disapproving way).

- "That's what you think."

Heldmann (1990) writes that most people respond to criticism with behavior they learned in childhood. She calls this behavior "The Four Don'ts": defend, deny, counterattack, and withdraw. You want to avoid these types of responses.

- Don't defend.
  Trying to prove to others that you really haven't done anything wrong can make you feel foolish, childish, and guilty, even when you haven't made a mistake.

- Don't deny.
  You may use denial because you truly haven't been responsible for whatever it is that you're being accused of. But repeated denial can also make you feel like a child again ("Did not!" "Did too!").

- Don't counterattack.
  You may strike back at the person with BPD to try to win the argument or vent your feelings. But when you do this, you'll fall into the projection and projective identification trap that the person with BPD has unconsciously set for you.

- Don't withdraw.
  When loved ones of people with BPD realize that defend, deny, and counterattack don't work, they often withdraw. Some clam up completely. Some leave physically. Some learn to dissociate. There is nothing wrong with leaving if you feel attacked. In fact, there are times when it's a good thing to do (see chapter 8). The damage comes from remaining passive and silent, absorbing the other person's criticism while your sense of personal power and self-esteem deteriorate.

Defusing Techniques

Following are some of Heldmann's better choices for responding. These disarm your critics and enhance and empower you. If you use these suggestions, speak sincerely, naturally, and neutrally. Avoid being flippant or counterattacking. Also, use them cautiously, since you never know how the other person will respond. The same technique, used on two different days, may spark different reactions.

Agree with Part of the Statement

CRITICISM: "I see you're going out with your friends again" (said in a disapproving way).

RESPONSE: "Yes, I am going out."

CRITICISM: "When I was your age, I never would have gone on a date looking like that."

RESPONSE: "No, you probably wouldn't have" (said in an agreeable way).

CRITICISM: "I can't believe you won't let me go out with my friends just because you found some pot in my room. If you weren't my mother, my life would be so much better."

RESPONSE: "True, I'm not going to let you go out with your friends because you've been smoking pot."

Agree with the Possibility That Your Critic Could Be Right

CRITICISM: "I had an affair. Big deal!"

RESPONSE: "Some people might not think it was a big deal if their husband had a affair. But I'm not one of them."

CRITICISM: "How can you even suggest not inviting Mom to the party? So she acts a little strange, sometimes. She's still your mother!"

RESPONSE: "Yes, she is still my mother. And some people would invite all their relatives, no matter how they act. But I believe that Mom has a choice about how she wants

Speak sincerely, naturally, and neutrally; avoid being flippant or counterattacking.

127

to behave. If she's going to choose to say outrageous things that hurt people's feelings, I don't feel comfortable inviting her."

Recognize That the Critic Has an Opinion

CRITICISM: "Children belong with their mother, not their father. And I know the judge will see it that way too."

RESPONSE: "I can see you have strong opinions about custody. The judge may see it the way you do. Or she may not."

CRITICISM: "If anyone has BPD, it's you, not me."

RESPONSE: "I can see that you disagree with the therapist's opinion that you have BPD."

Use Gentle Humor When Appropriate

CRITICISM: "I can't believe you forgot to buy charcoal. How are we going to grill the fish?"

RESPONSE: "Well, we've always been meaning to try sushi" (said without sarcasm).

Practice defusing responses in less threatening situations first. And no matter what happens, congratulate yourself for your efforts.

In this chapter, we've given you the foundation you'll need to make important changes in your relationship with your loved one with BPD. In the next chapter, we'll show you how to actually discuss this with them. Make sure that you understand the information presented in this chapter thoroughly before you go on.

You should have a clear understanding of the following:

- the factors that can trigger BPD behavior, along with the concept that while you may trigger the behavior, you are not to blame for it

- how the person with BPD may trigger you with fear, obligation, and guilt

- how personal limits (boundaries) help relationships

- the personal limits that you would like the person with BPD to observe

- the futility of discussing your "rights" to set limits—the question is not about "rights" but about your personal feelings about how you want to be treated

- guidelines for good communication

In the next chapter, we will go over how you can begin to effectively assert your needs with the person with BPD.

CHAPTER 7

Asserting Your Needs with Confidence and Clarity

I told my wife over and over again how much I loved her, that I would never leave her, that she was a beautiful and intelligent person. But it was never enough. If a female salesclerk's fingers brushed mine as she was giving me change, my wife would accuse me of flirting. Trying to fill the emotional black hole inside a person with BPD is like trying to fill the Grand Canyon with a water pistol—except the Grand Canyon has a bottom.

—From the Welcome to Oz
internet support community

You can respond to someone with BPD in two primary ways: like a sponge or like a mirror. It is common for the same person to react both ways—sometimes absorbing, sometimes reflecting.

Stop "Sponging" and Start "Reflecting"

Some people absorb the projections of their loved one with BPD and soak up their pain and rage (sponging). These people may be under the illusion that they are helping their loved one. But in fact, by not reflecting the person with BPD's painful feelings back to their rightful owner (mirroring), they are rewarding them for using these defense mechanisms. This may make it more likely that their loved one will continue to use them in the future.

People who act like sponges say they feel like they are trying to fill a black hole of emptiness inside their loved one. But no matter how much love, caring, and devotion they provide, it is never enough. So they blame themselves and work even more frantically. At the same time, the person with BPD feels the terrifying pain of the aching cavity and urges their loved one to work even harder and faster at filling the hole. If your loved one with BPD is the acting-out type, they may castigate you for being lazy or indifferent to their anguish. If they are more prone to acting in, they may tearfully beg you to help end the suffering.

But it's all a diversion to keep you both from addressing the real issue: the emptiness belongs to the person with BPD, and the only person who can fill it is themselves.

Stay Focused and Observe Your Limits

Don't get caught up in the person with BPD's accusations, blaming, impossible demands, and criticism. Instead of soaking up the other person's pain, try to:

- Maintain your own sense of reality despite what the other person says.

- Reflect the pain back to its proper owner—the person with BPD.

- Express confidence that your loved one can learn to cope with their own feelings.

- Offer your support.

- Make it clear that your loved one is the only person who can control their feelings and reactions.

> The emptiness belongs to the person with BPD, and the only person who can fill it is themselves.

- Show by your actions that there are limits to the type of behavior that you will and will not accept.

- Communicate these limits clearly and act on them consistently.

You may also need to take steps to protect yourself or your children—not because you are judging or labeling anyone else's behavior, but because you value yourself and your feelings. These steps might include:

- Remove yourself or your children from an abusive situation.

- Let the person with BPD take responsibility for their own actions.

- Assert your own feelings and wishes.

- Disregard name calling or provocative behavior.

- Refuse to speak to an enraged person.

- Decline to let anyone else's public behavior embarrass you.

- Simply say no.

What Is Your Bottom Line?

You must know your own bottom line for different types of situations. It may be helpful to think through what you would do if anyone else besides your loved one with BPD were to act toward you in the same way. For example, what would you do if a stranger in the grocery store began talking to you in the same way the person with BPD does? If you would take steps to stop a stranger from treating you in this way, why not take steps to stop your loved one from doing the same? If you're concerned about the person with BPD's behavior toward a child, what would you do if your child's teacher behaved toward your child like your loved one does? Which do you believe is more potentially harmful: abuse from a teacher or abuse from a caretaker? Another way to think about these tough issues is to consider what advice you would give to a friend or loved one in your situation. Then ask yourself: is any of this advice applicable to you as well?

Avoid the words "all" or "never." Instead of thinking everything is "this way *or* that way," come up with three more alternatives.

If you find that you feel helpless in these situations, you may wish to work with a therapist to explore and set personal limits. This should help you in all your relationships—not just the one with the person with BPD.

Strategies to Help You Reflect or "Mirror" BPD Behavior

There are some specific strategies that you can use to reflect BPD behavior instead of absorbing its affects:

1. **Breathe deeply.** When stressed, people have a tendency to take shorter and shallower breaths. The fight-or-flight reaction kicks in, and it becomes hard to think logically. This can happen to the person with BPD as well. Taking slow, deep breaths can help you settle down and think logically instead of simply reacting emotionally.

2. **Keep seeing shades of gray.** Often, loved ones pick up the borderline defense mechanism of splitting, or seeing things in black and white. Keep in mind the subtleties inherent in all situations. Don't get drawn into the other person's extreme reactions; trust your instincts and form your own judgments.

3. **Separate your feelings from those of the person with BPD.** Earlier in this book, we explained that people with BPD often use projection to try to get others to feel their feelings for them. You may need to keep checking yourself to determine whose feelings are whose. If you start to feel helpless or angry, is it because the other person is projecting his or her own helplessness or anger onto you?

4. **Validate your own opinions and keep an open mind.** The person with BPD may state "facts" you know to be untrue or may assert opinions that you strongly disagree with. Yet people with BPD can be perceptive. So objectively consider what the person with BPD is saying. If, after reflecting, you still disagree, then remind yourself that your version of reality is equally as valid as anyone else's. Your feelings need to be validated just as much as those of the person with BPD.

5. **Be aware of timing.** There are good and bad times to bring up certain subjects. If, for any reason, the person with BPD is feeling rejected, abandoned, or invalidated by other life events, they may react strongly to what you have to say. So you may want to postpone the conversation for a calmer time.

6. **Be aware of your own moods.** If you are feeling vulnerable, lonely, or sad—or even tired or hungry—you may wish to wait until you are feeling stronger.

7. **Remember that you have a choice about your feelings.** The choice of how someone feels is largely up to them. For example, if your daughter says, "You're the worst mother in the world," you can choose to believe it and feel guilty or you can depersonalize these words because you know they're not true.

> Don't get drawn into the other person's extreme reactions; trust your instincts and form your own judgments.

Acknowledge Before Disputing

People with BPD may unconsciously revise their version of the facts to fit their feelings about a certain situation. While it may be tempting to argue about the facts with your loved one, doing so neglects the real root of the issue: their feelings. Consider the following example of how to address the person with BPD's feelings without agreeing with or arguing over his or her version of the facts.

Fact: Cynthia, the mother of a teenager who has BPD, Jessie, occasionally has a glass of wine at night when a friend comes over for a visit.

Feelings: When Cynthia has friends over, Jessie feels ignored, depressed, and angry.

Jessie's "Facts": Because of shame and splitting, Jessie doesn't take responsibility for her own negative feelings. Instead, she accuses her mom of causing them, actually convincing herself that Cynthia has a drinking problem. To Jessie (and other people with BPD), if an explanation *feels* right, it *is* right. Facts that don't fit a person with BPD's theories may be denied or ignored.

If Jessie accuses her mom of being an alcoholic and Cynthia immediately begins defending herself (a natural response), Jessie will interpret this to mean, "You are wrong and bad for feeling this way." She will then become even angrier at having her feelings invalidated. Furthermore, the real issue—

Jessie's feelings of abandonment—would not be addressed. So nothing would be resolved.

By addressing Jessie's feelings before disagreeing with her facts, Cynthia will be able to share her version of reality at a time when Jessie is more open to hearing it. In the example that follows, notice how Cynthia allows Jessie to fully express her feelings before she presents the facts as she sees them. Cynthia doesn't begin by addressing whether she is or is not an alcoholic, because that would be dealing with facts. In Jessie's borderline world, feelings are all that are important right now.

Jessie: (*angrily*) You've been drinking out here on the porch with your friends for hours. You're just a drunk!

Cynthia: You seem angry and upset.

Jessie: You bet I am! How would you feel if your mother was an alcoholic?

Cynthia: (*sincerely*) I wouldn't like it at all. It would make me feel scared and worried that she wouldn't be able to take care of me. Is that how you feel?

Jessie: I'm just mad! I am calling the child-abuse hotline tomorrow. I'm telling them that my mom lies around the house drunk all day!

Cynthia: No one would want a mom who lies around the house drunk all day. It sounds like that's what you think I do. You have a right to your own feelings and opinions. I see things differently, though, and I also have a right to my feelings and opinions. The way I see things, I am quite busy all day, and I drink pretty infrequently. And when I do, I don't do it to a state of drunkenness. I don't feel drunk right now, and I don't believe I'm acting drunk either.

Jessie: You've had too much to drink. You're acting just like Grandpa when he is drunk. Why do you need to sit around the house with your friends? I hate your friends. They're just a bunch of stuck-up bitches.

Cynthia: I know you don't like my friends. You have a right to your opinions about them. We don't always have to like the same people.

Jessie: I don't see why they have to come over all the time.

Cynthia: I know that it seems to you like they're here all the time. Actually, I haven't seen Ronnie and Marta for several weeks. I have a good time with them, and I also have a good time with you when we go shopping and do stuff together, like yesterday when we went to pick up your dress for the prom and stopped for hamburgers and milk shakes. We had a good time, remember?

Jessie: (*calmer*) Yeah. But I just wish you didn't have to drink with them.

Cynthia: (*understandingly*) Yes, I know you don't like it.

Notice that Cynthia reflects Jessie's feelings without agreeing that drinking is the same as being drunk. Of course it's frustrating to be the subject of wild accusations that don't make any sense. It's not fair. Cynthia may go upstairs and grit her teeth with a knot inside her stomach. She may wish that Jessie lived somewhere else. But she has succeeded in talking with her daughter about the real issue that's upsetting her. In addition, Cynthia has expressed her own opinions and observations without invalidating Jessie's. That's quite an accomplishment.

In these kinds of situations, it's helpful to remember the developmental levels that you learned in chapter 3. Jessie looks like a young adult. She sounds like a young adult. But emotionally, Jessie is a small, vulnerable child, feeling forsaken by a mother whom she believes doesn't know or care she exists. But instead of crying for her mommy the way a toddler would, Jessie shouts and threatens. Her childlike feelings bring about very real adult consequences. Such is the nature of BPD. You may make things harder for yourself if you expect adultlike behavior from someone who is currently incapable of it or if you censor your negative feelings and scold yourself for having them.

Expect the unexpected. Accept your feelings for what they are and know that they're normal for people in your situation. See through a person with BPD's exterior and realize that right now, they may not be capable of what most people would consider "normal" behavior.

Prepare for the Discussion

Talking with the person in your life who has BPD about your personal limits is something you can and should prepare for. Following are some tips for communicating about your limits:

- Be specific.
  "I would like you to respect me more" is ambiguous. What exactly is respect, and how do you know when you're getting it? "I would like you to stop blaming me for your physical illnesses," is specific and measurable.

- Communicate one limit at a time.
  The person with BPD may be treating you in a variety of ways you find intolerable. But asking them to stop blaming you for all problems, to stop raising his or her voice, and to stop calling you names may be too much for the person with BPD to process all at once. Choose one to start with.

- Begin with the easy stuff.
  Telling someone to stop calling you names may be simpler than asking them to stop blaming. You can increase your chances of success—and build your confidence—by starting with something easier.

- Practice with a good friend.
  Role-play the situation with a friend. Do this a couple of times, changing the person with BPD's responses each time. Don't feel you have to rush; take as much time as you like to think and respond, both during the role play and the real event. Things will come together, and it will get easier. It just takes time.

- Think about the rewards.
  Maintaining your personal integrity leads to feelings of strength, self-respect, confidence, hopefulness, and pride.

Determine Your Reality and Stick with It

Often, the truth is not so clear cut. Many people we interviewed who love someone with BPD told us they had trouble trusting their own perceptions of reality because their loved one was so convincing in their insistence that they were right and the interviewee was wrong.

Let's look at Sara and her mother with BPD, Maria. Sara tells Maria that she will no longer stay on the phone when Maria blames and criticizes her. Sara also puts limits on the number of times per week that her mother may call her.

"I would never do that to my mother!" Maria snaps. "How can you refuse to talk to your own mother on the phone? How can you hurt my feelings like this? How could I raise such an ungrateful, selfish daughter?"

Sara's father, George, agrees. He takes Sara aside and says, "That's just how your mother acts, Sara. She can't help it. Be a good daughter and make things right with your mother."

Sara feels confused. Is she being bad and selfish? Does she owe it to her mother to stay on the phone, even if she feels a horrible tightness in her chest when her mother berates her?

When the person with BPD or other people around them make counter-moves, you will need to return to the belief that you have a right to all of your opinions, thoughts, and feelings. Good or bad, right or wrong, they are part of you. You also need to keep in mind the personal limits you've set for yourself.

Asserting Your Reality Statement

If Sara decides to debate proper phone etiquette with her parents, she will be avoiding the real issue: as an adult, she is responsible for making her own choices about how she wants to be treated.

Sara says, "Dad, I appreciate the fact that you have different beliefs about me asking Mom to observe phone limits. I understand that the two of you might do things differently. But I am not you—I am me. And to respect myself and my own feelings, I need to limit phone calls to once a week and not stay on the phone and listen to criticism and blaming that makes me feel bad."

Reality statements help you and the person with BPD find the grays in between the black and white of your "truth" and theirs. The two of you may negotiate. For example, Sara and her mother may ultimately agree on phone calls twice a week instead of once a week.

> When the person with BPD or other people around them make countermoves, you will need to return to the belief that you have a right to all of your opinions, thoughts, and feelings.

Shift Responsibility Back

Once you've asserted your reality statement, you must shift responsibility for the person with BPD's feelings and actions back to them. You can let the person with BPD know that you support them, but ultimately they are the only person who can make themselves feel better.

Even if the person with BPD acknowledges that they have borderline personality disorder, it is usually unwise to make this shift by bringing up the diagnosis. This may be viewed as dismissive and disrespectful.

Here is a more positive way of shifting, using the example of Sara and her mother: "I understand, Mom, that you disagree with my phone limits. I can see it's upsetting to you that I have feelings about the negative things you say to me when we talk on the phone. Hopefully you will realize that I still want to talk with you, but not if you're criticizing and blaming me. I care about you and I want to hear from you—I just want to be treated with respect."

> You must shift responsibility for the person with BPD's feelings and actions back to them.

Share the Responsibility

Let's say that your daughter with BPD is upset with you because you forgot to pick up a book from the library for her as you promised. But her reaction is out of proportion. She insists that you "always" forget these kinds of things, that you must have forgotten because you don't care about her, and that you wish she was dead.

In this instance, you might want to share the responsibility rather than just shift it. As you read this, remember that you've already gone through the process of paying attention, understanding fully, and so on.

Here's what you might say: "I know you feel very hurt and angry that I forgot to pick up the book. And you've said you feel that I 'do this all the time' and that 'this means I don't love you.' I can try to make up for forgetting the book by saying I'm sorry and offering to pick it up tomorrow—which I've done. And I can point out the times I have remembered to do you favors. And I can tell you that I do love you—which I do, very much. That's all I can do. I can't change the past. I can't make you believe that I love you. I know it hurts and you're mad. You can choose to keep thinking these things, or you can choose to try to calm down, accept my apology, and see where we can go from here."

If you've made a mistake and the person with BPD is upset, you should share the responsibility.

Build Communication Skills

When the person with BPD is not agitated, you can pursue the issues even further than Cynthia was able to do with Jessie and attempt to clarify and even resolve issues. When engaging in this type of discussion, it is essential that, when it is your turn to listen, you really listen. Here are some tips:

- Don't think about what you are going to say.

- Do not become defensive and tune the person out, even if the person with BPD is accusing you of things you never did or said. You'll have the chance to address this later.

- Pay attention to the person's words, body language, expressions, and tone of voice. This will help you validate his or her feelings. People with BPD are not always in touch with their own emotions, and by listening closely, you may be able to hear beyond the words and detect the feelings that lie beneath the surface.

It is also important that you understand fully what the person with BPD is upset about. Sometimes the person with BPD will say something or accuse you of something that makes no sense to you. It's easy to get frustrated and angry, which simply escalates the situation if the person with BPD feels invalidated and misunderstood.

Remember that you and your loved one may be speaking two different languages. Try to stay calm and gently ask the person to clarify what they mean.

Following is an example of how to go about better understanding the person with BPD, in a conversation between Tara and Cory. No matter how angry or upset Tara gets, Cory remains calm and composed.

Tara: I know you're having an affair.

Cory:	(*surprised*) What makes you think that?
Tara:	Because you don't love me anymore, you never loved me, and you want to leave me.
Cory:	Whoa, let's take those one at a time. Why do you doubt my love for you?
Tara:	You don't spend enough time with me, for one thing.
Cory:	You said I don't spend enough time with you. Can you tell me what you mean?
Tara:	You know what I mean!
Cory:	No, I'm not sure I do. But I want to understand. Can you help me?
Tara:	Last Saturday, you went out with your friends to a movie without me.

In this situation, asking Tara to elaborate gave Cory some much-needed information. If he had immediately responded by denying the affair, they probably would have fought at length without uncovering the real issue—Tara's fear of abandonment, sparked by Cory going out with friends.

Validate Your Loved One's Emotions

If you want the conversation to facilitate change, you must validate your loved one's emotions. This combines the paraphrasing and reflective listening skills you learned in chapter 6.

Lynn

When I finally got counseling, it was like a miracle to be given permission to feel my feelings and to be told those were healthy, intelligent reactions to have, given the situation I had been in. My family had been telling me I shouldn't feel the way I did, which just made me angrier and more upset.

The feelings of the person with BPD may not make sense to you, but they do make sense to them. Here are some guidelines for how to address them:

- Don't judge the person's feelings, deny them, trivialize them, or discuss whether or not you think they are "justified."

- Restate the person with BPD's feelings; dig a bit beneath the surface for feelings that may not be as obvious.

- Ask the other person if your perceptions are correct.

- Show the person with BPD you are hearing what they are saying.

- Avoid sounding patronizing or condescending, or the person with BPD may get enraged because you don't sound like you are taking his or her concerns seriously.

> If you want the conversation to facilitate change, you must validate your loved one's emotions.

This conversation demonstrating validation is a continuation of the one between Tara and Cory:

Tara: Last Saturday, you went out with your friends to a movie without me.

Cory: You sound really upset and angry—both about me going out to the movie and about thinking that I don't love you. I can see that from the tone of your voice and the expression on your face. Tara, I can understand if you thought I didn't love you, that would be upsetting. If that were true, it would be more than upsetting—it would be devastating. Are you feeling hurt and sad right now?

Tara: Yes!

Express Your Reality Statements

After you have validated your loved one's feelings, assert yourself with "my reality" statements. In this example, Cory's reality is straightforward: he knows that he asked Tara if she wanted to go to the movie, and she refused. And he knows that indeed, he does love her. In this case, he could say, "Tara, it's true that I did go out with friends. You didn't want to go, so I went by myself. I had a good time—I enjoy being with my friends. But that doesn't mean I don't love you—I do, in fact very much."

Some reality statements will be factual (e.g., "When I said that I smelled something burning, I wasn't commenting on your cooking. I was just noticing a burning odor"). Other reality statements will reflect your opinions (e.g., "I don't believe that wanting to see a movie with friends is selfish. I think that even when two people are married, it's good for them both to have other friends and pursue their own interests").

Express your reality statement clearly. The person with BPD may try to argue with you about who is "right" or who is to "blame." Some of these arguments may be illogical; for example, one person with BPD insisted that she was justified in punching and kicking her husband because he had called her "violent." Resist the temptation to justify, overexplain, or debate. Simply stay focused on your message, for example, an appropriate response to an accusation would be: "I understand that you feel this way, but I see it differently." Repeat it as often as is necessary.

> Resist the temptation to justify, overexplain, or debate. Simply stay focused on your message.

Ask for Change

Once you know what your personal limits are, it's time to communicate them. But before you do, be clear on what you can reasonably ask for—and what you can't.

It is reasonable to ask the person with BPD to change their behavior. Chances are your loved one acts differently with you than they do in front of friends, when out in public, or when at work. If someone with BPD can control their behavior under some circumstances, it's likely they can control it in others.

Of course, people with BPD may need help in order to change their actions. If the person with BPD seeks help, they may have a much easier time observing your limits. But as you know, this is a decision people with BPD must make for themselves.

But while it's reasonable to ask someone to change their behavior, it isn't reasonable for you to tell someone how they should feel. In other words, you can ask your loved one not to yell at you, but you can't tell your loved one not to be angry. You can request that your loved one not call you more than twice a day, but you can't tell them not to feel alone and panicky when you're not around. If people with BPD could change their feelings through sheer willpower, they would have done so already!

In *The Dance of Anger* (1985), Harriet Goldhor Lerner writes:

> Most of us want the impossible. We want to control not only our own decisions and choices but also the other person's reactions to them. We not only want to make a change; we want the other person to like

the change that we make. We want to move on to a higher level of assertiveness and clarity and then receive praise and reinforcement from those very people who have chosen us for our old familiar ways.

While it's reasonable to ask someone to change their behavior, it isn't reasonable for you to tell someone how they should feel.

Communicate Your Limits

Pick a good time to talk—a time when both you and your loved one with BPD are feeling grounded and in good spirits. When things are going well, you might not want to bring up difficult issues because you don't want to spoil the mood. You will need to overcome this urge to leave well enough alone.

BPD researcher Marsha M. Linehan (1993b) has developed a communicating style known as DEAR, which stands for describe, express, assert, and reinforce. Following are each of the steps and how you can use them to explain your personal limits.

Describe

Describe the situation as you see it without exaggerating, making judgments, or explaining how you feel about it. Be as objective and as specific as you can. It may help to pretend you are a video camera capturing the action exactly as it happens. Do not use judgmental or loaded words or phrases. Do not claim that you are privy to the person's inner motivations or feelings, although you can say that it "appears as if" the person was upset, angry, and so on.

For example, you can say, "Yesterday, we were driving home from our vacation. Around lunchtime, we began talking about when we were going to stop to eat when you began speaking to me in angry tones that got louder and louder. You seemed to be very upset about something that had happened the day before. After about ten minutes, I asked if we could continue the conversation at another time. Then you continued to yell at me. After several more minutes, I asked again if we could talk about this after we got home. You refused and swore at me and called me names."

Describe the situation as you see it without exaggerating, making judgments, or explaining how you feel about it.

Express

Express your feelings or opinions about the situation clearly. Take responsibility for your own feelings; do not say, "You made me feel this way." Instead say, "I felt this way." You may need to do some thinking beforehand to determine your exact emotions.

For example, you can say, "When you were shouting at me, I felt very bad. I was afraid because I didn't know what you might do or say next. I felt helpless because there was no place for me to go because we were in the car. I felt sad because you were angry at me. And when I asked you to stop and you didn't stop, I became mad because you were not responding to me. I also felt concerned because our son was in the back seat, and I was worried about how the argument was affecting him."

> It's very difficult for people with BPD to understand that you can be angry or upset with them and still love them. You may wish to remind the person with BPD that even though something is bothering you, you still care about them deeply.

Assert

Assert your limits, making them simple. Again, explain that you've decided on this limit not because it is right, expected, normal, or how the other person "should" act. Instead, you want this because it is your personal preference, it is how you would like to be treated, and it is behavior that makes you comfortable.

For example, you can say, "I do care about your feelings, and I do want to resolve our difficulties. When things get intense and we start yelling at each other, I may need to stop the conversation and return to it later when we have both calmed down. This is something I need to do to make myself feel better."

Again, the person with BPD may try to engage you in a debate about what is right or wrong or who is at fault. Once more, resist the temptation to justify, overexplain, or debate. Listen carefully, then repeat your message: "I hear what you're saying and understand that you think it's all my fault. However, I see things differently. My firm position is that this kind of behavior toward me is unacceptable, and I want it to stop."

Reinforce

Reinforce the benefits of your limits, if appropriate. Explain the positive effects of getting what you need. If appropriate, help the person with BPD see the negative effects of the status quo, too.

> Explain that you set a limit because it is your personal preference; it is how you would like to be treated; and it is behavior that makes you comfortable.

For example, you can say, "When we resume the conversation, I can be in a better position to hear your concerns because I feel calm and more centered. And we will not get bogged down in angry conversations that do not seem to resolve anything and leave us both upset."

Don't threaten your loved one in an attempt to control their behavior. For example, let's say that you and the person with BPD are attending your grandma's eighty-fifth birthday party. They see that everyone else is dressed very nicely and get mad at you because you dressed informally in shorts and a faded T-shirt. They scream at you, calling you a slob in front of everyone. A natural—but unhelpful—response would be to say in an angry tone of voice, "If you don't stop it right now, I'm walking out the door!"

Instead, make it clear that you are not acting against the other person, you are acting for yourself. For example: "I am extremely uncomfortable when you yell at me—especially when other people can hear. It makes me feel angry and helpless. I am asking you to stop this right now, so we can keep on having a good time at the party." You may need to assert your wishes and reinforce the positive consequences (e.g., "we can keep on having a good time") more than once.

Don't threaten your loved one in an attempt to control their behavior. Instead, make it clear that you are not acting against the other person; you are acting for yourself. You may need to assert your wishes and reinforce the positive consequences more than once.

You may also wish to bring up the negative consequences: "If you don't stop this, I am going to have to go somewhere else and take a break." Then do it if the person with BPD still doesn't respond.

Be Prepared for Countermoves

When one person gives up ineffective fighting and makes clear statements about their own needs, desires, and beliefs, the other person usually shifts their behavior in response. This happens in all relationships. But when one of the people has BPD, it is crucial to anticipate the ways in which they might react to the changes you are making.

People with BPD try to manage their pain through their interactions with other people. As we have explained, projections, rages, criticism, blaming, and other defense mechanisms may be attempts to get you to feel their pain for them. When you assertively redirect the pain back to the person with BPD so they can begin to deal with it, you are breaking a contract that you didn't know you signed. Naturally, the person with BPD will find this distressing. The person with BPD will probably make a countermove. This is an action designed to restore things to the way they were. Countermoves also help people justify their actions, both to themselves and to you. This element is crucial because it seems to make the blackmail acceptable—even noble. Your ability to withstand these countermoves will determine the future course of your relationship.

According to Harriet Lerner (1985), people react to limit setting in three predictable and successive steps: mild disagreement, intense disagreement, and threats. (Be aware that someone with BPD, however, may skip right to threats.) In our discussion of these steps, we will focus on mild and intense disagreement. In chapter 8, we'll discuss unsafe threats.

How to Respond to Mild Disagreement

Following are some countermove tactics discussed by Susan Forward and Donna Frazier in *Emotional Blackmail* (1997):

- **The spin:** The blackmailer tells you that their motivations are pure and honorable, while yours are underhanded, unscrupulous, and self-serving. (It's common for loved ones who set limits to be split into the "bad" person.)

- **Labeling:** The blackmailer calls you names that reinforce their "spun" viewpoint and undermine your sense of reality. Many of these are actually projections.

- **Pathologizing:** The blackmailer tries to convince you that you are not just acting bad—you are bad (or sick, messed up, damaged, etc.). The higher the stakes, the more likely it is that this will happen. Many people we inter-viewed told us that their loved one with BPD accused them of having BPD themselves.

- **Enlisting allies:** The blackmailer asks other people to pressure you. This seems to be most common when the person with BPD is a parent. In one case, a mother with BPD showed up at her daughter's door with four relatives to back her up.

People react to limit setting in three predictable and successive steps: mild disagreement, intense disagree-ment, and threats.

When responding, it's important to stay away from arguments about whether your limits are right or wrong. Here are some sample responses to some typical statements:

Person with BPD: You're a bad (selfish, etc.) person for making this request.

Their Loved One: I understand you think that I'm a bad person, but I feel good about myself and I'm proud that I respect myself enough to set this limit.

Person with BPD: You must hate me.

Their Loved One: No, I don't. In fact, I care about you so much that I want to work together to make our relationship better. I also care for and respect myself, which is why I'm bringing this up.

Person with BPD: You're manipulative and controlling.

Their Loved One: I understand that you think I'm manipulative and controlling. I feel it's your job to make choices and decide how you want to act. And it's my job to think about the things I'm comfortable with and the things I'm not. I've thought about this a great deal, and this is very important to me and my own self-respect.

Person with BPD: You shouldn't feel that way.

Their Loved One:	Perhaps if you were in my position, you wouldn't feel this way. We're two different people and we each have our own beliefs, feelings, and opinions. I am asking you to respect my feelings, even if you don't share them.
Person with BPD:	You're the child. I'm the parent.
Their Loved One:	I am your child. And I'm not a little girl (boy) anymore. I'm an adult, and it's time for me to make my own decisions based on my own feelings and beliefs. You may not agree with me, and that's your right. It's my right to act in ways that respect myself.

Other nonargumentative responses include:

- That's your choice.

- I would like to talk about this later when things have calmed down.

- I need to think about this more.

- There are no villains here. We just see things differently.

- I'm not willing to take more than 50 percent of the responsibility.

- I know you don't like this, but it's not negotiable.

- I know you want an answer right now, but I need time to think.

- I won't be put in the middle. You need to work that out with them.

How to Respond to Intense Disagreement

When the person with BPD increases the intensity of their responses, the implicit message is: "You are taking away my method of coping, and I cannot stand these feelings—so change back!" If the person with BPD shouted before, they may now rage out of control. If he previously accused you of being selfish, now he may call you the most self-centered, egotistical, and controlling person in the world. If she coped by using violence—either against herself or others—the violence may become more severe. Chapter 8 will address how to protect yourself from violence.

Remember Countermoves Are Normal

It is important to remember that countermoves are not a sign that what you did was wrong or did not work. It means that you have asked the person with BPD to do something difficult. Nobody likes doing things that make them uncomfortable.

It is possible that over time, your limit setting will lead to the person with BPD taking a hard look at themselves and deciding to seek help. Or the person with BPD could devalue you, accuse you of abandoning them, and claim that they never want to see you again. Or he could do both.

> Countermoves are not a sign that what you did was wrong or did not work. It means that you have asked the person with BPD to do something difficult.

Whatever happens, it is possible that it would have happened eventually anyway. Your actions may just have accelerated the pace of things.

Persisting

If Your Limits Aren't Observed

If you want your loved one with BPD to change, you have to be willing to make some changes yourself if they do not observe your limits. Think about the things you can do, not the things you feel you can't do. Be creative. Here are some examples:

- You can change the subject or refuse to discuss the matter.

- You can leave the room or hang up the phone.

- You can change your phone number or change the door locks.

- You can go in your room and shut the door.

- You can be with the person only when a third party is present.

- You can refuse to read the person's mail or email. You can change your email address.

- You can stop the car or refuse to drive with the person.

- You can say no firmly without changing your mind.

- You can ask for help from therapists or friends, even if your loved one with BPD doesn't want you to do so.

- You can call a crisis line or shelter.

- You can call the police and get a restraining order.

- You can stop seeing the person for a while or break off the relationship altogether.

- You can find alternative places for a child to stay (e.g., a group home, with a distant relative, etc.).

- You can take steps to protect children from abusive situations (e.g., taking the kids out when your loved one is raging, reporting child abuse, and seeking sole custody).

Naturally, all of these things will be perceived as abandonment by your loved one with BPD. That's why you may need to gently point out that you are not acting against the person; you are acting for yourself. Explain that your limits are essential to the health of the relationship and that you are asking your loved one to observe them so you can be with them for a very long time.

Consistency Is the Key

Within reason, we suggest you observe your limits in a gentle way every time—even when you're tired or when you'd rather avoid a fight. You may not always be able to take immediate action, but you can't let unacceptable behavior go unnoticed or you may actually reinforce it. Again, preparation is key. Think through the "what ifs" and decide ahead of time, if you can, what steps you will take in each case.

Use Caution and Seek Help

BPD is a serious personality disorder. It is crucial that you seek outside help from a competent mental health professional if you have any reason to believe that the countermoves may be more severe than you can handle alone. Here are some specifics on getting help:

- **Consult a qualified professional.** If children are involved, we strongly suggest that you consult with a qualified mental health professional about how to best protect children under difficult circumstances. It is essential that this person be knowledgeable about both BPD and issues involving children. If this person's recommendations go against your gut instincts, you may wish to get a second opinion. Remember, each person with BPD is different, and each child is different.

- **Seek legal counsel if needed.** If you are a parent who is worried about visitation, custody, or false accusations, we strongly recommend talking with an attorney who is familiar with personality disorders before you make any sudden moves. It is crucial that anyone you consult with is familiar with these types of situations and has dealt with them successfully.

> Observe your limits every time—even when you're tired or when you'd rather avoid a fight.

- **Prepare emotionally.** If the person with BPD is your parent and you were physically or emotionally abused as a child, we suggest that you work with a mental health professional to make sure that you are emotionally ready to ask your parent to observe your limits and that you are prepared for any response they might have.

Whatever your circumstances, you may need a great deal of love, support, and validation as you stand up for yourself. Some of the important people in your life may be able to support you; ask for their help. Other people may disagree with your actions because they feel it threatens their own relationship with the person with BPD, or because it contradicts their own firmly held beliefs about how things should be. This is normal. Acknowledge their right to have their own opinions and express your desire to keep your relationship with them separate from your relationship with the person with BPD.

Measure Your Success by the Things You Can Control

The person with BPD may or may not respond as you would like during any one particular conversation. This is beyond your control. So measure your success by the factors you *can* control. Ask yourself:

- Did you respond as an adult, not as a child?

- Did you act in a way that demonstrates your self-respect?

- Were you clear about your position?

- Did you remain focused, even if the person with BPD tried to draw you off track?

- Did you remain calm and composed?

- Did you refuse to be baited and drawn into a losing argument?

- Were you considerate of the other person's feelings, even if they did not give you the same consideration?

- Did you maintain a firm grip on your own reality while maintaining an open mind toward the person with BPD's concerns?

If you can answer yes to any of these questions, pat yourself on the back.

We've covered a great deal in this chapter. Don't try to absorb it all at once. It may seem overwhelming now—but you can change the way you interact with the person with BPD. Just remember these key points:

- You're asserting your limits for the long-term health of the relationship—not just for yourself.

- Be a mirror, not a sponge.

- Stay on track. Don't let the person with BPD distract you from your communication goals.

- Feel good about the steps you've taken. You've come a long way.

In the next chapter, we'll discuss what to do when the person with BPD's behavior becomes unsafe.

CHAPTER 8

Creating a Safety Plan

Yeah, make your arm bleed, bang your forehead on the headboard, harder, harder! Scream at those you love until they slink off terrified of you, the traitors! Burn your fingers on the stove, prick your hand with a pin over and over and over and over. Take those pills. Buy more, stock up. This might just be the big eclipse.

—Melissa Ford Thornton, *Eclipses: Behind the Borderline Personality Disorder*

Rages, physical abuse, self-mutilation, and suicide threats are the most isolating, frightening kinds of behaviors you must contend with from the person with BPD in your life. Sometimes loved ones of people with BPD also rage, become abusive, or consider suicide themselves. The keys to managing these difficult situations are planning and obtaining outside help. Hopefully your behavior will encourage your loved one to get the professional assistance they desperately need.

Out-of-Control Rages

Borderline rages can be terrifying. The person with BPD may be completely out of control, acting on impulse, and heedless of the consequences of their behavior.

Karen Ann

When I am angry, I can't think rationally. I'm possessed by emotions that cause me to act out viciously. The feelings overpower me, and I have to lash out to let them escape. It's an attempt to protect myself, knowing that what I am doing will drive a person further away.

Dick

When I rage at people, they are no longer real people with real feelings. They become the object of my hatred and the cause of my distress. They are the enemy. I get paranoid and believe they want to hurt me, and I am determined to strike out to prove control over them.

Laura

I think that borderlines are concerned about only one thing: losing love. When I am cornered, I get very scared, and I show that by getting angry. Anger is easier than fear and makes me feel less vulnerable. I strike before being struck.

Rage and Logic Don't Mix

In our interview with clinician Jane Dresser, RN, she said, "When someone with BPD is highly emotionally aroused, do not expect them to act in a logical way. It isn't going to happen, not because they're not willing to, but because they cannot."

Dresser notes that when people who have experienced trauma are emotionally aroused, the logic centers of their brains do not seem to function as well. This finding is not a surprise to you, as most people who love someone with BPD find reasoning with an enraged loved one pointless and frustrating. The time for rational discussion is later, when both of you have calmed down.

When someone with BPD is highly emotionally aroused, do not expect them to act in a logical way.

Dresser also points out that because some people with BPD do not have the capacity to regulate their emotions, all anger has the same intensity. A mild irritation seems indistinguishable from an impassioned fury. Dresser suggests, "Sometimes it's important to ask the person with BPD, 'On a scale of 1 to 10, how mad are you?'"

What to Do

During a rage, the best thing to do is temporarily remove yourself and any children from the situation. In our interview with Margaret Pofahl, ACSW, she suggested that you say calmly, "I will not discuss this further with you if you continue to yell and scream at me. I am willing to be supportive if you can calmly tell me what it is that you want or need." Note that you've given the person with BPD a choice and made it clear that their actions will be responsible for your temporary withdrawal. If the raging continues, immediately retreat to safer ground. Here are some ways to do this:

- Retire to a room that is off limits to everyone else.

- Call a friend and go to their house.

- Call a relative and have them come to your house.

- Take the kids and go to a movie.

- Put on some headphones and listen to music.

- Take a taxi home.

- Turn on the answering machine or disconnect the phone and take a hot bath.

- Refuse to read the person with BPD's letters or email.

Sometimes it can be helpful to ask the person with BPD, "On a scale of 1 to 10, how mad are you?"

If the person with BPD routinely loses control, think through your options now and make concrete plans for the next time they fly into a rage. Make arrangements to leave quickly if you need to: for example, know the location of your purse or wallet, or have the phone number of a friend written near the phone.

What Not to Do

It's important that you don't continue to ignore or accept rages. Realize that extreme rage directed at you or your children is verbal and emotional abuse. Even if you think you can handle it, over time it can erode your self-esteem and poison the relationship. Seek support immediately.

It is in your own best interest not to respond to borderline anger with rage of your own. Cory F. Newman, PhD, said during our interview, "This will escalate the pattern of hostility and coercive control. When you fight fire with fire, the problem gets worse and nothing is resolved." Remember that the person with BPD may be trying to provoke you into anger, consciously or unconsciously. If you find yourself losing control, stop and leave the scene. If you do get angry, however, don't be too hard on yourself. It's human nature to want to fight back. Just tell yourself that you'll try to be calmer next time.

"When you fight fire with fire, the problem gets worse and nothing is resolved."

You probably know how to fight back and say hurtful things, and retaliation can be tempting in the face of a rage. However, try not to push the person with BPD's shame or invalidation buttons if you can help it. Comments like, "You have no right to be angry" can make things worse. You can't control the person with BPD's actions, but with the knowledge that you handled their rage well, you can feel good about yourself.

Don't take out your frustration on other people. This is another reason why enduring abusive behavior is a bad idea. When you try to swallow your feelings, they usually end up surfacing elsewhere in a way you didn't expect. This can leave you even more isolated in the long run.

Set Personal Limits Around Rages

What you learned in the last chapter about setting limits applies when it comes to rages, too. If possible, try the following:

- Discuss your limits with the person with BPD beforehand so the two of you have a shared understanding of what steps you're going to take the next time this happens.

- Set this limit when things are on an even keel, using the communication tools described in the last chapter.

- Assure them that if you leave, you will be back.

- Explain that the person with BPD has some control in the matter: If they choose to calm down, you will stay. If they choose to rage at you, you may leave and return when things are calmer. The decision is theirs.

Before you implement the plan, review the information in chapter 7 about responding to countermoves. You must be prepared for any escalation. And remember the importance of consistency. In our interview with therapist Margaret Pofahl she said, "If you say today that you are not going to take angry blaming, then tomorrow you cannot take it, either." Otherwise, you may intermittently reinforce the behavior.

The person with BPD may apologize sincerely—and then repeat the behavior the next time they get angry. This may be because the person with BPD doesn't have the tools they need to calm down and choose another course of action. If the person with BPD won't seek help or keeps repeating the behavior, you may need to decide what you will and will not accept in the relationship. It's up to you.

Suggestions from People with BPD

Many people with BPD have given us suggestions to pass on to readers like you, who must bear the brunt of borderline rages. Evaluate these recommendations in light of your own unique circumstances. Because each person and situation is different, these suggestions may or may not work for you. You may wish to discuss them with a therapist.

Chris

When people try to calm me down, it only makes me feel more angry and invalidated—like they are telling me that I shouldn't feel the way I do. I feel this way even if I intellectually understand that they did not mean things the way I've interpreted them.

Laura

The only thing that helps me get less angry is when my husband says to me, "I know you are scared, not angry" and gives me a hug. At that moment, my anger melts away and I can feel my fear again. Reacting in anger only makes it worse.

Jean

If a person with BPD is being dangerous, others better stay away until things are safe. Let them know that anger is okay and normal

If the person with BPD won't seek help or keeps repeating the behavior, you may need to decide what you will and will not accept in the relationship. It's up to you.

but that they need to express it in ways that do not attack another person's self-esteem.

Annie

When I am angry, the best thing someone can do to make me feel better is to listen to me. A lot of current literature on BPD encourages others to ignore what the borderline is saying because supposedly they do not know what the truth is or they are "manipulative." My anger is caused by others not listening to me or believing me. It makes me feel as if I don't exist.

Physical Abuse

In our interview with Don Dutton, a psychologist and researcher at the University of British Columbia, he estimated that about 30 percent of men who batter their partners or children have BPD. The percentage of physically abusive women who have BPD is probably much higher.

Take all forms and instances of physical violence very seriously—even if it has never happened before and you doubt that it will happen again. The potential is there for the violence to escalate. Children who witness violence experience many of the same ill effects as those who are directly abused. You must be prepared.

Space limitations prevent us from listing all the steps that victims of domestic violence should take to protect themselves and their children. But the information is widely available from shelters, crisis intervention programs, and online. Search under "domestic abuse" or "crisis intervention" in the yellow pages of the phone book or using a search engine. Plan what you will do if the situation arises again. Find out your legal options.

Male Victims

Family violence is recognized as a serious problem for women. The subject of battered men, however, often remains quiet or is viewed as a joke: a cartoon image of a heavyset woman in curlers and a robe wielding a rolling pin while a tiny, undignified man covers his head with his hands and runs away.

But men have reported being slapped, scratched, punched, clawed, and stabbed with small objects by their loved one with BPD. One man was tripped and fell down a flight of stairs.

Mike

Sometimes when my ex-wife was in a rage, she would claw me, smash me across the side of the head, and punch me in the chest. I'm six feet three inches tall and weigh 215 pounds. Yet she could knock the wind out of me. My father taught me not to hit a woman. So what was I supposed to do?

Men who are physically attacked by women may not see themselves as having a problem. More often, they see the woman as the one with the problem. Many men also believe they should suffer in silence to "protect" the abuser or avoid being embarrassed.

When men do realize they need help, they are often unable to find it in a society that does not believe or understand their complaint as credible. This hurts them and denies the violent women the opportunity to get help of their own.

If you are a man who is being battered, we have some suggestions for how you can address and cope with the situation:

1. Do not, under any circumstances, hurt the other person. This goes double if you are bigger or stronger than the person with BPD. Maintain control of yourself and remain calm at all times—especially when talking to authorities.

2. Organizations involved with domestic violence vary tremendously as to their attitudes about the physical abuse of men by women. However, reports of battered men are not as uncommon as you might think. (Some come from men battered by other men, usually a gay partner or male relative.) If you're being battered, don't wait for an emergency to discover the attitudes of the police, justice system, and social service agencies in your town. Talk to someone now.

3. Consult with legal resources about documenting the abuse and protecting yourself and your children. Know your legal rights and responsibilities. Don't make assumptions or go on advice from a friend of a friend. Find out the facts and be assertive about using your resources to protect yourself.

Self-Mutilation

You may feel frightened, angry, frustrated, disgusted, and helpless in the face of a loved one who mutilates themself. Responding to such behavior requires a balancing act: you should be concerned and supportive without unintentionally rewarding the behavior or making the person feel even more ashamed.

What Not to Do

- Don't take responsibility for someone else's actions. You did not cause this to happen. If an event that involved you preceded the episode, recall the difference between causes and triggers (chapter 5).

- While you can do your best to provide a safe environment, realize that you can't remove every potentially sharp object in the house or watch the person with BPD twenty-four hours a day. As the mother of a teen with BPD says, "If my daughter is determined to hurt herself, she will."

- Don't try to be the person's therapist. Leave that to the professionals.

- Don't keep weapons such as guns in the house.

- Don't define someone with BPD in terms of the self-mutilation. It is something they do, not who they are.

- Don't dwell on the details of self-injury when discussing it with the person. Self-harm can be addictive; you don't want to trigger the behavior. In our interview with Cory F. Newman, PhD, he said, "Addictive behaviors can be cued, such as when a cigarette smoker craves a smoke when he hears someone else talking about lighting up. However, this doesn't mean that it's your fault if the person with BPD engages in self-mutilating behavior after you confront them about it. I am merely stating that you have to handle dynamite with great care."

- Don't moralize, preach, or act disgusted. One woman who hurts herself says, "My friends lecture me about self-injury—as if I didn't know it was wrong. What if I were overweight? Would they follow me around and slap my hand every time I reached for a candy bar?"

- Don't say things designed to evoke shame or guilt, such as "How could you!" The person with BPD already feels ashamed.

- Don't make threats in an angry or controlling way ("If you do this again I'm leaving you!"). This may come across as punishing. Even if you choose to set this limit, it should come across as something you are doing for yourself, not something against the other person. For example, during times when you're both calm, you could explain which actions you cannot tolerate and which of these will force you to leave the relationship.

What to Do

- If the person with BPD threatens harm to themselves (or others), notify their therapist (if they have one) at the earliest possible time. You, your loved one, and the therapist may all want to meet to discuss how you will handle self-harm in the future. If this is not possible, seek professional help on your own to discuss how to handle the situation. If you believe that the person with BPD may be a danger to themself or others, they may need to be evaluated for hospitalization.

- Remain calm and speak in a calm and matter-of-fact way. In *Lost in the Mirror* (1996), Richard Moskovitz says, "Since self-mutilation usually occurs when the person with BPD feels out of control, it is important that those around them do not add to the inner chaos with their own panic" (Moskovitz 1996). Moskovitz points out that although the behavior may be shocking and new to you, it may have been going on for a long time.

- Seek appropriate medical treatment for the person with BPD if warranted. You may wish to call medical professionals to obtain their advice. In our interview with Elyce M. Benham, MS, she said, "This also needs to be handled in a supportive, yet composed and factual manner. What I usually say is, 'Let's take care of this' or 'I'm going to take you to the doctor and have them check this out.'"

- Help the person with BPD put together a support team so you don't feel overburdened and exhausted. The first person should be their therapist, who can work with them to reduce self-harm.

- Empathize with and listen to the person with BPD. Show that you are trying to understand how they feel. Ask questions in a concerned way, such as, "How are you feeling?" and "Is there anything I can do?" Don't underestimate the person with BPD's fear, anguish, and inner turmoil. Imagine the worst you have ever felt, and then triple it.

- Emphasize messages of love and acceptance for the person, while making it clear that you wish they would find another way of handling problems. One person with BPD suggests saying, "I feel helpless and angry when you hurt yourself. I want to understand this, even though I don't fully. But I know I don't want you to do this anymore, and if you feel those urges again please talk to me or call your therapist."

- Stress the positive and offer encouragement (e.g., "Before you did this, you went fourteen days without cutting yourself, and I know you can get back on track.").

- Suggest alternatives to self-harm such as squeezing ice, plunging their hands into very cold water, heavy exercise, biting into something strongly flavored (hot peppers or unpeeled lemon, lime, or grapefruit), or other activities that produce an intense sensation that is not harmful. However, realize that using these alternatives—or not—is up to the person with BPD.

- Refuse to be put in no-win situations—for example, promising not to seek outside help because the person with BPD is embarrassed and ashamed. This is unfair to you both. If the person with BPD insists that you keep the self-mutilation a secret from people who could help, point out that you are not qualified to handle this on your own. (See the upcoming section for no-win situations involving suicide threats.)

If you start to feel consumed by your loved one's behaviors, step back. You may be exaggerating the influence you have on their self-mutilating behaviors. The best way to be there to support them in the long run is to make sure that, in the short run, you're taking care of yourself.

Set Personal Limits Around Self-Harm

As with rages, planning and setting limits beforehand is the key to reclaiming your own life when someone you care about hurts themself. Make sure that you can follow through with the consequences that you set.

Penny

My therapist taught me to tell my friends that if I contacted them before doing anything self-destructive, they could talk to me and reassure me if they wanted to do so. But if I contacted them during or after doing something like drinking or cutting, they were to simply say, "Penny, I love you, but I'm absolutely not going to deal with you when you're like this." Then they were to hang up and refuse to accept any contact with me while I was in that condition.

They wouldn't feel pressured to be my caretakers, and so our friendship would have a better chance of surviving because of less stress placed upon it. It also kept my self-destructive behavior from being reinforced, because drinking and cutting would no longer be rewarded with solicitude from my friends. A phone call before the fact has so far been sufficient to prevent relapses. I dread the dial tone and what it represents enough to find other ways of coping. Plus, my friends have said that this contingency plan relieved them considerably because they knew they wouldn't have to feel guilty about abandoning me.

Karen

My husband Eric's self-harm used to hurt me more than it hurt him. He sensed this and when nothing else worked and he felt awful and couldn't get what he wanted, he would self-harm. The guilt trips were powerful and controlling my life. But I refused to keep being put in this position. I told him clearly when he was calm that I was not taking responsibility for his actions. If I saw blood, I was calling an ambulance and leaving. If I stayed and soothed him, I would be enabling him. He knows that if he doesn't want to be alone, he has to maintain that boundary. Eric's therapist and I each made separate contracts with him not to self-harm. He values his honor and honesty, so this works.

Suicide Threats

Research over the past twenty years shows that about ten percent of people with BPD attempt suicide. According to Beth Brodsky and John Mann (1997), when compared to people with depression or schizophrenia, people with BPD are more likely to make nonlethal suicide attempts, constantly think of suicide, and make repeated suicide threats. The presence of other illnesses such as major depression, substance abuse, and eating disorders seems to magnify the likelihood of actual suicide.

If the person with BPD really wants to die, you need assistance beyond what we can provide in this book. Please seek immediate professional help. You may also wish to call a local crisis line or hospital emergency department and ask for guidance. Then, keep the phone numbers of these people and places right by the phone.

Feeling Manipulated by Suicide Threats

When the suicide threats appear to be an attempt to scare you or make you do something you don't want to do, your sympathy and concern may begin to dissolve into anger and resentment. For example, many former partners of someone with BPD said that when their relationships ended, the person with BPD implied that they would kill themselves if the partner did not return. If you've been on the receiving end of these kinds of threats, you know how guilty, confused, and worried they can make you feel.

Compared to people with depression or schizophrenia, people with BPD are more likely to make nonlethal suicide attempts, constantly think of suicide, and make repeated suicide threats.

In their book *Choosing to Live,* Thomas Ellis and Cory Newman (1996) explain:

> The sense of collaboration and togetherness you once had with the suicidal person diminishes, while the uncomfortable power struggle increases. Comments like, "If you really cared whether I lived or died, you would come back to me" and "You make me want to die" have something in common: they make someone else's decision whether to live or die conditional on your response. This is unfair to both parties.

Sometimes the person with BPD will try to make you believe that you are responsible for their misery and that you will be to blame if they kill themself. Remind yourself that you are not threatening the other person with homicide—the other person is threatening suicide. You're dealing with someone who needs immediate professional attention much more than they need your capitulation.

What Not to Do

Newman and Ellis suggest avoiding the following actions with someone threatening suicide:

- Don't fight.
  Don't get into an argument with the person with BPD about whether they are serious about wanting to die—even if you're angry and feel like venting. The person may attempt suicide simply to prove you wrong.

- Don't accuse.
  Don't confront the person with BPD and accuse them of manipulating you. Again, this may turn into a power struggle. If the person with BPD is asking you to do something that is against your better judgment, follow your instincts. However, if the two of you are in a session with a mental health professional, it can be helpful to talk about how this behavior is making you feel.

- Don't give in to threats.
  Be extremely cautious about relenting just to prove that you really care. Contrary to what an angry, distraught person with

BPD may be telling you, you don't have to prove anything. Say Ellis and Newman, "When you give in to the threats, you will still be angry, the person with BPD will still be at risk for self-harm at any time, and the underlying issues will not have been addressed. Plus, it is likely that the same scenario will repeat itself again and again" (1996).

- Seek help for yourself.

   If you have a history of complying with demands because you believed that suicide was imminent, we suggest obtaining professional help for one or the both of you before the next crisis occurs.

What to Do

Suicide threats that feel manipulative are the ultimate in no-win situations. Whether you comply with your loved one with BPD's wishes or not, the risks are unacceptable. So, Ellis and Newman say, the best thing to do is to simply refuse to be put in this position, despite their attempts to make you feel responsible for their life and death. Just say no, following the guidelines below.

Express your support and concern for the person with BPD while firmly maintaining your personal limits. You can do both, even if the person with BPD thinks otherwise. You can accomplish this with mirroring responses that put the choice of life or death back where it belongs—with the person with BPD—while stating as strongly as possible that you care about the person with BPD and you want them to choose life and seek help.

Ellis and Newman give these sample responses, which we have paraphrased:

In response to, "I'll kill myself if you leave me":

Express your support and concern for the person with BPD while firmly maintaining your personal limits.

"I'm not breaking up with you to be cruel. I'm very, very sorry that this hurts you. I want what's best for you in the future, but I just can't be part of it. And even if I were to stay with you, that wouldn't solve our problems. For one thing, your life's worth should be based on much more than just being in a relationship with me. Secondly, I know that you know deep inside that our relationship shouldn't be based on me staying because I'm afraid of you dying and you staying because you think you can't live without me. That's not healthy. I care about you. And because I care about you, I want you to live. And I want you to find your own happiness, and your own life's worth, without me."

In response to, "If you really cared whether I lived or died, you would come home every weekend":

"The fact that I love you and am concerned about you is already beyond doubt. I feel like I have proven my love time and time again, and I suspect that even if I did come home every weekend, that wouldn't be enough for you. I want to see you, and I do plan on coming up once a month or so. The fact is that I can't visit every weekend because I have my own family now and my own life to attend to. Perhaps the answer is that you need more things to do on your own, or more friends you can get together with on Saturday and Sunday. You used to talk about a lady you played cards with from your church; have you seen her lately?"

These statements should be accompanied by statements that show that you are taking the threats of suicide very seriously. Show warmth and concern in your voice and actions. For example, you might say, "We have to get you to the hospital. This is a matter of life and death." Show that a serious threat warrants a serious response. In this way, you give appropriate attention to the person with BPD's cry for help while making it clear that you aren't qualified to give the professional help that is necessary in such extreme situations.

In certain circumstances, you may wish to enlist the support of other people in your loved one's life: parents, relatives, friends, teachers, and so on. Don't keep this kind of behavior a secret; find other people who are willing to support you both.

When the Person with BPD Is Your Child

When a child or teenager becomes a danger to themselves or others, parents are often at a loss as to where to turn for help. Believing the child's behavior is always their responsibility, they may tolerate behaviors they would never accept in anyone else. If your child is violent to themself or others, it's all right to ask for help from therapists and other outside authorities, family and friends, crisis hotlines, treatment centers, and support groups.

Admission to a Treatment Facility

Admission into a treatment facility is usually voluntary; the child must agree to treatment. However, if professionals believe that the child is a danger to themself or others, they and the police can authorize a legal commitment that can last from twenty-four to seventy-two hours.

Sharon, who manages an internet support group for parents of children with BPD, says that some parents in her group are concerned that a child may be discharged before the parents feel the situation is really safe. In one instance, a prematurely discharged child took an overdose of pills and ended up back in the hospital. As a last resort, Sharon advises simply refusing to take the child home—even if the hospital protests. This, she feels, gives parents additional time to make other arrangements such as residential care. However, the laws about this vary from state to state, and even from county to county. In some areas, you might be charged with neglect. So seek legal advice from a qualified professional as soon as possible.

> You have been doing the best you can with the resources available to you.

Police Intervention

You can call the police to intervene if the child is becoming violent or threatening. As with most police and 911 calls, response time is based on the perception of immediate risk. If you explain that the threat of harm is clear and present, the response may be quicker.

Sharon suggests telling the police as soon as possible—beforehand, if possible—that the child has a mental disorder. "Otherwise they will assume this is just another rebellious teen getting out of hand," she says.

Christine Adamec, in *How to Live with a Mentally Ill Person: A Handbook of Day-to-Day Strategies* (1996), suggests that you immediately give police a "crisis information" form you have prepared ahead of time and kept in a safe place. You can find a copy of the form in her book. This form consists of:

- a brief medical history

- the diagnosis and its definition

- the names of the child's doctors

- names of the medications the child is taking

When the police arrive, they will first contain the situation and then discuss alternatives. If the crisis has passed, no further intervention may be made. If parents choose to press charges, the police will explain the procedure.

According to Sharon, parents in her group who were concerned that the child would become violent after the police departed insisted that the authorities take the child to a safer environment.

If the child's behavior continues to escalate and the child is not agreeable to treatment, they may be placed in juvenile detention overnight or be treated as "allegedly mentally ill" and placed under emergency psychiatric detention at the nearest county-operated hospital.

Unsafe behavior is probably the most difficult aspect of caring about someone with BPD. But by planning for it and asking for outside help, you can defuse its power and make it a lot less frightening.

CHAPTER 9

Protecting Children from BPD Behavior

My narcissistic father never spoke to me about my mother's borderline behavior. He emotionally abandoned me when I was still in grade school. I wish he could have shown me unconditional love. I wish he had not left us alone with her and her moods.

I am glad I was born. But sometimes I wish I wasn't. I am still on an emotional roller coaster; I am still that child looking for the unconditional love I never got. It is too late for me, but it is not too late for the other kids of people with BPD out there.

—Joan

Many people with BPD never act out in front of their children. Others feel the urge but consciously make an effort to shield their children from their BPD behavior. Indeed, people with BPD who are aware of their issues and work to overcome them can be excellent parents—better parents, even, than those who don't have the disorder but aren't as introspective.

However, some people with BPD are unable or unwilling to adjust their behavior around their children. Perhaps they raise their voices more than they should. Or they may experience states of depression that leave them unable to focus on their children as much as they would like to. At the other end of the spectrum, BPD can cause parents to be extremely abusive or neglectful.

As you read this chapter, keep in mind that not all people with BPD act out toward their children. In addition, borderline behaviors directed toward children can vary greatly in their intensity depending on the situation and the person involved.

Typical Problems with BPD Parents

As we said earlier in this book, in some ways people with BPD are emotionally and developmentally similar to children. Like children, they:

- may find it difficult to set aside their own needs to focus on those of others.

- may not be able to adequately consider the children's needs, feelings, and wishes.

Borderline behaviors directed toward children can vary greatly in their intensity depending on the situation and the person involved.

- may be so preoccupied with their own emotional difficulties that they overlook their children's emotional needs.

- may also resent that the children's needs and feelings are different from their own and may therefore ridicule, invalidate, or dismiss them. If the child is happy when the parent is sad, this may be taken as a sign of disloyalty and insensitivity.

Problem: Difficulty Separating Relationships with Children from Problems with Others

Some parents with BPD find it difficult to separate their relationships with their children from their problems with others. For example, they may have a hard time acknowledging that their children can have their own positive relationships with people they may not like. They may also try to get back at others through their children. Some parents with BPD try to force children to choose between a relationship with them and being true to themselves; for example, they may tell a child they are selfish for wanting to spend time with friends.

Problem: Inconsistent Parenting

Other parents with BPD are inconsistent with their parenting. They may vacillate between over-involvement and neglect, depending upon their moods and emotional needs at the moment. They may only pay attention to the children when the kids are doing something to meet the borderline parents' needs. Some parents with BPD try to cope with their own feelings of inadequacy by demanding that their children be perfect. Children may then feel worthless when something goes wrong. They may also try to get their emotional needs met through the children in ways that are inappropriate (e.g., having a ten-year-old sleep in the same bed or miss a classmate's birthday party because the parent with BPD doesn't want to be alone).

Problem: Unpredictable Love

Some people with BPD alternate between taking too little and too much responsibility. For example, a parent with BPD may ignore the negative effects of their actions on the children but then feel guilty or depressed when a child gets a bad grade.

Other parents with BPD may treat their children as if they are all good or all bad. This can hurt children's self-esteem and make it difficult for them to develop a consistent sense of self. BPD parents may turn their love off and on; their children thus learn not to trust them—and, sometimes, not to trust anyone else either. The person with BPD's behavior may be so unpredictable that their child's focus becomes stabilizing the parent and trying to anticipate the parent's moods and actions—to the detriment of the child's normal development.

Children of parents with BPD are often "parentified," according to Kimberlee Roth and Freda B. Friedman, PhD, coauthors of *Surviving a Borderline Parent: How to Heal Childhood Wounds and Build Trust, Boundaries and Self-Esteem*: "[T]hat is, they learn to act as caretaker, perhaps for their siblings or for their parent(s). Many adult children have trouble recalling times when they just felt like fun-loving, silly kids."

Problem: Feeling Threatened by a Child's Normal Behavior

Parents with BPD may feel threatened by children's normal behavior. As children grow and become more independent, the parent may feel abandoned and subsequently become depressed and may rage at the children. The parent with BPD may also unconsciously try to increase a child's dependence. Children thus may have a hard time separating from the parent or feeling

"Many adult children have trouble recalling times when they just felt like fun-loving, silly kids."

competent at handling their own lives. When children become angry them-selves, the parent may act in invalidating ways or rage back, thereby escalating the situation.

Problem: Inability to Love Unconditionally

Some parents with BPD may have a hard time loving their children unconditionally. They may need the children to be perfect to make up for their own feelings of inadequacy. When children disobey, the parent may feel unloved, become angry or depressed, and withdraw their love. Children learn that their parent's love is conditional. Parents with BPD may need to believe that their children are stupid, failures, or unattractive so they don't have to be alone with similar feelings about themselves. Also, this conditional love allows the parent to feel more competent than someone else in their life.

Problem: Feeling Threatened by a Child's Feelings and Opinions

Parents with BPD may need their children to be just like them and may feel threatened when children have different feelings and opinions. This par-enting trait is also common in people with narcissistic personality disorder. In *Trapped in the Mirror: Adult Children of Narcissists* (1992), Elan Golomb writes:

> The pressure to conform to expectations is like the water in which a fish swims, so relentless and uniform that the child is hardly aware of it. [These children] feel as if they do not have the right to exist. Their selves have been twisted out of their natural shape since any move-ment toward independence is treated as a betrayal that can cause the parent irreparable harm.

Though Golomb writes about another disorder, the effect on children is similar. Some parents with BPD may be physically or emotionally abusive or neglectful. Their impulsive behavior may threaten the safety or well-being of their children, or they may hit or slap the children. The parent with BPD may also call the children damaging names or tell them outright that they are bad and unworthy. This sabotages the child's self-concept, self-esteem, and self-worth. In a less directly abusive but equally damaging way, the parent may be unable or unwilling to protect children from the abuse of others, either because they feel that doing so might threaten their relationship with a partner or because the parent is too consumed by their own problems. Children often interpret this as a reflection of their own lack of self-worth.

Potential Consequences of Uncontrolled BPD Behavior

In our interview with Andrew T. Pickens, MD, he said, "Parents who verbally abuse their children will cause emotional damage. How much damage depends on many factors, such as the inherited temperament of the child, the amount of love and empathy given to the child by other adults, the age of the child (the younger the child, the more vulnerable they are), the intensity of the abuse, and other factors."

Janet R. Johnston, PhD, the executive director of the Judith Wallerstein Center for the Family in Transition, said in an interview that the impact of BPD behavior on children varies according to the behavior of the parent and the temperament of the child. For example, if a parent with BPD who primarily acts in is matched with a child who has a "caregiver" personality, the child may feel responsible for keeping the parent alive and happy.

Sela

My three-year-old, Bess, watched when the ambulance took me away after I had taken too many pills. She plays quietly with her toys when I lie in bed, so depressed that I can barely get up to feed her. When I even pretend to cry, her eyes well up with tears. Her first full sentence was, "Is Mommy okay?" When I am happy and beginning to pull out of the black pit, she grows and changes at lightning speed, as if to make up for the time she has lost trying to cope within my shadow. I am determined to get through this horror so I can be a real mommy, not a burden to her.

A primarily acting-out parent combined with a more assertive child could create a unique type of chaos. When one mother raged, her son would write phrases like "Shut up!" and "I hate you!" on pieces of paper and throw them at his mother.

Many studies have shown that BPD tends to run in families. Whether the tendency is due to genetics or environmental factors, such as learning behaviors from a parent with a mental illness like BPD—or some combination—is still not fully understood. Children who do not develop BPD themselves may still be at risk for developing BPD-related traits such as:

- difficulties regulating their emotions.

- problems with eating disorders, addictions, and substance abuse.

- tendencies to over-idealize or devalue people.

- feelings of shame, emptiness, and inferiority. This tendency may result from biological factors as well as environmental ones.

Children who do not develop BPD themselves may still be at risk for developing BPD-related traits.

A study published in the *Journal of Personality Disorders* found that BPD symptoms in a mother are related to interpersonal and family relationship problems and a fearful attachment style in the parent's adolescent children, and that these children are at risk of psychological and social problems in settings outside the family, too (Herr, Hammen, and Brennan 2008).

According to MaryBelle Fisher, PhD, when a parent has BPD, the normal formation of the child's identity may be derailed. In our interview with Fisher she said, "The child's 'self' becomes a mechanism to regulate the borderline parent rather than an internal, cohesive event."

In *Surviving a Borderline Parent* (2003), Roth and Friedman write:

But who *are* you? As the child of a parent with BPD and/or other emotional and cognitive difficulties, it may be surprisingly difficult to answer this question. You likely didn't have much mirroring, or validation, when you were young, which babies need in order to know where they stand in the world, that their feelings and observations and perceptions are healthy and normal. Without that early mirroring, it was difficult to see yourself, to know yourself... As a child, you wanted to please. If Mommy wanted a little ballerina for a daughter, you tried hard to excel in ballet class, even though you really wanted to be out playing kickball or at home reading a book. If Dad needed someone to guide him into the house when he was too drunk to find his way from the garage, you probably associated being a good person with downplaying your own feelings and needs.

Elan Golomb (1992) says:

To grow up as a whole person, children in their formative stages need the experience of genuine acceptance; they have to know they are truly seen and yet are perfect in their parent's eyes; they need to stumble and sometimes fall, only to be greeted by a parent's commiserating smile. Through parental acceptance, children learn that their "is-ness," their essential selves, merit love.

Similarly, Roth and Friedman list "six seeds to grow a healthy child" in *Surviving a Borderline Parent* (2003):

1. support

2. respect and acceptance

3. voice

4. unconditional love and affection

5. consistency

6. security

People with BPD "likely didn't receive them or have them modeled by their own parents when they were children, so they didn't have an appropriate, healthy point of reference. And with a fragile sense of self, they may not have been able to ask for help or accept their own shortcomings," the authors write (Roth and Friedman 2003).

Children with BPD parents may also receive a distorted view of how interpersonal relationships work. For example, one of Fisher's patients feels that he can't become emotionally involved with anyone because he's afraid the other person will take over his life. He stays on the edges of all his relationships, and his emotional life is very sterile.

Children whose borderline parents vacillated between extreme love and raging or abandoning behaviors often have particular difficulty developing trusting relationships with others. They may unconsciously set up tests designed to prove the other person's love, or they may feel abandoned because of small or imagined rejections.

Matthew McKay and his coauthors in *When Anger Hurts Your Kids: A Parent's Guide* (McKay et al. 1996) summarize studies showing that children of angry parents grow up to face more severe problems than those raised in less angry homes. In women, effects include:

> Children whose borderline parents vacillated between extreme love and raging or abandoning behaviors often have particular difficulty developing trusting relationships with others.

- depression

- emotional numbness

- painful yearnings for closeness and intimacy

- a sense of powerlessness

- a limit of achievement in school and work

In men, the primary outcome seems to be difficulty sustaining emotional attachments.

Practical Suggestions for Protecting Children

Most BPD parents love their children very much and worry about the effects of their borderline behaviors. Many parents told us that the knowledge that they could be harming their children gave them the courage and determination to recover from BPD. If the person with BPD has a similar attitude, then it will be easier to be supportive, set limits, and help them in their efforts to improve parenting skills.

However, if the person with BPD refuses to admit that their behavior is abusive and damaging to the children, or if they are unwilling to change, then you may wish to take a more assertive role. Keep in mind that while borderline behavior can be difficult for adults to cope with, it is much harder for children. They have no sense of perspective, little experience, and little or no intellectual understanding of BPD. Furthermore, they are dependent on their borderline parents to meet their most basic physical and emotional needs.

Your ability to shield children from these behaviors will depend on many factors, including your legal and emotional relationship to the child, the nature of your relationship with the person with BPD, the laws in your locality, and your willingness and ability to set limits. In general, however, the closer you are to the person with BPD and the children, the greater an impact you can have—and the greater your responsibility. Following are some suggestions.

> Keep in mind that while borderline behavior can be difficult for adults to cope with, it is much harder for children.

Determine Your Priorities

Some people don't take action because they fear harming their own relationship with the person with BPD. They're afraid that if they set limits regarding children, the person with BPD will rage at them, belittle them, or cut them out of their life.

Only you can decide what risks you can afford to take. Whatever you decide, you must be able to live with the long-term consequences.

> Be honest with yourself; don't downplay or explain away the negative effects of the person with BPD's behavior toward the children. One father justified his inaction by telling himself that his children would learn a valuable lesson from their stepmother's rages: that the world can be a bad place. These justifications may make things easier on him, but they do nothing to shield his children.

Set a Good Example

Children mostly learn by observation. What you do is more important than what you say. That's why mentors and role models "can play a large role in modeling healthy behavior, providing insight into a parent's emotional challenges or simply removing a child periodically from a dysfunctional home," write Roth and Friedman in *Surviving a Borderline Parent* (2003).

Watching you put the steps discussed in this book into practice is also a powerful way for children to learn the basics of detachment, self-care, limit setting, and so forth. Of course, the opposite is also true: if you model less-healthy coping mechanisms, they may learn those as well.

Sam, for example, was embarrassed when his children witnessed fights between him and his wife. He mistakenly believed that his wife's behaviors reflected negatively on him. So he did everything he could to keep the peace—including allowing her to be verbally abusive. If he protested, his wife would call him names and make angry accusations. When this happened in front of the children, he felt ashamed.

Sam's intent was to be kind and responsible. But his children learned that when their mom acted

Children mostly learn by observation. What you do is more important than what you say.

out, it was their job to absorb it. They began to believe that she must be right about what she was saying, because if she were wrong, they believed their dad would say so.

If Sam had used limit setting and mirroring techniques and defused the situation, while simultaneously keeping his limits in place, the children could have learned an important lesson: although their mom acted in unhealthy ways sometimes, she was responsible for her own behavior.

We have two additional ideas for demonstrating healthy behavior in front of children:

- First, make sure that you hold to your limits in front of the children. Explain, "Mommies sometimes get mad, and it's okay to be mad. But it wasn't okay for Mommy to scream at Daddy."

- Second, if the person with BPD is often unpredictably moody, don't let his or her moods affect everyone else or spoil the children's plans. Show children that it's all right to be joyful and have fun even when a parent is feeling down. Try not to cancel fun activities with your kids when your partner is feeling upset.

Enlist the Support of the Person with BPD

Janet Johnston and Vivienne Roseby, in *In the Name of the Child: A Developmental Approach to Understanding and Helping Children of Conflicted and Violent Divorce* (1997), say that people with BPD want to feel support, caring, and acknowledgment that they try their best. But even if you couch your criticisms and suggestions in a supportive way, whatever you say may be interpreted as devastating criticism.

Johnston has three suggestions for overcoming this:

1. Appeal to the person with BPD's natural inclination to want the very best for their children. In other words, don't imply that their parenting may be poor. Simply point out that certain actions are good for kids and some are potentially damaging.

2. Emphasize that parenting is the toughest job there is and that all parents need some help now and then.

3. If the person with BPD had an unhappy childhood, appeal to their desire to give their own children a better experience.

MaryBelle Fisher, PhD, advises approaching the person with BPD when they are calm and starting out by acknowledging their genuine love for and dedication to their children: "Build an alliance with the person by emphasizing the positives and the areas in which you agree. Appeal to their sense of fairness. Don't blame, shame, or attack, which simply makes people defensive."

Two examples of shaming phrases are, "What's the matter with you?" and "How could you do that?" Instead, you might say something like: "It's so hard to bring up kids these days, and I know you want the best for Tim. But we just can't ignore that you seem to be losing control with him sometimes. I can certainly understand what a handful he is after you've come home from a long day at work. And I know you've been under a lot of stress lately. But the other day it looked like you were about to hit him, and I'm very concerned about that. We need to figure out a strategy that allows you to do something differently when you're losing it—perhaps call someone or go somewhere. A lot of people find it helpful to get some outside advice from a counselor about how to make things work out better."

Assist the person with BPD in obtaining help and building a network of support. Offer positive feedback and constructive comments rather than criticism and blame. Fisher says, "Tactfully work with the parent so [they don't] become alienated. There's a tendency for people to close ranks and think, 'Mom's the problem,' and leave it at that. Instead, say, 'Mom's the problem, but how do we maintain respect for her and the integrity of the family?'"

Ask the person with BPD how and when they would like feedback about parenting. Above all, try to enlist their support in helping the children adapt to having a parent who loves them but sometimes can't regulate their own emotions.

> Assist the person with BPD in obtaining help and building a network of support.

Strengthen Your Own Relationship with the Children

Whether you're a parent, family member, or a friend of the family, you can make a big difference simply by increasing the amount of quality time you spend with the children.

> Ask the children questions about what's going on in their lives. Be involved. Give them lots of hugs—even the older ones, if they let you. Consistently show them love and affection.

If appropriate, try to subtly counteract the types of behaviors that concern you. For example, twenty-seven-year-old Lisa was concerned that her boyfriend's daughter didn't have enough privacy at home. At the time, the ten-year-old girl, Stephanie, was sleeping in the same bed as her mother, who had custody. Whenever Lisa was with her boyfriend and Stephanie was visiting, Lisa would take special care to respect Stephanie's boundaries and give her as much privacy as possible. She also spent time developing a trusting relationship with the girl. Eventually, Stephanie insisted on having her own space at home.

Listen to the children nonjudgmentally. Help them trust their own perceptions. Encourage them to talk about their feelings, which may range from grief to rage. They may even be angry at you—perhaps because it feels safer than being angry at the person with BPD. Let them know that their feelings are normal. Be as consistent as you can. Keep your promises. Let the children know they can count on you. Encourage them to call you when they need to and let them visit as often as feels comfortable for you.

> Encourage other adult relatives to develop relationships with the children as well. Grandparents, aunts, uncles, in-laws, and friends of the family can all make a real difference in children's lives. Everyone involved should make it clear that they are not taking sides, but they are offering their love and support to both parent and child.

Encourage Independent Thinking and New Experiences

Children who feel dependent on their parent with BPD can benefit from interaction with other parents and children. Provide experiences without the BPD parent and reward children's natural curiosity and sense of adventure. Encourage kids to follow their own interests and dreams.

In our interview with Fisher she said, "Take care not to wrench the child from the BPD parent. If Janey doesn't want to go somewhere without Mommy for several hours, don't force it. But you might take Janey on a short walk and point out that Mommy's going to be there when she gets back."

If you are a co-parent, and the parent with BPD objects to the child's independence, you may need to set some limits: "Hanna really is old enough to go on a sleepover at her friend's house. I know that this upsets you, but I feel very strongly that we need to encourage her normal friendships with other children. I gave her permission, and she is going to go. Maybe the two of us can go out to dinner and a movie that night."

Help Children Depersonalize Their Parent's BPD Behavior

Most children believe that everything is their fault. So you'll need to help them depersonalize their parent's behavior—especially if the parent outwardly blames the children.

Rachel Reiland is the author of the book *Get Me Out of Here: My Recovery from Borderline Personality Disorder* (2004). Here, she explains how her husband, Tim, helped their children depersonalize the disorder.

Help children trust their own perceptions.

He would tell our kids, "Mommy is sick. Not the kind of sick that makes your throat or tummy hurt, but the kind of sick that makes you very, very sad. Mommy was in the hospital because there was a special doctor to work with this kind of sickness, a doctor who would help Mommy get better and not cry so much or get so mad. Mommy didn't get so mad or cry because of anything you've done, kids, but because she is sick. Mommy loves you so much, and you two make her so happy that you are one of the biggest reasons she can smile or laugh at all." He said this over and over again. And it really made a difference—you could see the relief in their eyes.

Jennifer

When my husband yelled at our children for ten minutes for disturbing him when he was reading the newspaper, I told the kids: "I know that Dad is upset because of what you did. But understand that Dad is really upset about more than that. We can tell by the way he's reacting so strongly. He could have asked you quietly to talk to him later, but instead he got really excited and yelled. That's just way out of proportion to what you did. Even though Daddy is grown up, sometimes he loses control. Remember when you got really upset yesterday when I said you couldn't have candy at the grocery store? You started to cry and you couldn't stop, and Mommy had to calm you down. Daddy's reaction is kind of like that. But how he acts is his responsibility; you aren't to blame.

Older children, of course, may understand this intuitively. However, even if a child realizes intellectually that the BPD parent's behavior is not their fault, the child may still feel responsible on some level. Your own close relationship with the child is your best guide to helping them understand their parent's behavior and handle their own feelings.

Set Limits with the Person with BPD Concerning Children

Rachel Reiland

Tim set firm limits with me regarding the children. In the worst of times, there were out-of-control episodes of rage and hysterics. Tim knew my actions scared the hell out of our kids. So he'd pull me aside and let me know, quite firmly, that the kids were listening and scared by it. "You're not going to put the kids through this," he would say. "You're out of control. Why don't you just go upstairs?" I almost always did. And the few times I didn't, he'd find a place to take the kids until things calmed down.

Like most borderlines, I had moments of control and moments of loss of control. My husband's firm reminders were not just limits but reality checks, pulling me out of childish regression long enough to realize that I had adult responsibilities and that my behavior could have an impact on my kids. It might not have been enough to get me to snap to and think rationally, but it was enough to get me to take it elsewhere.

Children are unable to set limits for themselves; therefore you will need to do it for them.

Some parents with BPD, however, will not be as agreeable. When one father came home and discovered that his wife had just hit their son on the head and called him a disparaging and inappropriate name, he soothed his sobbing son and took his wife out to their planned dinner. As they ate and drank, he gently suggested that hitting and name calling were not the best ways for her to express her frustration. The mother agreed, but excused her behavior by saying, "I had a headache." The father then felt frustrated that his wife didn't understand the seriousness of the problem and was shrugging off responsibility for her actions.

There are times when making gentle suggestions to the person with BPD is the best course of action. This was not one of them. In this case, the father could have postponed the dinner and addressed the problem on the spot, explaining the damage that her behavior could do to their son, insisting that this never happen again, and working with the mother to help her find other ways to cope with her frustrations.

Take all physical and emotional abuse of children very seriously the first time you see or hear of it. Ignoring it may give the person with BPD permission to do it again. And once you set limits regarding the children, observe them consistently.

Seek Therapy for the Children

Children can benefit tremendously from working with a therapist who is experienced in treating people with BPD and their families. Signs that children may benefit from therapy include the following:

Take all physical and emotional abuse of children very seriously the first time you see or hear of it. Ignoring it may give the person with BPD permission to do it again.

- **Difficulty coping with painful feelings:** Intense or long-lasting feelings of sadness or other distressing emotions; recurring thoughts of harming themselves, others, or animals.

- **Self-defeating behaviors:** These include actions that lead to problems at home, at school, or with friendships (e.g., substance abuse, fighting, unusually poor grades, and other unmanageable behavior). In younger children, signs may include frequent, unexplainable temper tantrums or persistent disobedience or aggression.

- **Unexplained physical problems:** Marked change in sleeping or eating habits; hyperactivity.

To find a child therapist, ask your pediatrician for a referral or call a local helpline or the National Alliance on Mental Illness. Interview clinicians by phone or in person to make sure you feel confident in them.

Remove Children from Abusive Situations

You may need to take the children and withdraw when situations become unsafe. Before you retreat, ask the person with BPD to speak with you out of earshot of the children. Like Tim in the preceding example, point out that children should not be exposed to this behavior and offer to discuss the situation later, just the two of you. Or offer to take the kids elsewhere to give your partner some time to calm down.

Remove the Child from the Situation

If the person with BPD remains out of control, take the kids shopping, out for ice cream, over to a relative's house, to a park, to the movies, to a children's museum, to the playground, to the zoo, and so on. If the person with BPD frequently acts out in front of the kids, you may wish to prepare ahead of time by generating a list of things to do and places to go, keeping a few of the children's things packed and ready to go, and/or making arrangements with friends or relatives to be "on call" to help.

Involve Children in Activities

When children are older, help them become involved with rewarding after-school activities. This accomplishes four things:

1. It minimizes the children's exposure to the behaviors.

2. It boosts their confidence and self-esteem.

3. It puts them in contact with other caring adults.

4. It takes some of the pressure off you.

If You Seek a Divorce

If you have decided to seek a divorce from your spouse who has BPD, you may be worried that you won't be there to run interference if your spouse becomes abusive. This fear is much more common among men than women—and justifiably so.

Men who sought custody told us they faced three major obstacles:

1. The court system is often biased in favor of mothers. This is changing, albeit slowly.

2. The court system, by and large, is unconcerned with the type of emotional abuse we've been discussing in this chapter. Judges, lawyers, and activists tell us that while physical abuse can be verified and measured in court, emotional abuse cannot. Judges know that parents battling for custody often make false or exaggerated claims. So unless you have expert testimony (which can be expensive) or credible witnesses, judges may discount or ignore even what you believe to be extreme emotional abuse.

3. Some borderline soon-to-be-ex-wives, frantic at the prospect of losing custody and furious at their husbands for abandoning them, engage in dishonest tactics to discredit their spouses. Their strategies included denying visitation, filing for restraining orders, and making false accusations of sexual abuse of the children.

For the sake of your children and yourself, if you are a man seeking custody, it is absolutely critical that you obtain legal help as soon as possible from an attorney who has much experience with issues surrounding men and custody, as well as with dealing with the kind of tactics we've just described.

As an attorney, mediator, and therapist, William A. Eddy has an international reputation as an expert in legal disputes with high-conflict personalities—especially those with borderline and narcissistic personality disorders. His book *Splitting: Protecting Yourself While Divorcing a Borderline or Narcissist* (2004) reveals how to find such an attorney—and much more—in sections on Preparing for Court, the Court Process, and Special Issues. (*Splitting* is available from www.BPDCentral.com.)

Eddy says, "Managing high-conflict people usually involves using skills [that] are the opposite of what one feels like doing. Learning these skills takes time and practice but can make an amazing difference in resolving, managing, and containing high-conflict disputes" (2003).

Eddy's main message in the book, as well as accompanying audio, is that the divorce process sets the stage for the non-borderline's relationship with their child post-divorce, and the key is what he calls the "assertive approach": one that is sensitive without being passive and persistent without being aggressive.

When people go to court, says Eddy, the judicial system can actually encourage splitting. "When people go into court, they enter an adversarial decision-making system that is splitting people into 'all good' or 'all bad'.... This reinforcement of splitting can be extremely threatening to the fragile identity and embedded insecurities of [someone with BPD]. It allows their daily exaggerations and fears to be taken seriously and provides them a forum for putting all of the blame on the 'bad spouse'" (Eddy 2003).

The assertive approach contains five tenets:

1. **Think strategically, not reactively.** Stop and think when you are angry. Don't act impulsively.

2. **Choose your battles.** Talk to your attorney about which issues need a response and which don't. Some provocative letters, for example, often don't need a response.

3. **Don't make yourself a target.** When in court, expect that innocent things you've said and done may be twisted for adversarial purposes. Keep your composure.

4. **Be very honest.** Things that are half-true are harder to deny than statements you can prove to be totally false. You need that credibility to counter emotional blaming.

5. **Gather evidence that shows the true nature of your spouse's behavior patterns.** Some of the most useful evidence may appear during the actual court case.

Talking to Younger Children

Johnston and Roseby (1997) advise fathers of children aged four to six to simply give the children good, positive messages like, "That's not true. Daddy loves you very much no matter what anybody says." She advises, "Don't worry about undoing what their mother is saying; they're too young to understand motivation and they can only hold one set of information in their minds at a time."

Whatever you say, do not denigrate the other parent.

Talking to Older Children

When the children are older—aged eight to ten—they have the ability to sort out different perspectives. Your goal is not to put the children in the middle by telling them "your side of the story," but to give them factual information that will gently guide them to believe the truth. Remind them of all the loving things you've done together, using concrete examples from the recent past. Help them explore their feelings and assure them of your love. Whatever you say, do not denigrate the other parent.

Here is an example of what you might tell a young child. The central message to a teen will be the same, but the language you use will be different:

"You know, divorce is a very hard on moms and dads. When people break up, everyone's feelings get hurt. And I think that right now Mommy is very mad at Daddy. And when your mom is mad, she tends to think very bad things about people. Remember the time that I came home late on your birthday? Your mommy told you that I was out with my friends, and when I came home, you found out that a nail punctured my tire. That night, I gave you a basketball for a present and we went to the playground and played and had a lot of fun. I loved you back then, and I love you today, and I will always love you, no matter what anybody tells you. And if you feel scared, call me up right away, and I will give you a big hug over the phone, day or night."

Abe

A few weeks ago I was on vacation with my three kids (without my wife). I told them that they may have heard bad things about me from their mother. I told them that they didn't have to believe what she says— that they can believe what they feel or see is true. I also told them that I wouldn't force them to see things my wife's way or my way—that they get to decide on their own what is true. And if they decide to have an opinion that's different from mine, I will still love them and I won't get mad at them. I could tell that this really helped my kids a lot.

For Those Considering Having Children

In this chapter, we've provided a variety of suggestions for protecting children from borderline behavior. We would like to close with this thought: if you and your partner with BPD don't have children but are considering doing so, we suggest postponing having a family until your partner is well into their recovery.

If you and your partner with BPD don't have children but are considering doing so, we suggest postponing having a family until your partner is well into their recovery.

Here's why: having their emotions invalidated is one of the biggest triggers for people with BPD (chapter 6). Yet children constantly invalidate their parents—it's what being a child is all about.

When parents set necessary rules and boundaries, children don't thank their parents for providing guidelines. They cry, scream, and may shout, "You're the worst parent in the world!" When parents feel hassled and ask their children to give them some peace and quiet, children may instead demand that the parent read them a book or take them to the mall.

Just when parents want closeness with their children, the children may decide to assert their independence. Parents may teach their children certain values that their children choose to reject. And children usually don't appreciate the sacrifices their parents make for a long time—often not until they're grown and have children of their own.

Parenting is the toughest job in the world. Constant invalidation is part of it. Make sure that you do what's best in the long term for you, your partner, and any children you might bring into the world.

PART 3

resolving
special issues

CHAPTER 10

Waiting for the Next Shoe to Drop: Your Borderline Child

Laurie, Whose Daughter Has BPD

My daughter Maria is 21 years old now, but when she was 14, I found out she was having sex, skipping school, smoking, drinking, ignoring any rules, sneaking out, having boys over, refusing to do homework, and going to school and changing into inappropriate clothing that wasn't what she left the house in. I was called by security at the mall when she tried to shoplift some jewelry. But she had enough money in her purse to pay for it! I took her to numerous therapists and worked with school counselors. We are not rich, but we did all we could think of, short of sending her to an inpatient facility. In hindsight, I wish we had sent her there when she was a teenager.

I also tried to hide her problems from others, but now I wish I had been honest and let other people know what was going on. That is the only thing that really affects her—she hates feeling embarrassed. Of course I would have been embarrassed, too, but it would have been worth it if it helped.

Now my daughter continues to live in chaos, and she has a two-year-old daughter living in a nasty apartment. I've been so worried that I called the child protective services hotline myself, but since Maria isn't a raging drug addict, they won't do anything.

My advice to other parents is this: If your child has serious problems, get as much help as you can when your child is young, and if that means inpatient treatment, then do that. I wish I had known back then that Maria had borderline personality disorder, and I wish we'd had therapists who had identified this problem and helped Maria. They mostly blamed me for the problem, but I was running myself ragged trying to help her.

Parents need help. Yet many mental health professionals still believe that only adults should be diagnosed with BPD. Some think it's legitimate to diagnose people under 18, but then won't disclose such a diagnosis to parents because they feel it is too stigmatizing. But it is no more ethical to keep silent about a mental health diagnosis than a physical one, whether the person with the illness is an adult or a child.

Here is what often happens with a young person who has BPD:

Their parent takes them to expert after expert. Each time they get a different diagnosis, from ADD to "He's just a bad kid." Then, finally, an expert declares the child bipolar, because both BPD and bipolar disorder involve changing moods. But the two disorders are very different, and so are the treatments. (See the box on page 54 for a detailed discussion of these differences.) Meanwhile, both the parent and the child become ever more frustrated.

Contrary to what some clinicians think, the *DSM-5* does *not* forbid diagnosing children with BPD, or a variety of other mental disorders. Furthermore:

- The National Institute of Mental Health has posted the following information about BPD online: "Recognizable symptoms typically show up during adolescence (teenage years) or early adulthood. But early symptoms of the illness can occur during childhood."

- A detailed report to Congress on BPD, issued by the Substance Abuse and Mental Health Services Administration (SAMHSA), states:

   Although a diagnosis of BPD is seldom made in children and adolescents, research overwhelmingly demonstrates that BPD symptoms and risk factors can be observed in even very young children. Self-injuring behaviors are often present in persons with BPD and can emerge as young as ages 10-12 years. To avoid years of disability and impairment, a focus on early detection of BPD is essential. Many of the consumers

> *[patients] and family members we interviewed lamented the years lost due to the absence of early detection and intervention or to multiple misdiagnoses.*

- Psychiatrist Blaise Aguirre, medical director of a BPD unit for adolescents at McLean Hospital and the author of *Borderline Personality Disorder in Adolescents*, writes: "Two things are absolutely clear. First, adults with BPD almost always recognize that their symptoms and suffering started in childhood or adolescence. Second, some adolescents have symptoms that are so consistent with BPD that it would be unethical not to make the diagnosis and treat them accordingly."

Here is another reason why it so crucial that kids with BPD be diagnosed before they become adults: when a child turns 18, they can vote, join the military, drive a car, and generally become part of the adult world. More notably, at that point their parents no longer have any legal authority over them. All too often, parents can do little more than watch in dread as their adult children with BPD become sicker and sicker, and more and more out of control.

Ava, Whose Daughter Has BPD

When Karen was 16, sometimes she didn't like to see the psychiatrist, but I could usually convince her to go. But now that she's 18, I can't make her get the treatment she urgently needs. Nearly everyone can see she still needs help—with the one exception being Karen herself.

Comparing Kids with BPD to Normal Adolescents

Some clinicians argue that it is impossible to differentiate the average adolescent from a teenager with BPD. That is patently false. Just as talented clinicians can sort out clients who are temporarily depressed from those who suffer from clinical depression, a good mental health professional can differentiate between normal adolescent behavior and BPD behavior.

Your child may dye their hair blue, wear it in a Mohawk, and pierce their body in a few places that you don't approve of. They may roll their eyes at you, refuse to clean their room, and sometimes storm off to their room and slam the door. But this is all just surface stuff, typical of many teenagers.

In contrast, some adolescents with BPD will repeatedly become rageful. They may hurl objects, physically hurt others or themselves, and terrorize their siblings (and possibly their teachers or parents).

Similarly, many adolescents experiment with mood-altering drugs. But smoking weed now and then is far different than developing a dependence on meth or heroin. (Addiction is common among children with BPD.)

Many adolescents briefly entertain thoughts about hurting or killing themselves, especially when their lives are going badly, but few act on those thoughts. In contrast, young people with BPD are at high risk for cutting themselves and/or attempting suicide.

In their book *Stop Walking on Eggshells for Parents: How to Help Your Child with Borderline Personality Disorder Without Sacrificing Your Family or Yourself,* Randi Kreger, Christine Adamec, and Daniel S. Lobel compare typical adolescents and teenagers with BPD in detail. We've compressed examples from that book and put them in the chart below:

COMPARING TYPICAL ADOLESCENT BEHAVIOR WITH BPD BEHAVIOR

Typical Teen	Teen with BPD
May try cutting themselves once because other teenagers they know have tried it. It hurts, so they stop.	May try cutting themselves. They discover that it makes them feel more real and more alive. Over time, cutting becomes part of how they cope when they feel overwhelmed or upset.
May bust curfew occasionally, or even repeatedly, arriving home at midnight instead of at 11 PM. They are remorseful or apologetic.	They stay out all night, come in at 5 AM or later, and tell their parents that it's none of their business what they do.
No longer sees their parent as infallible or heroic, but as a normal human being.	Sees their parent as either perfect or the worst parent ever, based on whatever that parent did most recently (e.g., cooked their favorite supper, or complemented them, or criticized them, or said no to one of their requests).

Tries marijuana a few times.	Considers marijuana too lame. Tries meth, ecstasy, oxycodone, or some other potentially dangerous or addictive drug. Says they want to feel different and better.
Has an argument with their boyfriend and is very upset. Tells parents, "You can't possibly understand how I feel."	Has an argument with their boyfriend, is very upset, and believes that their boyfriend now despises them. Tells parents, "It's because I'm worthless and evil. But actually, *he's* the worthless and evil one. I hope he dies."
Is angry with parents for restrictions, such as a limit on phone time until their grades improve.	Rages at parents for the phone restrictions, and says to them, "If you don't give me my phone back, I'm reporting you to Child Protective Services for abuse." When the parents don't lift the restrictions, the child *does* call CPS, which launches an investigation into the family.
They are upset with their mother after a disagreement. They kick a door hard, scuffing the paint.	Is in a rage with their mother after a disagreement. Throws several glasses at a door, shattering them. Perhaps purposely, steps on a piece of glass and begins bleeding profusely. Mom must call 911.

Treatment for Adolescents with BPD

When normal adolescents get older, they grow out of their adolescent behavior. But young people with BPD do not change their behavior—or that behavior can get much worse—unless they receive treatment.

Effective treatment for teenagers with BPD typically includes one or more of the following:

- dialectical behavioral therapy (DBT)

- cognitive behavioral therapy (CBT)

- a skilled therapist's own mixture of treatment styles

- medication

Let's look at each of these in detail.

Dialectical Behavior Therapy (DBT)

Dialectical behavioral therapy has been effectively adapted for adolescents, and is often used with teenagers who cut themselves or are suicidal. When employed by a trained professional, DBT helps a teenager to accept that their reality, as they perceive it, may be very different from how others see them and their situation. They aren't expected to conclude that their own views are wrong. They simply learn to accept that others can have completely different views. Experts say that DBT allows teenagers to better accept their feelings; it also helps them to use thinking to change those feelings.

Unregulated emotions can be a major problem for most people with BPD. When an adolescent with BPD has emotions that run amuck, they may often behave impulsively and self-destructively. They simply don't know how to cope with their intense emotions. DBT can help them learn to cope with and manage those feelings.

Cognitive Behavioral Therapy (CBT)

CBT is a very frequently used therapy in the United States. It is based on the premise that many people suffer from irrational ideas that they use as operating principles in their lives—to their detriment. Over time, a good CBT therapist learns a client's most common cognitive distortions. One such common distortion is *catastrophizing*, in which someone imagines that if they fail at a goal, then it will destroy their life. So, for example, a teenager with BPD who received an F on a math test might tell themself that life as they know it is over. Their therapist will help them realize that, although failing a math test is not good, it is not a genuine disaster. Furthermore, there are actions they can take, such as getting tutoring in math and spending more time working on it, that can create better outcomes in the future.

Personalized Treatment Combinations

Most therapists use a combination of therapies. For example, a therapist may use CBT and some aspects of dialectical behavior therapy (DBT), such as validating the emotions of the client. Other therapists might use a combination of acceptance and commitment therapy, solution-focused therapy,

EMDR, or one of many others. A good therapist pays close attention to each client and bases their therapy on the needs of that client.

That said, some excellent therapists are specialists in a single form of therapy. If a particular type of therapy works well for your child, there is no need to ask for or require additional therapeutic approaches.

Medication

A bit shockingly, no medications have been FDA approved for the treatment of BPD in adults *or* children. Instead, psychiatrists use medications "off label" to treat specific issues and traits. Any decision on medications for your child needs to be made by a qualified and skilled clinician—in consultation with you, of course.

Below, in brief, are the medications that are typically prescribed, alone or in combination, for teenagers with BPD, according to Blaise Aguirre, MD, author of *Borderline Personality in Adolescents*. (It is worth noting that, to date, all studies on these drugs and their effects on BPD have been conducted on adults.)

MEDICATIONS USED TO TREAT BPD IN YOUNG PEOPLE

Type of Medication	Examples	Effects
Antipsychotic medications (neuroleptics) in small doses	Olanzapine, Abilify, Seroquel, Risperdal	Reduces anxiety, paranoia, anger/ hostility, depression, and interpersonal sensitivity
Antidepressants	SSRIs, including Prozac, Zoloft, Paxil, fluoxetine, and fluvoxamine Tricyclic antidepressants such as Imipramine	Reduces anxiety, depression, and rapid mood shifts; may have an energizing effect
Mood stabilizers	Depakote, Topamax, Lamictal	Decreases irritability, anger, and impulsive aggression.

Keep in mind that all of these drugs have side effects—unfortunately including, in some cases, suicidal feelings. Also, ideally, one physician should be in charge of *all* your child's medications, including both psychiatric medications and those for other illnesses.

For a more detailed guide to medications for adolescents with BPD, consult Blaise Aguirre's *Borderline Personality Disorder in Adolescents*.

Because children with BPD typically end up seeing multiple clinicians over time, many are prescribed a cornucopia of meds. If this is the case with your own child, you will need to manage them all. It's critical to create (and, as needed, update) a written document detailing all your child's medications, including, for each med:

- Name (ideally, both the brand and generic names)

- Current dosage (amount and frequency)

- Previous dosage (if applicable)

- Purpose

- Side effects (both potential and observed)

- Your best judgment of its effectiveness (or lack of it)

Whenever your child sees a new clinician, it's vital that you provide that professional with this information on all their current medications.

Finding a Skilled Treatment Professional

It's probably not going to be easy to find a talented mental health professional who has the ideal combination of skills, training, and experience. Ideally, you want a therapist who:

- is experienced in treating people—including young people—with BPD

- is willing to talk honestly and openly with you about your child—though without violating the confidentiality of individual sessions with them

- is clear on what their goals are for your child, and how many sessions may be needed to make progress

If a therapist assumes that you or somebody else has abused your child, and no such abuse has occurred to the best of your knowledge, consider this a big red flag. While some young people with BPD have been abused or neglected—just as some kids in every group have—most have not. A therapist should be your child's advocate, but never your avowed enemy.

In addition, any therapist you choose should assume that your child *can* make progress. A therapist who believes that people with BPD can never improve in any way, and thus are doomed to failure, is the wrong therapist for your child.

BPD is a challenging disorder to treat, but it is definitely treatable with the assistance of a dedicated and talented therapist. While you shouldn't ask or hope for a quick fix for all your child's problems, if a therapist does not have an underlying hopeful philosophy, then they're not the right person to help your child.

Lastly, follow your instincts. If a professional appears on the surface to be okay, but something in you screams, *No, no, no!*, listen to that inner voice. Something may be off, even though you don't know just what. Trust your gut.

Some questions you may wish to ask a potential therapist:

1. Do you think that children or adolescents can have symptoms of borderline personality disorder? (The correct answer is of course *yes*.)

2. Will you and I meet periodically to talk about how things are going? Can I call you with concerns? (The answers to both should be *yes*, unless your child is 18 or older).

3. Do you think you can help my child? (Although nobody can give a guarantee in therapy, good answers include *yes, probably, very likely,* and *I'm confident that your child can make progress*.)

4. Do you think that all young people with BPD have been abused? Or do you see the disorder as the result of nature as well as nurture? (The answers should be *no* to the first question and *yes* to the second.)

5. What kinds of therapy do you use to help your clients? (Good options are DBT, CBT, EMDR, ACT, and/or some other treatment that has proven effective for people with BPD.)

Your Spouse and Your Family

Having a child with BPD takes a toll on any marriage. You and your partner will need to approach parenting as a team. This includes regularly supporting each other, especially when one partner feels overwhelmed or discouraged. It also means sharing—or trading off—tasks and responsibilities, so that one of you does not bear the brunt of raising a child with BPD. And it means getting clearly aligned on all aspects of parenting, so that your child does not split the two of you and find a way to turn one against the other. Raising a child with BPD is a long roller coaster ride—but it's so much easier when you are sitting together in the same seat.

Raising a child is expensive; raising a child who has BPD typically entails a great deal of additional expense. If your child needs to enter a residential treatment program, a hefty co-pay may be required, even if you have excellent health insurance. If your child needs to see multiple professionals, this can mean multiple bills to pay. This is a given, not something that could have been avoided with the right planning or strategy or attitude. Accept it; do your best to manage it; know that you may need to make some very difficult (and even heart-wrenching) choices; and remind yourself that your situation is not unique. Countless other parents of kids with BPD must face similar choices.

If you have more than one child, it's important to take all your children's needs into account. It can be tempting to focus most or all of your attention on your child with BPD, because they have the biggest needs. But just because your other kids are better behaved and more self-sufficient, this doesn't mean that they don't need your love, attention, and support. They do.

It's extremely common for siblings of children with BPD to complain that they receive almost no attention from their parents. Often this complaint is justified. Or, they may not overtly complain, but that doesn't mean that everything is fine. Inside, they may feel lonely and angry.

We know how much of a balancing act this can be. Sometimes you may feel that the whole task of raising a child with BPD is beyond you. That's normal. Everyone with a child with BPD feels that way at times. You are *so* not alone.

When the situation gets really tough, remind yourself—and, if necessary, your partner—that the situation you're in is not your fault. BPD has a large biological component, involving both brain chemistry and brain structures. Those are, and always will be, beyond your control.

Also reach out to other parents who have kids with BPD; don't go through this alone. (See Appendix C for specific resources.) We also recommend that you see a therapist yourself to help you stay grounded, focused, compassionate, and realistic.

Kids, BPD, and Boundaries

Adolescents in general are not great with personal boundaries. They will almost always see their momentary desires as more important than anything you might be involved or concerned with.

Teenagers with BPD will usually be highly disrespectful of others' boundaries, including yours. This means that you (and your partner) need to be especially careful, consistent, and insistent on setting and holding personal boundaries with your child. These boundaries need to be very clearly communicated, very clearly drawn, completely consistent, and utterly unambiguous (e.g., being home for supper by 7:00 PM means that 7:01 is too late, even if the 5:00 PM movie your child goes to see ends later than they expected).

Your child will test, push against, argue against, and violate (or try to violate) those boundaries, over and over again. You will need to hold those boundaries firmly, establish clear consequences for violating them, and then follow through with those consequences—every single time. This careful attention to boundaries will help to keep your family from being enveloped in chaos.

Never set a consequence you can't or won't follow through on. And you *must* be consistent—as consistent as you were when your child was an infant, and you put them in their car seat every time you took a drive. With a child who has BPD, following through inconsistently is worse than setting no limit at all.

No matter how much your child pleads and begs and promises to be good—or rages at you for being worse than a Nazi—if you do not hold a boundary firmly, or follow through consistently with a consequence, they will learn that what you say doesn't really matter. So hang tough throughout the tears and yelling and accusations.

Remember, by setting boundaries and consequences, you are not directly trying to change your child's behavior. The boundary is for *you*; it's an action *you* take to keep your family safe and secure.

So, for example, if your child abuses their car privileges, take the car keys away from them, just as you said you would. And think of that action not as an attempt to control or punish your child, but as a way to preserve your family's stability and integrity.

Take Charge of Your Child's Care and Treatment

Over time, your child may see many clinicians, receive more than one diagnosis, and be involved with a variety of agencies, clinics, and programs. Like it or not, you (or you and your partner) need to be the CEO of your child's treatment and care. You will need to do the planning, the scheduling, the coordinating, the budgeting, the reminding, the talking with professionals, the decision making, and, usually, the driving. Don't expect anyone else to take on these roles—or to take charge—because it's not going to happen. Keep careful track of everything in writing. And remember that nobody cares about your kid more than you do.

We recommend that you keep an ongoing log of relevant events, incidents, and changes in your child's life. This will help you see patterns in their behavior. It will also make it easier to retrieve answers to questions that other people, such as clinicians and social workers, may have about your child.

Below is a typical page from one such parental log. Your own log can of course take any clear and readable form that you like.

Date	System or Place	Note
11-5-20	Clinic	Appointment with Dr. South. She increased Mark's Prozac to 40 mg.
11-5-20	School	Met with Ms. Gwande, math teacher. She said Mark has missed six assignments this term, was tardy three times, and sometimes is "mouthy."
11-15-20	Clinic	Family therapy today. Worked on expectations—ours and Mark's.
12-4-20	Home	Major fit of anger from Mark. Threatened suicide but calmed down after one hour. Said we didn't trust him. We told him we don't, because he missed curfew by two hours last night.
12-6-20	Police	Mark was picked up for underage drinking and released to us. He was with two girls he'd just met.
12-7-20	Home	We found cuts on Mark's wrist. Superficial bleeding. Mark cried hard and said he felt bad about scaring us.

Working with Clinicians

Many parents feel intimidated by mental health professionals. But remember this: although they are helping your child, they work for you and your family. Respect their professional opinions and expertise, but don't always assume they are right. Listen with an open mind; ask questions; and challenge them, or ask for more details, if and when something doesn't sound right or make sense to you.

Ultimately, you (or you and your partner) need to decide what is best for your child, whether it's a new medication, a different type of therapy, or any other option that a professional might recommend.

It's important to pay attention to your gut. No matter how hard someone is pressing you, if your inner voice says that something feels *so* not right, do not agree. This goes especially for any diagnosis of mental illness. As a parent who knows your child inside and out, you may be a better judge than a clinician who only has a short time to evaluate them. And remember: the final decisions are yours (or yours and your partner's) until your child turns 18.

Consequences, Yes; Hovering, No

A helicopter parent hovers around their child most or all of the time, then swoops in and saves them from unpleasant consequences when anything, however minor, goes wrong—or looks like it *might* go wrong.

It's easy to fall into this role when your child has serious mental health problems. *Resist this temptation.* Children—including kids with BPD—need to learn from their mistakes. And everyone falls down a few times before they learn to ride a bike. Unless your child's health or well-being is genuinely in danger, back off and let them learn from life.

However, do reward your child when they do something right. And if they aren't doing something right, give them an incentive to change their behavior. Better still, promise and give them a reward if they change, and a negative consequence if they don't.

For example, imagine that your son Jack has been late to school multiple times. Tell him that if he gets to school on time every day during the week, he can stay up as late as he wants to on Friday night. But if he is late even once during the next week, he must take the dog for a long walk every day after school for the next week. (Tailor the reward to your child, of course. If they really like walking the dog, make that the reward.)

Parenting Tips from the Experts

In their book *Parenting a Teen Who Has Intense Emotions*, Pat Harvey and Britt H. Rathbone provide a wealth of useful advice. We strongly recommend this book, and we also want to call your attention to their acronym of what they call BALANCED, effective parenting. Each letter in BALANCED stands for a crucial helpful concept. With their permission, we've listed these points below, and provided a few of our own thoughts for each one.

BALANCED stands for:

- **B**e willing to change

- **A**cceptance is necessary for change

- **L**earn new skills and strategies

- **A**cceptance leads to less suffering

- **N**ote the validity in multiple points of view

- **C**hanging behaviors is hard and necessary

- **E**valuate pros and cons

- **D**istract temporarily from stressful situations

Be Willing to Change

To help your child, at times you will need to learn new ideas and throw out old ones. For example, if your child is screaming at you, it may seem natural and appropriate to shout back. But your shouting can escalate your child's behavior. Instead, speak softly. This goes against the grain, but try it.

Acceptance Is Necessary for Change

Part of making a change is first accepting how things are now. If you always wanted your child to get high grades, but they're earning Ds and Fs, the first step in helping them improve is accepting that these grades reflect their current effort and level of engagement.

Learn New Skills and Strategies

You can help your child better cope with their BPD symptoms if *you* learn new and better ways of coping with their illness. For example, you might take a workshop in basic mindfulness techniques, or more effective listening skills.

Acceptance Leads to Less Suffering

When you accept that your child has serious problems—and that most or all of them are not your fault—you relieve yourself of an enormous burden. Also, once you know and accept that your child has BPD, you don't have to spend any more time wondering what the problem is. So you can move on to creating a plan and developing specific strategies to help your child.

Note the Validity in Multiple Points of View

Instead of spending your time and energy trying to change your child's viewpoint to match your own, consider it as simply one way (among many) of looking at things. So long as that viewpoint is no threat to anyone, let them have their own beliefs and opinions—which will likely change over time anyway.

Changing Behavior Is Hard and Necessary

Changing is almost never quick and easy. This is equally true for you *and* your child. But until people change what they do or say, nothing can improve.

This doesn't mean that every change you hope for is doable, especially if your child fervently resists most or all of them. Yet we can assure you that *some* positive change is possible. Even if your child's illness grows worse, there are things *you* can do to better manage your relationship with them.

Evaluate the Pros and Cons

When making decisions about your child, don't focus on a single benefit or drawback. List all the pros and cons of an issue, then weigh them against one another. This will help you more clearly see what to do next.

Distract Temporarily from Stressful Situations

When your child is at their worst—screaming at you, telling you that you're the worst parent ever, and repeating unreasonable demands—say something completely beside the point to distract them. "Who owns that cool red convertible going down the street?" "I'm *so* freaking hungry; I have to eat something right now!" These may sound like silly distractions—and they are—but, surprisingly, they often work.

Try distracting yourself, too, when you feel trapped or hopeless. Instead of dwelling on your situation, take a walk, or see a movie, or call a friend (but don't talk about your child).

Christine Adamec, co-author of *Stop Walking on Eggshells for Parents: How to Help Your Child with Borderline Personality Disorder Without Sacrificing Your Family or Yourself*, has some invaluable insights of her own for the parents of young people with BPD. We've summarized some of her key points below. You'll notice that a few of these echo suggestions provided earlier in this chapter.

1. *Validate your child every day.* Here are some good ways to do this:

   - Be fully present when they speak, and listen intently. Then summarize what you heard in your own words, and let your child correct you, if necessary.

   - When they express an emotion, say that you understand why they feel that way, and that you've felt that way too (assuming you have).

   - Match or reflect their mood. If they're happy, act happy with them; if they're depressed or sad, show that you can *feel* their emotions with your body language, voice, and facial expressions.

   - If you can guess what they are feeling but are not revealing—for instance, if they are overtly angry, but you sense sorrow behind that anger—mention that emotion as well.

   It's critical to understand that validation has nothing to do with the reason *behind* your child's emotions, which might make no sense to you. It also has nothing to do with how realistic or appropriate those emotions seem to be. If your child is absolutely furious that 3 + 3 = 6, then the truth is that they're angry—and that is what you validate. Validation is *only* about feelings. It might help you to imagine, "*If* this were true, how would I feel?" (Remember, for people with BPD and NPD, feelings equal facts.) One mother said that when she finally started validating her son with BPD, he cried tears of happiness.

2. *Don't blame yourself.* It's not your fault that your child has issues. Don't spend even one minute feeling guilty, or wondering what terrible thing you did to make them the way they are.

3. *Keep a written chart (or list) of your child's moods—especially of their prevailing mood during each part of the day.* This may help you find patterns, like a detective finds clues. Those patterns, in turn, may help you better address issues as they arise—as well as anticipate some potential future problems.

4. *Find at least one good mental health professional—one who thoroughly understands BPD—for your child.* It's not enough for a therapist to be talented and caring; they must also be deeply familiar with the disorder—and they must have worked with many other young people with BPD. This is important, because what typically works with normal adolescents often will not work with young people with BPD.

5. *Find a good therapist—one who thoroughly understands BPD—for yourself (or yourself and your partner).* Again, only someone intimately familiar with the illness will deeply understand what you are feeling and going through—and will be able to offer wise recommendations and guidance.

6. *Don't be a martyr.* It's easy for *any* parent to sacrifice too much, do too much for their kids, and not give their children the opportunity to learn to do things for themselves. This is particularly true for parents of a child with BPD—especially when that child is screaming, raging, and insisting that they can't possibly do what you insist that they do. Hold the line. Protect your child from physical harm, but also let them fail, or suffer the painful consequences of an action, inaction, or decision.

7. *Surprise your child,* especially if they are angry or acting out. If they are raging at you, tell them a silly joke, or happily sing a few bars of a song. If they are accusing you of something, raise your eyebrows, bug out your eyes, and say in a childlike voice, "Eeeeeeeeeeeeek! I'm a monster!" Confusion is better than rage.

8. *If your adult child is living with you and won't follow your household rules, kick them out.* Give them reasonable notice, of course. And, if they let you, help them make the move, and be emotionally supportive throughout the process. But you should kick out *anyone* who won't follow your household rules. You are not being

a bad parent by setting and maintaining this healthy boundary. If your child tries to emotionally blackmail you, don't give in. If and when evicting your adult child from your home becomes necessary, hold firm. Change the locks on your doors if you have to. Turn off your phone when you go to bed. If genuinely necessary, call the police. Then enjoy your freedom from your adult child's illness. You deserve to have a life.

CHAPTER 11

Lies, Rumors, and Accusations: Distortion Campaigns

Hell hath no rage like a borderline scorned.

> —From the Welcome to Oz family member support
> community, www.BPDCentral.com.

Some people that we interviewed told us that they have been falsely accused of harassment and abuse by the person with BPD in their lives, been the subject of damaging rumors, and even faced legal action brought against them without legitimate cause. We call these distortion campaigns.

Jerry

My soon-to-be-ex-wife got a protection order and had me evicted from my own home. She cut me off from our daughters and told all the neighbors that I am violent. They won't even look me in the eye. She systematically sought out the people in social and professional organizations I belong to and attempted to turn them against me. She told my boss that I was impotent—and that I gave her herpes! She told her lawyer that I raped her ten years ago because we had had sex when she didn't want to—and she hadn't even told me she wasn't in the mood! I haven't seen the woman *in months, nor have I called her. In the meantime, I am paying $3,500 a month for support. I can't sleep at night thinking of the injustice of it all. I am terrified of what she will allege next week in court.*

Here are other examples of distortion campaigns:

- Valerie's mother, Hannah, told family members that Valerie had stolen money from her and had been violent on several occasions. Family members refused to speak with Valerie. Hannah made the accusation after Valerie told her she couldn't visit her over Christmas.

- Judy was stalked by her former friend, Elizabeth, who sent threatening letters to herself in Judy's name. Elizabeth would then call Judy's answering machine and beg her to "stop threatening her." The matter ended up in court, where Elizabeth broke down under questioning and insisted that Judy had "forced" her to write the threatening letters to herself.

- Majel's son, Rick, was engaged to a woman with BPD named Jeri. Jeri began telling Rick that Majel had made some highly negative comments about him to her when no one else was around. Although these comments were pure fabrications, Rick felt torn and didn't know whom to believe—his mother or his fiancée.

Not all people with BPD distort the truth. Many would never do such a thing. We are not invalidating the experiences of people with BPD who have been victimized; we are merely validating the experiences of those who have been falsely accused. All types of people, both those with and without mental disorders, may make false claims.

Motivations for Distortion Campaigns

Several theories account for what might motivate someone with BPD to engage in a distortion campaign.

Abandonment and Anger

We have explained that BPD does not cause fundamentally different behavior but behavior that is very far to one side of the continuum. Or, as one person with BPD put it, "Borderlines are just like everyone else—only more so."

We all experience feelings of loss and rejection when relationships end or are threatened. These emotions are especially intense when the other person decides to leave and we want the relationship to continue. Many distortion campaigns seem to revolve around either real or perceived abandonment, loss, and rejection—terrifying issues for people with BPD.

Divorce—the issue in Jerry's case—is an example. Hannah may have felt rejected when her daughter decided not to come home for Christmas. Elizabeth may have felt humiliated when her friend Judy terminated the friendship. But sometimes the perceived loss is not so apparent. Jeri, for example, may have felt that her own relationship with her fiancée Rick was threatened by his close relationship with his mother, though he had love enough for them both.

> Many distortion campaigns seem to revolve around either real or perceived abandonment, loss, and rejection—terrifying issues for people with BPD.

Johnston and Roseby in *In the Name of the Child* (1997), explain how grief can manifest itself as anger:

> Loss—whether that of a loved one, the intact family, cherished hopes and dreams, or the threatened loss of one's own children—evokes powerful feelings of anxiety, sadness, and fear of being abandoned and alone. Some people have difficulty acknowledging these feelings. Instead, they seal over their grief with anger and try to prevent the inevitable separation by embroiling their spouse in unending disputes. Fighting and arguing are ways of maintaining contact (albeit of a negative kind). Even throughout the fighting these same individuals harbor reconciliation fantasies. People who have suffered a dramatic loss in the past (e.g., parental death or divorce) may be also reacting to these earlier, unresolved traumas.

Identity and Aggression

A woman whose husband divorces her loses her identity as wife; a woman whose children are grown may feel as if she's lost her identity as mother. In the face of real or perceived losses, people with BPD may feel:

- empty

- insignificant

- helpless

- unable to survive

Johnston and Roseby believe this may lead people to adopt a false front of being fiercely independent, refusing to negotiate lest they lose part of themselves. (They call this, "I fight, therefore I am.") People may also become overly dependent and clingy—or alternate between aggression and cliginess. People with BPD who see themselves as victims may thus feel that distortion campaigns help give them an identity.

Shame and Blame

Divorce and relationship problems can also spark feelings of rejection, which in turn evoke feelings of inadequacy, failure, shame, and humiliation. As you know, people with BPD often feel awash in shame and have low self-esteem. They may then try to cover up with a mask of absolute competency. Johnston and Roseby say that this exaggerated sense of failure may lead people to try to rid themselves of all blame by proving that the other person is totally inadequate or irresponsible.

> People with BPD who see themselves as victims may feel that distortion campaigns help give them an identity.

The authors write, "The fragile self-esteem of these people depends on keeping all sense of failure outside the self. So they present themselves with a self-righteous air of angry superiority and entitlement and accuse the ex-spouse of being psychologically and morally inferior" (Johnston and Roseby 1997).

When a psychologically vulnerable person with BPD views the spouse's desertion as a total, devastating attack, they may develop paranoid ideas of betrayal, exploitation, and conspiracy. Johnston and Roseby write, "As the spouse surveys the rubble of their marriage, they begin to rewrite history and perceive their partner as having intentionally plotted and planned from the outset to exploit and cast them off" (Johnston and Roseby 1997).

At that point, they say, the "betrayed" spouse may respond aggressively with a counterattack that becomes the central obsession in their life. The spouse, along with any allies, is viewed as dangerous and aggressive. Having been wronged, these people feel justified in seeking retaliation. Or, more urgently, they believe in launching a preemptive strike. Their motto is "attack before being attacked."

Assessing Your Risk

In analyzing dozens of distortion campaigns, we noticed several similarities:

- People with BPD who set up distortion campaigns often claimed to have had a history of being victimized by others. Sometimes, they even described how they sought revenge against people who they said had victimized them in the past.

- The people with BPD often possessed the ability to appear calm, logical, and persuasive under certain circumstances. However, when under emotional distress or alone with loved ones, they appeared to lose contact with reality or become paranoid.

> The "betrayed" spouse may respond aggressively with a counterattack that becomes the central obsession in their lives.

- Those victimized by distortion campaigns often viewed themselves as protectors and caretakers. As a result, they had great difficulty looking out for their own best interests. Many overlooked warning signs, disregarded admonitions from friends, denied what was happening, and refused to take precautions or defend themselves.

It is hard for most people to accept that someone they love could do something to hurt them. If love for the person with BPD, or happy memories of the good times you shared, are preventing you from protecting yourself, it's essential that you understand that the person with BPD may not feel the same way. Splitting may render them unable to remember the good feelings they had for you or to see you as a whole person with both good and bad qualities. As a result, the person with BPD may view you as an evil monster who deserves to be punished. The sooner you realize this, the better chance you have of emerging from a distortion campaign with your dignity and rights intact.

Most complaints of distortion campaigns came from men and women who had recently broken up or asked for a divorce from a partner with BPD. Parents of children with BPD were the second most frequent source of complaints, followed by children of parents with BPD.

Combating Distortion Campaigns

First, an important disclaimer: Each person's situation is different, and each person with BPD is unique. The right approach for one person could be totally wrong for another—even if the situations seem similar. The following guidelines may help.

> Before you take action, consult with a qualified mental health professional who is familiar with your unique situation. If the allegations involve the law, it's vital that you discuss the situation with a qualified attorney as soon as possible.

Secondly, recognize that BPD is a mental disorder. People who have it deserve to be treated with sensitivity, respect, and dignity. Protect yourself, but don't try to hurt the other person out of spite or revenge. For example, it might be prudent to remove your clothing and personal belongings from the house before asking for a divorce. However, hiring a moving company and taking half of everything the two of you own is probably going too far. In fact, it might understandably trigger a hostile response.

Reduce Your Vulnerability

The best way to handle a distortion campaign is to prevent it from happening. If you can't do this, be proactive and protect yourself as much as you can—legally, financially, and emotionally.

Some distortion campaigns seem to occur for no discernible reason. But others seem to be triggered by actions the person with BPD perceives as hostile. Start with these steps:

> Be proactive and protect yourself as much as you can—legally, financially, and emotionally.

- Consider any major actions you may be taking that involve the person with BPD—anything from setting limits to seeking a divorce. What kind of reaction might you anticipate from them?

- Consider yourself: what are your vulnerable areas, and what could you do ahead of time to guard against any actions the person with BPD may take? Hope for the best; prepare for the worst. Many have found that typical areas of concern include their finances, children, property, job, reputation, and friendships.

- Formulate a plan and implement it before you take any action that could trigger the person with BPD.

Consider the example of Lyndia and Elicia. Lyndia needs to tell her daughter, Elicia, that Elicia can't come home from the residential facility for the upcoming weekend. The last time Elicia came home for a visit, she threatened to burn down the house if Lyndia wouldn't let her spend the night with her drug-abusing boyfriend.

Lyndia knows from experience that after Elicia hears the news, she will immediately go to her counselors, grandparents, and anyone else who will listen and possibly believe Elicia's story, and tell them that Lyndia hates her (and always has) and that her behavior is spotless and that Lyndia is a bad parent.

So before Lyndia tells Elicia the news, she communicates the reasoning for her decision to anyone who might become involved. By the time Elicia speaks with them, they will already know what is going on.

Consider Not Responding

There may be times when responding in any way at all simply prolongs the person with BPD's abusive actions. That is because this entire matter may be an effort on their part to keep you engaged in the relationship. Any response—particularly an emotional one—may reward the behavior.

Think through the short-term and long-term ramifications of the other person's actions. If the consequences are insignificant or simply embarrassing—or if you believe the person with BPD is trying to goad you into more contact with them—it may be best to simply let the matter go.

Answer Questions Without Being Defensive

Alison was alternately suicidal and incensed when Luke broke up with her. She called Luke at work several times a day, screaming at him and begging him to take her back. When Luke had his work number changed, Alison retaliated by calling Luke's boss, David, and informing him that Luke often snorted cocaine while at work. "Luke's a crack head," she insisted. "Don't trust him."

Naturally, David confronted Luke with Alison's accusation. Several years earlier, Luke had tried cocaine at work when it was offered to him by one of the stagehands. But it happened just once. Other than that, Luke was a responsible employee and did not drink or use drugs on the job.

Luke owned up to what he had done but emphasized that it had happened just once. Luke also explained what was going on without intruding upon Alison's privacy any more than was necessary. Luckily, David understood and did not fire Luke for violating the company's drug policy.

A person with BPD may also tell family, friends, and acquaintances untrue things about you. Before you decide whether to respond, ask yourself what you hope to achieve. Do you want to clear your name? Or is there something tangible at stake, such as the loss of friendship of people who are important to you?

When consequences of the person with BPD's actions are relatively minor, it may be best to act in a way that reveals the lie for what it is. For example, if they tell the neighbors that your new wife is a shrew, it may be best to simply let them meet her and make their own decisions. However, if the person with BPD tells the neighbors you've been arrested for battering her and their opinion matters a great deal to you, you may wish to try to set the record straight.

> When consequences of the person with BPD's actions are relatively minor, it may be best to act in a way that reveals the lie for what it is.

When talking with people about false accusations, keep the following guidelines in mind:

- Act calm, composed, and in control—no matter how upset you feel.

- Validate the other person's concerns before explaining the facts. Say that if the rumors had been true, it would be a very serious matter.

- Do not disparage the person with BPD—no matter how much you think they deserve it. Instead, sincerely express your concern for the person with BPD or acknowledge your own confusion about why they would say such things. Be cautious about discussing BPD or any other psychological problem—people may misunderstand and think you are trying to belittle them.

- Realize that you cannot control what other people think about you. Say what you need to say and then let it go.

Benjamin

Here's what I said to a neighbor who wrongly believed I'd been violent toward my former wife: "I'd like to clear the air about something. It may make you a bit uncomfortable, and I understand that because it makes me uncomfortable too. But it's important, so I'm willing to stick my neck out. I heard that my former wife, Kassidy, told you that I was arrested for battering her. Someone told me that she had some cuts on her arm and she was showing them to people and saying that I attacked her. I wouldn't blame you if you felt horrified and didn't want to talk to me. If I thought that someone I knew had done such a thing, I would probably avoid them too. But it never happened. The divorce hasn't been easy, it's true. But I never did anything remotely like that. And I'm very concerned for Kassidy's sake—both that she would tell this to people and that somehow her arm is being cut.

"I'll understand if you feel confused and wonder about what really happened. But we've known each other for a while, and I did want to set the record straight with you. I appreciate your listening."

Prepare for False Accusations of Abuse from Children with BPD

Children who falsely accuse parents of abuse is a growing phenomenon. Reasons for doing this include revenge for perceived abuse, retaliation for being treated "unfairly," and an attempt to split their parents' loyalty to one another.

Dealing with False Accusations

As you may suspect, an angry child's phone call to 911 or to the local child protection agency can have devastating effects on the family. Typical investigations can often take more than a month to complete. In the meantime, the accused parent is often ordered by the court to stay away from the child and temporarily live outside the family home. The child is often required to remain with the other parent, who experiences the conflict of trying to be supportive and loyal to both the child and to a spouse or partner. The family's friends, relatives, and employers may be caught in the same trap of feeling they must either demonstrate support for the child or loyalty toward the accused parent.

In our interview with attorney Charles Jamieson, he advised that the parents of a child who makes false accusations do the following:

- Keep detailed records documenting the child's diagnosis or BPD behaviors. Examples include letters from school authorities, medical records, court papers, and reports that unsubstantiate prior allegations. This will enhance your credibility.

- Keep a diary of your activities, including where you were, who you were with, and what you did. If allegations come weeks or months after the supposed event, this may provide you with an alibi.

- Ask your other children if they would be willing to help explain your innocence to the authorities.

- If necessary, make sure that a third party is present when you are with the child.

- Take all accusations seriously. They may quickly snowball out of control. If you need to, hire an attorney who specializes in false allegations.

Coping with Your Feelings

From an emotional perspective, there are some things to keep in mind that can help you cope with the situation. Usually, false accusations center around abuse or neglect. Therefore, they are followed up with investigations by your county's social service department or child protection unit. While the investigation will seem to be accusatory, remember that the investigation is merely a fact-finding process. Only hard evidence can be used to render charges.

Remember that being defensive and uncooperative can hurt your case. Do not take questions personally; keep telling yourself that the process is necessary to ferret out real cases of abuse. In some cases, parents may be separated from their children while the investigation is going on. Siblings of the child with BPD need to know that the separation is temporary and that they may be asked questions during the investigation. Stress your love for them and the need to answer the legal authorities' questions honestly.

Finally, remind yourself that BPD is a mental illness. Anger toward your child is normal; however, remember that the illness is really to blame—not the child.

If your child is trying to hurt you by mounting a distortion campaign, you might consider them to be your enemy. In reality, your enemies are:

- **denial:** doing nothing about the problem in hopes that it will go away

- **wishful thinking:** doing nothing because you're sure that a miracle will occur and your child will have a change of heart

- **emotionality:** reacting emotionally rather than remaining calm and thinking through logical solutions to your problem

- **martyrdom:** doing nothing because you can't bear to hurt your child's feelings, which you may think are more important than your own

Being defensive and uncooperative can hurt your case.

- **isolation:** trying to handle the problem by yourself instead of asking for help

- **legal delays:** not hiring the right attorney before you lose legal rights and the situation becomes critical

Most people find that if they react quickly and logically and obtain the right legal help when needed, distortion campaigns sputter and fail. The truth has a way of revealing itself, and lies are eventually exposed for what they are. By acting appropriately, you can help that occur sooner rather than later.

> The truth has a way of revealing itself, and lies are eventually exposed for what they are.

CHAPTER 12

What Now?
Making Decisions
About Your Relationship

People who care about someone with BPD are usually in a great deal of pain. Staying in the relationship as it is seems unbearable. But leaving seems unthinkable or impossible. If you feel this way, you are not alone. Nearly everyone we spoke with echoed the same sentiments. But you do have options, even if you can't see them right now. This chapter will help you think through your choices and come to a personal decision that feels right for you.

Predictable Stages

People who love someone with BPD seem to go through similar stages. The longer the relationship has lasted, the longer each stage seems to take. Although these are listed in the general order in which people go through them, most people move back and forth among different stages.

Confusion Stage

This generally occurs before a diagnosis of BPD is known. In this stage, you might struggle to understand why your loved one sometimes behaves in ways that seem to make no sense. You might look for solutions that seem elusive, blame yourself, or resign yourself to living in chaos.

> You do have options, even if you can't see them right now.

Even after learning about BPD, it can take weeks or months to really comprehend on an intellectual level how the person with BPD is personally affected by this complex disorder. It can take even longer to absorb the information on an emotional level.

Outer-Directed Stage

In this stage, you might:

- turn your attention toward the person with the disorder

- urge the person with BPD to seek professional help, attempting to get them to change

- try your best not to trigger problematic behavior

- learn all you can about BPD in an effort to understand and empathize with the person you care about

It can take a long time to acknowledge feelings of anger and grief—especially when the person with BPD is a parent or child. Anger is an extremely common reaction, even though most people understand on an intellectual level that a person's BPD is not their fault.

Yet because anger seems to be an inappropriate response to a situation that may be beyond the person with BPD's control, loved ones often suppress their anger and instead experience depression, hopelessness, and guilt.

The chief tasks for loved ones in this stage include:

- acknowledging and dealing with their own emotions

- letting the person with BPD take responsibility for their own actions

- giving up the fantasy that the person with BPD will behave as we would like them to

Inner-Directed Stage

Eventually, loved ones of someone with BPD look inward and conduct an honest appraisal of themselves. It takes two people to have a relationship, and the goal in this stage is to better understand your role in making the relationship what it now is. The objective here is not self-recrimination but insight and self-discovery.

Decision-Making Stage

Armed with knowledge and insight, you might struggle to make decisions about the relationship. This stage can often take months or years. In this stage, you need to clearly understand your own values, beliefs, expectations, and assumptions. For example, one man with a physically violent wife came from a conservative family that strongly disapproved of divorce. His friends counseled him to separate from her, but he felt unable to do so because of his concern about how his family would react.

Be guided by your own values—not someone else's.

You may find that your beliefs and values have served you well throughout your life. Or you may find that you inherited them from your family without determining whether they truly reflect who you are. Either way, it is important to be guided by your own values—not someone else's.

Resolution Phase

In this final stage, you implement your decisions and live with them. Depending upon the type of relationship, you may, over time, change your mind many times and try different alternatives.

Beyond Black and White

It is easy to adopt the person with BPD's black-and-white way of thinking and believe you only have two choices—stay or go. But many other options also exist, for example:

- leaving the situation temporarily whenever the person with BPD violates your limits

- taking a temporary break (days, weeks, or months) from the relationship

- learning to depersonalize the person with BPD's actions

- remaining in the relationship but living apart

- making the relationship less close

- spending less time with the person with BPD

- achieving balance by cultivating your own interests, friends, and meaningful activities

- telling the person with BPD that you will remain in the relationship only if they are willing to work with a therapist or make specific changes; this means holding the person with BPD to any promise they make, and it may mean leaving if they violate such a promise

- putting off making a decision until you feel comfortable making one

- putting off making a decision until you see a therapist and work on some of your own issues

Questions to Ask Yourself

These are questions you should ask yourself about your current relationship with your partner. Most of these questions address important needs that should be met in relationships. The answers to these questions can provide you with some direction on how to proceed in the relationship. Generally, the more needs and wants that go unfilled and the more "unbalanced" the attention and energy in the relationship, the more likely it is that the relationship is unhealthy.

- What do I want from this relationship? What do I need from this relationship?

- How open can I be with my feelings with this person?

- Am I putting myself in physical danger by staying in this relationship?

- How will this decision affect any children?

- How does this relationship affect my self-esteem?

- Do I love myself as much as I love the person with BPD?

- Have I accepted the fact that the person with BPD will change only if and when they are ready to do so? Am I able to wait until that happens or live with things the way they are if it never happens?

- What practical considerations do I need to consider, particularly financial ones?

- Do I believe that I have the right to be happy?

- Do I believe that I am only worthwhile when I am sacrificing myself for others?

- When am I currently the most content: when I am with this person, when I am alone, or when I am with others?

- Do I have the energy and fortitude to go against my family or other people who might be upset with my decision?

- Am I truly making my own decision, or am I doing what other people want me to do?

- What are the legal ramifications of my decision?

- If a friend was in my place and told me the story of this relationship, what advice would I give them?

When Children Are Involved

One person we interviewed says, "I am not one who believes that unhappy people should stay together for the sake of the children. I think they would be far better off living with one happy parent than one miserably unhappy parent and one who is completely delusional."

While many parents worry about the effect of divorce on children, Janet R. Johnston, PhD, executive director of the Judith Wallerstein Center for the Family in Transition, said in our interview that studies consistently find that children's exposure to unresolved conflict and verbal and physical abuse is a better predictor of children's adjustment than the marital status of their parents.

According to Johnston, children do the best in a happy, intact marriage with both parents present; next best is a divorce in which the parents protect the children from conflict. Third best is an unhappy, intact marriage in which children are exposed to unresolved conflict and verbal abuse. Worst of all is a conflict-ridden divorce where the children are put in the middle.

Chosen Relationships

When it comes to chosen relationships, we found that the person with BPD's willingness to admit they had a problem and seek help was by far the determining factor as to whether the couple stayed together or not.

Of the hundreds of people we spoke with, when the person with BPD was truly committed to recovery, their partner was almost always willing to stand by them and help them through it. But when the person with BPD refused to take any responsibility for the couple's problems, no matter how hard their partner tried to rescue the relationship, the relationship usually ended.

Richard

I stayed with my wife for the same reasons I fell in love with her. She is bright, beautiful, witty, passionate, and fun. When we got married, I didn't know she had borderline personality disorder. In fact, I didn't know what BPD was until it was clinically diagnosed.

I knew early on that there were problems; sometimes they were frustrating; sometimes they made me angry. Sometimes they scared the hell out of me. No matter what, however, she was still the person I loved who just happened to have a mental illness. Even during the worst of it, I never considered leaving. I wasn't about to throw away a relationship so easily, especially one where so much of it was good. She was very sick, but I could always see the good in her.

After her four years of therapy and hospitalizations, our marriage is very close. The reward for loyalty has been great—the same passion, the same beauty, the same wit that attracted me to her in the first place are all there. But the fear and confusion of BPD are gone.

Rhoda

I have broken up with my BPD boyfriend many times. When he is able to see what he is doing, apologize for it, and tell me how he is going to change, I go back.

To me, he is worth it. He is a kind, beautiful, passionate, generous man. I have never met anyone in my life who has made me feel more loved. And he can't destroy me because he does not define me. I do. And I am very fortunate that his BPD is "moderate"—he is not prone to rages or violent outbursts, doesn't cheat on me, and makes a sincere effort to modify his behavior.

This relationship suits me because I sometimes have a strong need for privacy and solitude. I take the time to be alone and enjoy other things without him.

I am aware of the risks. But I love him and I plan to enjoy his presence in my life as long as I can.

Marie

My soon-to-be-ex-husband gave me a surprise visit this afternoon. The conversation started out all business and finances, but then the conversation changed. He said I hadn't given him a chance (twenty years of chances are obviously not enough). I guess he forgot he threatened to kill me in no uncertain terms. Silly me—can't I just get over the death threat? I could go on with the twisted logic, the convenient amnesia, and the transparent manipulation. But I will get to the point. Which is: there is no point. He just doesn't get it. It was my job to seek the proper ways to communicate with him. My job to set boundaries. My job to understand the illness. What was his part?

What kind of relationship can you have when one person must do all of the work? What kind of relationship is it when one person must have all of the understanding, have all of the forgiveness, and do all of the giving to the needy other?

He called me a few hours later and began sighing on the phone that he might as well quit his job. He told me he was eyeballing a handgun in the house where he now lives. It took every fiber of me to hang up—but I did hang up. I released him to his own pitiful misery. I didn't even know the power still existed within me. But it does. And it's perfectly okay for me to own my own feelings again.

As I'm writing this, I'm watching my eight-year-old fill a decorative birdcage full of oatmeal cookies. It's his science project. Why is this relevant? Because he's free and safe to be himself, without risk of raging or verbal abuse from someone he should have been able to trust. Because his mother is free and safe to just let him be an eight-year-old. Because we all have this option, and there should be no apologies forthcoming for an illness we did not cause.

Fill the birdcages with cookies, pour milk all over them, eat them with your fingers and make a big mess. Laugh until your sides ache, cry when something is wrong, spend some time doing absolutely nothing, say what you mean, and mean what you say. Invest in your own sanity for once.

Unchosen Relationships

With unchosen relationships, such as those with BPD parents, minor children, or minor siblings, sometimes the choice is not to stay or go as much as it is to set and observe your limits and not let the person with BPD's problems overwhelm your own life. But that doesn't mean you need to feel helpless and hopeless. While you may not be able to end the relationship or "break up," you can set limits on how much contact you have with that person and how much of your energy you invest in maintaining the relationship.

> With unchosen relationships, you need to be the one in charge. Identify your emotional and physical boundaries. Reinforce the limits you set in the relationship by consistent modeling and consistent responding to the disturbing behavior of the person with BPD. As an adult, when the relationship causes too much pain and your relative is unwilling to change, you have the option to temporarily or permanently step away.

Sylvia

I love my borderline son, John, very much. For many years, I lived or died depending upon how well he was doing. Was he drinking again? Getting involved with self-destructive women? Spending all of his money on things he didn't need? I continually gave him cash and provided him with a place to stay when yet another one of his roommates threw him out. I listened to him as he ranted and raved and blamed me and his father for everything that had ever gone wrong in his entire life.

Things changed after my husband had a heart attack. Paul is doing well now, but for a while, we weren't sure if he was going to pull through. This crisis helped me realize that I was concentrating on my son so much I was losing myself, my husband, and my relationship with my daughter.

I had to back away from my son's chaos. I set some personal limits around bailing him out and listening to his tirades. John wasn't happy about our new limits—he cut us off totally for three years. That was very painful. But eventually, John decided that having a relationship with us with limits was better than no relationship at all. We see him about once a month. There are phone calls, too. It's strained, but I can live with that.

I feel like a human being again, with goals, dreams, and happiness. Everyone benefited from the limits—even John, I think. He learned that he can manage to run his life without us.

I still wish that I could have a closer relationship with my son. I wish that he would take care of himself more and get help. But I've learned to accept that I can't change John. I can only love him and be the best mother I know how to be while still loving myself and caring for the rest of my family.

Healing and Hope

Whatever you decide, there can be healing and hope: healing when a relationship ends and hope for your loved one's recovery from BPD.

Many people from the Welcome to Oz online support group (www.BPD Central.com) resolved their relationship with the person with BPD in their lives years ago. But they stay on the list to provide support to others, and to assure them that life does, indeed, get better after a relationship with someone who has BPD.

Marilyn

It has been ten years since my divorce from my ex-husband, and I am still dealing with the aftereffects. I spent so much time trying to hide his behavior from others that it left its mark upon me. Trust in others, faith in the world... these were the things that were destroyed in me.

Yet now, in most ways life couldn't be better! I am a happy and confident person. The experience taught me many things about myself—things that I had avoided or would not admit to myself before that time. Now I use my energy to correct those things that I find negative or unhealthy. I live a more conscious life.

As far as not becoming bitter—I was angry for a long time, until I finally realized that my ex-husband had not deliberately set out to make my life miserable. It would have happened, to one degree or another, no matter whom he had married. Blaming him for who he is is futile and does not help the situation in any way. A few months after the divorce I was having dinner with my parents. My father began to denigrate my ex-husband. I looked at my father and said, "Why would you say such things? Why would you hate someone like him? Don't you understand he has harmed himself more than he has me?" Bitterness and anger are emotions that tie one to the past. Had I held on to negative emotions, I would never have been able to start my life again or ever be happy again.

The last thing my former husband ever said to me was, "I've never been happy, never in my life!" I'll never forget the tears that were streaming down his face. And I will never forget the pain and anguish in his voice. The isolation he felt and most probably still feels—his fear of being alone and isolated in the world—stills any feelings of anger against him. I had been happy in the past. I knew I would be happy again someday. Yet for someone like him, who had never known happiness—what of him? I abandoned him, just as he felt everyone else had done in his life.

I felt a sense of terrible guilt for a long time. But if I was to survive, I had to let go of it. I could not help this man, and I could not destroy myself.

And finally, Rachel Reiland, author of *Get Me Out of Here: My Recovery from Borderline Personality Disorder* (2004), posted this note to Welcome to Oz to show that recovery is indeed possible.

Rachel

There were plenty of times I felt far worse than when I started it all, and I wondered if I would have been better off never having known about my illness and never having entered therapy. My entire way of thinking had to be disassembled and rebuilt. And for someone inherently struggling with uncertainty about identity, there were dauntingly frightening times when I had disassembled the old ways of thinking but had not yet adopted new ones.

During that time, I looked into a dark hole of nothingness and wondered if I had any identity at all. Luckily, with the help of an excellent psychiatrist and the support of my husband and children, I recovered from BPD. Yet I know enough to realize that what happened to me doesn't always happen. Some people with BPD are unwilling to take the journey. Others are outright incapable of it. And thus I would never expect that everyone close to someone with BPD stay in the relationship. In some cases—perhaps many cases—it is necessary and wise to protect oneself and move on with life. Yet, at other times, if you hang around, you will be rewarded in the end with a relationship that is closer and better than you had dreamed possible.

One of the most profound lessons I learned in my journey was the incredible capacity that people have for goodness, that this world, despite its trials, pains, and injustices, is indeed a miraculous place. It is filled with as much love and kindness as it is with hatred. I have emerged from all of this with a view of life that will never, ever be the same as it was. And that has made all of the pain and struggle eminently worth it.

In this book, you've learned what BPD is, why people with BPD act the way they do, the part that you play in the dynamic, and how to take back control of your life.

But as complex as BPD behavior can be, obtaining knowledge is the easy part. Now comes the wisdom: taking what you've learned and applying it to your own life.

This may happen in many ways, including:

- questioning long-standing beliefs and values

- facing issues that you've been avoiding for years

- revisiting the unspoken "bargain" you've struck with the person with BPD: that their needs and views are always, always more important and more "right" than yours

No one can hold up this kind of bargain very long without seriously compromising their own mental health.

We can't promise that it will be easy. But we can promise that it will be worthwhile. In the process, you will find out what you really value and who you really are. You will discover strengths you didn't know you had. Few things in life are more important than this. As William Shakespeare said four hundred years ago:

> This above all, to thine own self be true,
> And it must follow as the night the day
> Thou canst not then be false to any man.
> [*Hamlet*, act I, scene iii, lines 78–80]

We hope that the knowledge and tools you've gained from this book serve you well on the rest of your journey.

Causes and Treatment of BPD

Much of the information in this appendix has been taken from *The Essential Family Guide to Borderline Personality Disorder* (2008), by Randi Kreger, the coauthor of this book.

Risk Factors for BPD

There is no single cause of BPD. Instead, there are several risk factors that, when present, increase the chances that a person develops BPD. The risk factors fall into two categories: biological and environmental. A biological vulnerability to BPD combined with a problematic environment can lead to the development of BPD. In some people, biological risk factors may predominate; for others, environmental risk factors will play a larger role.

Biological Factors

Malfunctions in neurotransmitter levels, as well as other abnormalities in the neurotransmitter system, can lead to problems such as impaired reasoning, impulsivity, and unstable emotions.

The physical brain, too, can be impaired. The amygdala controls the intensity of our emotions and our ability to return to normal after sharp emotions have been aroused. Brain scans show that in people with BPD, the amygdala is more active than those of control subjects.

Robert O. Friedel, MD, suggests that there is not a single, specific gene for borderline personality disorder. He says it appears that the genes that increase risk for the disorder may be passed on by those people who have the disorder itself, or a related disorder, such as bipolar disorder, depression, substance use disorders, and post-traumatic stress disorder.

Friedel says it's vital to understand that BPD is the result of instability in specific neural pathways in the brain, and problematic behaviors are not intentional or willful. Research will give us a better understanding of biological risk factors, which will result in more effective treatment.

Environmental Factors

It's a myth that BPD is a result of some form of childhood abuse. Yes, many people with BPD *have* been the victim of abuse, abandonment, neglect, or other mistreatment—sometimes for years. But we don't really know how many fit that pattern, because of flaws in research.

Studies only reflect people with BPD within the mental health system and who are suicidal and self-harming. They're not a true random sample of the entire population with BPD because the entire higher functioning population is excluded.

Another issue is that the claims of abuse are self-reported and may lack a standardized definition of abuse.

Environmental factors—abuse, neglect, childhood trauma of many different kinds—do appear to trigger BPD in someone who may be genetically predisposed to the condition.

Friedel calls these "environmental burdens." In addition to abuse, environmental burdens might include:

- ineffective parenting—anything from inadequate parental skills to mental illness or substance abuse

- an unsafe and chaotic home situation

- a clash between the disposition of child and parent

- the sudden loss of a caregiver or the caregiver's attention—even common things such as the birth of a new baby—which the child perceives as abandonment

Treatment

The great news is that new forms of treatment are showing success (more about that in a minute). But if you're eager to seek treatment for your loved one, make sure that they sincerely want to make changes for their own reasons—not just because you or someone else has given an ultimatum.

Medication

Medications help reduce BPD symptoms such as depression, mood swings, dissociation, aggression, and impulsivity. This kind of treatment is very complicated because the details of how brain chemistry provokes BPD symptoms can vary widely from one patient to the next. Doctors using drugs to treat BPD have to be specially trained, and patients need careful monitoring.

Common medications are:

- antipsychotics such as olanzapine (Zyprexa)

- antidepressants such as sertraline (Zoloft) or venlafaxine (Effexor)

- mood stabilizers like divalproex sodium (Depakote) or lamotrigine (Lamictal)

Psychotherapy

There are several structured programs just for people with BPD who are motivated to work on their problems. These structured treatments seem to produce better results than treatment as usual. This may be due to factors, though, that are not exclusive to these treatments, including:

- specialized clinician training, which gives them more effective tools

- clinician education, which gives treatment providers a more positive attitude about recovery and working with patients

- treatment twice a week instead of once

- the opportunity to interact with peers who have the same disorder

All of these treatments focus on problematic borderline behaviors. But they vary as to the importance of the healing relationship between the therapist and the patient. Ultimately, for most patients, the decisions about treatment come down to what programs are available, the best fit between therapist and client, health insurance coverage, and other factors.

Dialectical Behavior Therapy

Dialectical behavior therapy (DBT) is probably the best-known structured treatment for BPD. Developed by Marsha Linehan, PhD, DBT essentially teaches clients to accept themselves as they are—which then enables them to make changes in their behavior.

People enrolled in DBT programs typically attend weekly group skills training sessions to learn how to tolerate distress, regulate their emotions, become more mindful, and improve their interpersonal skills. They also meet weekly with an individual therapist.

Mindfulness is one of the core concepts of DBT (you can read more about it in Appendix B). Mindfulness is about being in the moment and observing what is happening around you, noticing your emotions without being consumed by them. People who consider entering DBT need to be willing to faithfully attend therapy and fill out daily diary forms. You can find out more about DBT, including finding a DBT therapist, at www.behavioraltech.com.

Mentalization Based Therapy

Mentalization based therapy (MBT) is a specific type of psychotherapy designed to help people with BPD focus on the following:

- making a distinction between their thoughts and those of others

- recognizing how thoughts, feelings, wishes, and desires are linked to behavior—something that is an element in most established therapies, though with MBT, it's the major focus.

The focus of MBT is on the interaction between the patient and the therapist—unlike DBT, which focuses on skills training. The goals of MBT include better relationships with others and improved control over emotions and behaviors. The relationship between client and therapist is considered a vital part of treatment, whereas DBT targets dysfunctional behavior.

Schema Therapy

According to its founders, "schemas" are entrenched, self-defeating life patterns that can occur when vital needs are not met in childhood. They say that our schema modes are triggered by life situations that we are oversensitive to (our "emotional triggers"). These can lead us to overreact to situations, or to act in ways that end up hurting us.

The goals of schema therapy include helping people access their true feelings, turn off the self-defeating schema modes, and get their emotional needs met in relationships.

STEPPS Group Treatment Program

STEPPS stands for "systems training for emotional predictability and problem solving." It is popular in the Netherlands and is meant to be used in addition to, not as a replacement for, traditional therapy. Like DBT, STEPPS has a skills-training approach. Family members are an important aspect of this program; they learn how to reinforce and support the patient's new skills.

This program has three stages: awareness of illness, emotion management skills training, and behavior management skills training.

Finding a Therapist

Unfortunately, these structured treatments are not widely available. They can also be expensive. Since each clinician has his or her own unique "brand" of therapy—even if they come from the same schools of thought—finding the right therapist is a bit like searching for a job.

Therapists who treat BPD should have several qualities:

- They believe recovery is possible.

- They know about the latest research and understand the role of brain disorder in people with BPD.

- They can articulate specific goals for therapy that are realistic, especially within the time limits that a health insurance plan might set for the therapy.

- They have support from their colleagues for treating BPD.

- They are confident in their own ability and they are savvy about how people with BPD can behave. They are compassionate toward their clients with the disorder but smart enough not to get sucked in emotionally by their dysfunctional ways of relating to others, including therapists.

One way to find a psychiatrist is to develop a list of the best hospitals in your community for psychiatric care. Make sure you include teaching hospitals. Then, call each one and speak to the psychiatric unit nurse manager or the medical staff administrative assistant. Ask for the names of psychiatrists who specialize in treating personality disorders—don't mention BPD specifically at this stage.

Then, check the names you're given against the directory for your insurance plan or HMO. Then call the individual clinician's office and ask the staff about his or her experience in treating personality disorders. Listen for the tone of their response, and choose those clinicians whose employees seem to be enthusiastic about their bosses. Once you find the right psychiatrist, you can ask for referrals to other types of clinicians, such as therapists.

Once you have narrowed the list to a few doctors, make an appointment and ask each doctor the following questions:

- Do you treat people with BPD? If so, how many have you treated?

- How do you define BPD?

- What do you believe causes BPD?

- What is your treatment plan for clients with BPD?

- Do you believe people with BPD can get better? Have you personally treated clients with BPD who have improved?

- How much do you know about the stresses of living with someone with the disorder?

Your goal is to pick someone with experience in treating personality disorders, who understands that some clients with BPD are high-functioning and can cause particular problems, and who understand the real causes of BPD. You want to be sure the clinician doesn't wrongly believe that BPD always results from parental abuse, for example.

Finally, you want one who offers a treatment plan that is flexible and has specific, concrete, attainable goals. The chapter Finding Professional Help in *The Essential Family Guide to Borderline Personality Disorder* (Kreger 2008) covers these topics and goes into more detail about finding unstructured therapy, including how to assess the quality of the therapy and the reputation of the therapist.

Practicing Mindfulness

Mindfulness for Friends and Loved Ones of People with BPD

One essential component of dialectical behavioral therapy (DBT) that has proven very effective for people with BPD is mindfulness. Treatment for BPD often begins with learning mindfulness skills, and the person with BPD repeatedly practices these skills throughout treatment (Linehan 1993a).

These same mindfulness skills can also be beneficial for those who are coping with the BPD symptoms of loved ones. In fact, for the past decade, the National Educational Alliance for Borderline Personality Disorder (NEA-BPD) has taught mindfulness skills in its Family Connections Program, which offers education, skills training, and support to family members of people with BPD. (To learn more about the program, visit www.neabpd.org /family-connections.)

Mindfulness is awareness without judgment. As mindfulness researcher Jon Kabat-Zinn notes, mindfulness is "the ability to be aware of your thoughts, emotions, physical sensations, and actions—in the present moment—without judging or criticizing yourself or your experience" (2005). Some people call this "being centered"; others call it encountering one's "true self."

People with BPD are often ruled by their emotions. This can lead them to destructive and impulsive actions such as drug use, risky sexual encounters, and self-injury. In DBT, the goal of mindfulness is to get people with BPD to recognize these patterns of strong emotions and risky behavior so they can act more thoughtfully and less impulsively. In DBT language, the goal of mindfulness is to practice and achieve "wise mind": a balance between "reasonable mind" and "emotional mind" (or, as some clinicians say, "emotion mind"). With a wise mind, we are able to experience life as it comes to us, and appreciate the ambiguity and the shades of gray that we often encounter.

We are in reasonable mind when we approach knowledge from an intellectual and rational point of view. In reasonable mind, our emotions are put away and our responses are planned and controlled. In contrast, we are in emotional mind when our thinking and behavior are controlled by our current emotional state. In emotional mind, rational thinking is difficult and facts may be distorted to match or validate our feelings.

With a wise mind, our emotions and thoughts work together. As a result, we act appropriately and smoothly—even if our life and relationships feel temporarily out of control.

When we are mindful, we are open to life on its own terms, fully aware of each moment as it arises and as it passes away.

In the *Dialectical Behavior Therapy Skills Workbook* (2007), Matthew McKay, Jeffrey Wood, and Jeffrey Brantley remind us that "to be fully aware of your experiences in the present moment, it's necessary that you do so without criticizing yourself, your situation, or other people." The creator of DBT, Marsha Linehan, calls this "radical acceptance" (1993a). (These two words also form the title of a 2004 book by psychologist and meditation teacher Tara Brach.)

Radical acceptance allows us to focus on the here and now and to avoid the mental and emotional traps of focusing on what might lie ahead or what happened in the past. This can be especially helpful when coping with the unpredictable and confusing behaviors associated with BPD.

Mindfulness—and DBT in general—help people with BPD stay off the emotional roller coaster associated with black-and-white thinking. Over time, people who regularly practice mindfulness tend to be better at enduring pain, solving problems, and not creating turmoil and stress in their lives and relationships. Notice, though, that the goal of mindfulness isn't to experience profound happiness or a life without stress or trouble.

We all have the capacity to be mindful. It's a skill anyone can learn. There's nothing mysterious about it. We simply pay attention to the present moment. When mental clutter appears, we let it appear and let it fade away again. Over and over, we return to the here and now.

This isn't usually as easy as it sounds, especially as we're first learning it. But everyone gets better at it with practice. In the process, we also learn a lot about ourselves, others, and our relationships.

Practicing mindfulness can help you achieve a better balance between your rational mind and your emotional mind. This puts you in a better position to respond wisely to distressing situations, in a balanced, healthy manner. You'll also make better decisions, improve your relationships, and optimize your potential for physical and mental relaxation.

The Dialectical Behavior Therapy Skills Workbook (McKay, Wood, and Brantley 2007) offers an excellent introduction to mindfulness as well as many suggestions and opportunities for practice.

Mindfulness Exercise #1: Focus On an Object

The purposes of this exercise are to focus your mind on a single object and to be aware of the mental energy needed to stay in the moment.

Find a place where you can be alone and away from TVs, radios, and other distractions and interruptions. Get into a comfortable position—either sitting or standing—that you can maintain for three minutes. Keep your eyes open and breathe normally.

Pick a nearby object that you can see clearly. This should be something you don't have a strong feeling about—a plant, a chair, a book, a cup.

For the next three minutes, focus your attention just on that object. If you like, look at it from multiple angles. Pick it up or run your hands over it. Smell it, if you're so inclined. Take in all the different sensory information about it.

When your mind wanders off—and it will—simply catch yourself and return your attention to the object. This may happen several—or more than several—times. There's no need to get frustrated or critical with yourself. Just keep coming back to the object.

Mindfulness Exercise #2: Watching Your Thoughts

The purpose of this exercise is to increase your awareness of your own mind and its thoughts. Over time, with practice, it will help you to not get stuck on, distressed about, or overwhelmed by a particular thought.

Again, find a spot where you can be free of distraction or interruption. Get in a comfortable sitting position, with your feet on the floor and your back straight. (This might mean sitting forward on the front part of your chair.) Breathe normally and keep your eyes open.

For five minutes, don't think—or not think—about anything in particular. Just watch your thoughts surface, swirl about, and float away. Don't try to hang onto them, push them away, or judge them. Let them come and let them go.

If your mind wanders or gets stuck on a particular thought, just notice that and return to quietly watching your mind. If you notice yourself getting judgmental ("I'm not very good at this" "Why am I having such awful thoughts?" etc.), just notice your judgment and return once more to watching your mind.

With practice, this skill will help you avoid getting stuck in obsessive thinking or worry. Paradoxically, it will also help you better focus on important tasks, concerns, or activities—doing your taxes, for example—when you need to.

Resources

Books and Audio About Both BPD and NPD

For Anyone

Stop Caretaking the Borderline or Narcissist: How to End the Drama and Get on with Life, *Margalis Fjelstad* (*Rowman & Littlefield, 2014*)

This book shows you how to get out of destructive interactions and take new, more effective actions to focus on your personal wants, needs, and life goals—while allowing the person with BPD or NPD to take care of themselves.

For Partners

Splitting: Protecting Yourself While Divorcing Someone with Borderline or Narcissistic Personality Disorder, Bill Eddy and Randi Kreger (New Harbinger, 2011)

This book is for anyone with a partner who has BPD or NPD, and who has thought seriously about divorce (or been threatened with it). It covers hiring a lawyer, understanding blamers and targets of their blame, preparing for a court battle, gathering evidence, succeeding outside court, and much more.

Dealing with High-Conflict People in Separation and Divorce, Bill Eddy (audio download available at stopwalkingoneggshells.com)

In this two-hour audio, Bill Eddy covers high-conflict divorce basics, including managing your case when you don't have an attorney; educating the court about high-conflict personalities; and how to handle false accusations.

Dealing with High-Conflict People in Separation, Divorce, and Co-parenting, Bill Eddy (audio download available at stopwalkingonegg shells.com)

This six-hour audio is the same as the previous item, but also offers information on custody and other child-centered issues for divorcing parents. Topics include determining if your child has been abused; managing your relationship with the high-conflict parent; managing your relationship with your children at different stages of the divorce; custody evaluations; types of custody arrangements; and requesting supervised visits.

For Parents with a Partner Who Has BPD or NPD (or Both)

Raising Resilient Children with a Borderline or Narcissistic Parent, Margalis Fjelstad and Jean McBride (Rowman & Littlefield, 2020)

If you are raising a child with a high-conflict partner, read this book—the first of its kind. With compassion toward everyone involved, the authors will help you to stop caretaking your partner, and to put your energy into protecting your children from high-conflict behavior. This book will also give you tools to be a better advocate for your child.

For Parents of a Child Who Has BPD or NPD (or Both)

Parenting a Child Who Has Intense Emotions: Dialectical Behavior Therapy Skills to Help Your Child Regulate Emotional Outbursts and Aggressive Behaviors, Pat Harvey and Jeanine A. Penzo (New Harbinger, 2009)

This is a guide to de-escalating your child's emotions and helping them express feelings in productive ways. It contains strategies for when your child's emotions spin out of control.

Parenting a Teen Who Has Intense Emotions: DBT Skills to Help Your Teen Navigate Emotional and Behavioral Challenges, Pat Harvey and Britt H. Rathbone (New Harbinger, 2015)

"DBT" stands for "dialectical behavioral therapy," an evidence-based form of treatment used for BPD. This book includes a step-by-step guide for handling disruptive, risky, and substance-abusing behaviors. Other topics include effective parenting; specific parenting strategies; anxiety; eating disorders; siblings; suicide; self-harm; and self-care for parents. (Note the similarity of the title of this book and the title of the previous one. The two books complement rather than duplicate each other, and we recommend both.)

When an Adult Child Breaks Your Heart: Coping with Mental Illness, Substance Abuse, and the Problems That Tear Families Apart, Joel Young, MD, and Christine Adamec (Lyons Press, 2013)

Topics include what can you fix and what must you let go of; what to do when your child gets violent; and how to help your child without destroying your own life or finances.

For Adults with a Mother Who Has BPD or NPD (or Both)

Understanding the Borderline Mother: Helping Her Children Transcend the Intense, Unpredictable, and Volatile Relationship, Christine Ann Lawson (Rowman & Littlefield, 2004)

This book divides mothers with BPD into four types, or symptom clusters: the waif, the hermit, the witch, and the queen (the mother who has both BPD and NPD). It will help you identify what's missing from your own early childhood development, and clarify what you can do as an adult to rectify that lack of early development and move toward a life of love and trust.

Books About BPD

For Anyone

Borderline Personality Disorder Demystified, Revised Edition: An Essential Guide for Understanding and Living with BPD, Robert O. Friedel, MD. (Da Capo Lifelong, 2018)

This is a great reference book for anything related to BPD from a psychiatric point of view. Friedel takes an exhaustive look at the history of BPD; risk factors; treatments; BPD and the brain; co-occurring disorders (mental illnesses that sometimes coexist with BPD); the typical course of the disorder; BPD in children; medications; and more.

The Essential Family Guide to Borderline Personality Disorder: New Tools and Techniques to Stop Walking on Eggshells, Randi Kreger (Hazelden, 2008)

This book covers the five basic tools you need to learn in order to cope with the person in your life who has BPD. These tools are: taking care of yourself, uncovering what's keeping you stuck, communicating to be heard, setting limits, and reinforcing the right behavior. It also has basic chapters that cover treatment, finding a therapist, and risk factors of BPD.

Loving Someone with Borderline Personality Disorder: How to Keep Out-of-Control Emotions from Destroying Your Relationship, Shari Y. Manning, PhD (Guilford, 2011)

Manning's book is for family members of people with the conventional form of BPD—those who apologize and feel bad when they hurt someone's feelings, seek therapy, have suicidal thoughts, and harm themselves. As with most books for the parents of folks with conventional BPD, much of this book is a how-to guide for helping your loved one. Manning's book also discusses the many faces of BPD within the mental health system; dealing with medical crises; and making decisions about hospitalization. It also has a chapter on handling your own emotions.

For Parents of a Child with BPD

Stop Walking on Eggshells for Parents: How to Help Your Child with Borderline Personality Disorder Without Sacrificing Your Family or Yourself, Randi Kreger, Christine Adamec, and Daniel S. Lobel (New Harbinger, 2021)

Originally published in 1999, this book is currently being extensively updated, and is scheduled to be published in late 2020. It is written for the parents of both minor and adult children. It gives a full explanation of why children can have BPD, and it offers a wide range of parenting tips. It will help you navigate government agencies, the mental health system, and school systems. Other topics include getting a diagnosis; hospitalization and residential treatment; maintaining your sanity during difficult situations; setting limits; and much more.

Borderline Personality Disorder in Adolescents: What to Do When Your Teen Has BPD (Second Edition), Blaise A. Aguirre (Fair Winds Press, 2014)

If you are the parent of a teenager, this is a must-have volume. This second edition covers diagnosing BPD in adolescents; the differences between BPD behavior and normal teen behavior; medications; how BPD develops; treatments; and tips and strategies for parents.

For Anyone with a Parent Who Has (or Had) BPD

Surviving a Borderline Parent: How to Heal Your Childhood Wounds and Build Trust, Boundaries, and Self-Esteem, Kimberlee Roth and Freda B. Friedman (New Harbinger, 2004)

This book offers step-by-step guidance to understanding and overcoming the lasting effects of being raised by a person suffering from BPD. It contains coping strategies for dealing with low self-esteem, lack of trust, guilt, and hypersensitivity. It will also help you decide whether to confront your parent about their condition.

Books About NPD

For Anyone

Disarming the Narcissist: Surviving and Thriving with the Self-Absorbed, Wendy T. Behary (New Harbinger, 2013)

This book will show you how narcissists view the world, how to navigate their coping styles, and why being a narcissist can be sad and lonely. It will help you learn to anticipate and avoid certain hot-button issues, and to relate to narcissists without triggering aggression.

Unmasking Narcissism: A Guide to Understanding the Narcissist in Your Life, Mark Ettensohn, PsyD (Althea Press, 2016)

This book will help you gain insight into narcissistic behaviors—and, ultimately, to break though the narcissist's defenses so you can develop a healthier relationship with them.

For Partners

Healing from a Narcissistic Relationship: A Caretaker's Guide to Recovery, Empowerment, and Transformation, Margalis Fjelstad (Rowman & Littlefield, 2019)

In this important book, Fjelstad clearly and powerfully lays out what you need to do for yourself to heal from a relationship with a narcissist. Sections of the book include "How Could This Be Over?," "Healing After the Crash," and "Empowerment."

No More Narcissists!: How to Stop Choosing Self-Absorbed Men and Find the Love You Deserve, Candace Love, PhD (New Harbinger, 2016)

This book will help you examine why you may be drawn to people with NPD; how to avoid following that pattern in the future; and how to move on to healthier relationships.

Other Recommended Books

When Your Adult Child Breaks Your Heart: Coping with Mental Illness, Substance Abuse, and the Problems That Tear Families Apart, Joel Young and Christine Adamec (Lyons Press, 2013)

The Betrayal Bond: Breaking Free from Exploitive Relationships, Revised Edition, Patrick J. Carnes (Health Communications, 2019)

Emotional Blackmail: When the People in Your Life Use Fear, Obligation, and Guilt to Manipulate You, Susan Forward and Donna Frazier (HarperCollins, 2019)

Toxic Parents: Overcoming Their Hurtful Legacy and Reclaiming Your Life, Susan Forward and Craig Buck (Bantam, 2002)

No More Mr. Nice Guy: A Proven Plan for Getting What You Want in Love, Sex, and Life, Robert Glover (Running Press, 2003)

The White Knight Syndrome: Rescuing Yourself from Your Need to Rescue Others, Mary C. Lamia and Marilyn J. Krieger (Echo Point, 2015)

The Dance of Anger: A Woman's Guide to Changing the Patterns of Intimate Relationships, Harriet Lerner (Avon, 2014). This book is also invaluable for men.

Get Me Out of Here: My Recovery from Borderline Personality Disorder, Rachel Reiland (Hazelden, 2004)

The Gaslight Effect: How to Spot and Survive the Hidden Manipulations Other People Use to Control Your Life, Robin Stern (Harmony, 2018)

The Buddha and the Borderline: My Recovery from Borderline Personality Disorder through Dialectical Behavior Therapy, Buddhism, and Online Dating, Kiera Van Gelder (New Harbinger, 2010)

Reinventing Your Life: The Breakthrough Program to End Negative Behavior and Feel Great Again, Jeffrey E. Young, PhD, and Janet S. Klosko, PhD (Plume, 1994)

BPD-Related Websites, Support Groups, and Organizations

StopWalkingOnEggshells.com

This site was established by Randi Kreger in 1995 and revamped in 2020. It offers a wide range of tools and information on BPD, including specialized e-books, audio downloads, and other materials on a great many topics.

Moving Forward

This is a family support, information, and education group for people who want to discuss and learn more about BPD—as well as a safe place to grieve, recover, heal, and grow. To join, go to movingforward@groups.io or https://groups.io/g/movingforward/join.

PsychologyToday.com

This site offers many blogs on personality disorders and high-conflict relationships. It also has a fantastic therapist directory, which you can search by therapists' geographic locations, specialties, interests, and types of health insurance accepted. You can also search by specific personality disorders.

Quora.com

On this free website, anyone can pose a question, and experts (and onlookers) will answer it to the best of their abilities. Co-author Randi Kreger has answered more than 800 questions about BPD and NPD on this site.

neabpd.org

The National Education Alliance for Borderline Personality Disorder works to raise public awareness, provide education, and promote research about BPD, as well as enhance the quality of life of those affected by BPD. It offers family education programs, annual conferences, regional meetings, and educational and research materials. Its conference videos and radio talks are mostly out of date, but some are valuable, especially if you are interested in medical information. If you have a child with BPD, we strongly urge you to view the advanced video on validation by Blaise Aguirre.

DisarmingTheNarcissist.com

This website, run by Wendy Behary, former president of the International Society of Schema Therapy, contains a state-by-state directory of schema therapists. These therapists are trained in treating people with both BPD and NPD.

BehavioralTech.com

This website focuses on dialectical behavior therapy, and contains a state-by-state list of DBT practitioners.

PDAN.org

The Personality Disorder Awareness Network (PDAN) is a not-for-profit organization dedicated to increasing public awareness of personality disorders, alleviating their impact on families, and intervening early to prevent these disorders from developing in children. PDAN offers a website with many useful articles, sells books for children about BPD, and has a presence on social media, especially Facebook.

bpdworld.org

This site offers BPD resources in the United Kingdom.

aapel.org

This is a site about BPD in French.

Are You Being Abused?

Some people with personality disorders are abusive to others—often to the very people who care about them the most. And, over time, some of the folks they abuse may get accustomed to that abuse, and begin to see it as normal—or, worse, as what they deserve.

The *Merriam-Webster Dictionary* says that being *abusive* means using harsh, insulting language; inflicting emotional cruelty; or acting wrongly or improperly.

Domestic abuse is abuse that occurs in a home, or within a family. *Physical abuse* (or, when it occurs within a home or family, *domestic violence*) is abuse that involves some form of physical assault, such as shoving, hitting, slapping, punching, or strangling.

When someone you care about has BPD or NPD (or both), your entire world can get turned on its head. At times, you may question what is true and what is a lie, or what is real and what is a fantasy. You may feel like you're being abused, but your loved one may say that *you're* the one abusing *them*.

This appendix will help you to recognize the truth about your relationship.

The lists below include many of the hallmarks of an abusive relationship—especially a relationship in which someone has BPD and/or NPD. Please go through each list and circle each item that you feel describes you, your loved one, or your relationship with them.

Do you…

- feel afraid of your loved one much of the time?

- avoid certain topics out of fear of angering them?

- feel that you can't do anything right for them?

- believe that you deserve to be hurt or mistreated?

- wonder if you're the one who is crazy?

- feel emotionally numb and/or helpless?

Does this person intimidate you by…

- yelling at you?

- humiliating or criticizing you?

- treating you badly in front of your friends or family?

- ignoring or dismissing your opinions or accomplishments?

- blaming you for their own inappropriate behavior?

- seeing you as their property, or as a sex object, rather than as a person?

Are you afraid of them because they…

- have a bad and unpredictable temper?

- hurt you, or threaten to hurt or kill you?

- threaten to harm your children, or take them away?

- threaten to commit suicide if you leave?

- force you to have sex with them?

- destroy your belongings?

Do they try to control you by…

- acting excessively jealous and possessive?

- telling you where you can and can't go, or what you can and can't do?

- trying to keep you from seeing your friends or family?

- limiting your access to money, your phone, or the car?

- constantly checking on you?

- insisting that you share your passwords with them?

If you are gay, bisexual, transgender, or ungendered, do they...

- threaten to out you?

- tell you that you have no legal rights?

- tell you that you're a deviant?

- justify the abuse by telling you that you're not "really" gay, bisexual, transgender, or ungendered?

Every item in each of the above lists is a form of abuse. The more of these that are part of your relationship with your loved one, the more abusive—and potentially dangerous—that relationship is.

If you circled one or more of the items in the above lists, we encourage you to speak with a counselor about your relationship soon. If you circled two or more, we *strongly* encourage such a conversation *very* soon. You may also need to quickly distance yourself from the abuser—and perhaps call the police or 911.

Remember, no matter what mental illness your loved one may have—and no matter what they may claim—their abusive behavior is still a choice.

It is STILL abuse, EVEN if...

- Physical violence has not occurred. Abuse can be emotional and verbal.

- Physical abuse has occurred only once or twice in your relationship. Multiple studies tell us that if someone injures a partner once, they are more likely than not to do it again.

- The incidents of abuse seem minor when compared to those you have read about, heard about, or seen on television. "I only slapped you once" and "I only threaten you when I'm drunk, never when I'm sober" are not justifications. Neither is "Most of the guys I know knock their wives around a little bit."

- The abuse stopped when you gave in, became passive, and let the other person limit how you express yourself, where you go, whom you see, or what decisions you make.

- You are a man and your abuser is a man.

- The person is a man, and says that men are naturally violent and can't stop themselves.

- You are a parent and the abuser is your child.

- You are bigger than your abuser.

- The person tells you they are deeply sorry, and that it won't happen again.

- The person says that they've been having a hard time, or have been under a lot of stress.

- The person tells you it's your fault.

- The person tells you that they did it because they love you so much.

The Domestic Violence Cycle

According to Cliff Mariani, author of the *Domestic Violence Survival Guide*, untreated domestic violence follows a predictable and escalating cycle:

- Phase One: a period of increasing tension as the abuse escalates and the abuser tries to control their victim. The victim's fear, obligation, and guilt often make these efforts successful.

- Phase Two: acute physical or emotional assaults, which seem to strengthen the abuser's power and control.

- Phase Three: deescalation and a return to a period of relative calm, sometimes accompanied by the abuser seeking forgiveness or expressing remorse. This usually creates a false sense of hope that causes the abuse victim to back away from any plans to leave, document the abuse, or pursue criminal charges.

- Phase Four: a return to Phase Two—the abusive "normality," interspersed with intermittent caring behavior.

If this cycle describes a relationship that you are currently in, seek help at once.

The National Domestic Violence Hotline, 1-800-799-7233, www.thehotline.org, offers confidential help and consultations by phone and live chat. The Hotline is open 24/7. All services are free, and the Hotline's advocates speak over 200 languages.

Domestic Violence Against Men

If you're a man in a relationship with a violent abuser, it's important to know that you're not alone. Domestic violence against men is much more common than most people realize—and it happens to men from all cultures and all walks of life, regardless of their ages, occupations, or sexual orientations.

According to recent statistics, as many as one in three victims of domestic violence are male. However, men are often reluctant to report domestic violence, or abuse in general, because they fear they won't be believed, or are scared that their abusers will take revenge.

They are also frequently embarrassed about being victims of abuse. Men often worry, *What will people think if they knew I let a woman—or another man—beat up on me?*, or *I don't want to be laughed at*, or *No one will believe me*.

But *we* believe you. We know of countless men who have been intimidated, threatened, and physically harmed—by women, by other men, and by their own children.

Another counterintuitive statistic: although we tend to associate stalking with men, women are just as likely as men to stalk someone with the intention of harming them.

If you are being abused by someone you care about, the best thing to do is visit your local police station when things are calm, and explain your situation. Show them any evidence or supporting material you have, such as police reports, bruises, or photos. If you know someone who has witnessed an incident in which you were abused, bring them with you and have them explain what they witnessed. Tell the police that you understand that they can sometimes have a tough job knowing who the abuser is—and that, because you are male, you're concerned they will assume it's you. But assure them that you are the victim, not the abuser, and explain that you may need their protection one day. This will prepare them should you need to call them in an emergency.

One final piece of advice:

If someone is abusing, threatening, or physically hurting you, *never* threaten them back, and *never* physically harm them (unless it is absolutely necessary as an act of genuine self-defense). If you do any of these things, your abuser will almost certainly exaggerate it, use it against you, and demonize you later on.

Document every incident of abuse as best you can. Explain to trusted professionals—your physician, a therapist, your spiritual leader—what has been happening. If and when your relationship with the abuser ends, your documenting what happened, and having shared your story with professionals earlier, could make the difference between winning and losing in court, or gaining or losing custody of your children.

References

Adamec, C. 1996. *How to Live with a Mentally Ill Person*. New York: John Wiley & Sons, Inc.

Al-Anon Family Group Headquarters. 1981. *Detachment*. Virginia Beach, VA.

Beattie, M. 1987. *Codependent No More*. Center City, MN: Hazelden.

Brach, T. 2004. *Radical Acceptance*. New York: Bantam.

Bradshaw, J. 1988. *Healing the Shame That Binds You*. Deerfield Beach, FL: Health Communications.

Brodsky, B., and J. Mann. 1997. "The Biology of the Disorder." *California Alliance for the Mentally Ill Journal* 8:1.

Cauwels, J. 1992. *Imbroglio: Rising to the Challenges of Borderline Personality Disorder*. New York: W. W. Norton.

DSM-V. 2013. *Diagnostic and Statistical Manual of Mental Disorders*. Washington, DC: American Psychiatric Association.

Ellis, T. E., and C. F. Newman. 1996. *Choosing to Live: How to Defeat Suicide Through Cognitive Therapy*. Oakland, CA: New Harbinger Publications.

Engel, B. 1990. *The Emotionally Abused Woman: Overcoming Destructive Patterns and Reclaiming Yourself*. New York: Fawcett Columbine.

Evans, P. 1996. *The Verbally Abusive Relationship: How to Recognize It and How to Respond*. Holbrook, MA: Adams Media Corporation.

Forward, S., and D. Frazier. 1997. *Emotional Blackmail: When the People in Your Life Use Fear, Obligation, and Guilt to Manipulate You*. New York: HarperCollins.

Gibran, K. 1976. *The Prophet*. New York: Alfred A. Knopf.

Golomb E. 1992. *Trapped in the Mirror: Adult Children of Narcissists in the Struggle for Self*. New York: William Morrow.

Gunderson, J. G. 1984. *Borderline Personality Disorder*. Washington, DC: American Psychiatric Press, Inc.

Heldmann, M. L. 1990. *When Words Hurt: How to Keep Criticism from Undermining Your Self-Esteem*. New York: Ballentine.

Herr, N. R., C. Hammen, and P. A. Brennan. 2008. "Maternal Borderline Personality Disorder Symptoms and Adolescent Psychosocial Functioning." *Journal of Personality Disorders*, 22(5):451–465.

Johnston, J. A., and V. Roseby. 1997. *In the Name of the Child: A Developmental Approach to Understanding and Helping Children of Conflicted and Violent Divorce*. New York: The Free Press.

Kabat-Zinn, J. 2005. *Wherever You Go, There You Are*. New York: Hyperion.

Katherine, A. 1993. *Boundaries: Where You End and I Begin*. Park Ridge, IL: Fireside/Parkside.

Kreisman, J., and H. Straus. 1989. *I Hate You—Don't Leave Me*. New York: Avon Books.

Kreisman, J., and H. Straus. 1989. *Sometimes I Act Crazy*. New York: John Wiley & Sons, Inc.

Kübler-Ross, E. 1975. *Death: The Final Stage of Growth*. Englewood Cliffs, NJ: Prentice Hall.

Lerner, H. G. 1985. *The Dance of Anger*. New York: Harper Perennial.

Leving, J. M., and K. A. Dachman. 1997. *Fathers' Rights*. New York: BasicBooks.

Linehan, M. 1993a. *Cognitive-Behavioral Treatment of Borderline Personality Disorder*. New York: Guilford Press.

Linehan, M. 1993b. *Skills Training Manual for Treating Borderline Personality Disorder*. New York: Guilford Press.

Links, P. S., R. J. Heslegrave, J. E. Milton, R. van Reekum, and J. Patrick. 1995. "Borderline Personality Disorder and Substance Abuse: Consequences of Comorbidity." *Canadian Journal of Psychiatry* 40:9–14.

Links, P. S., M. Steiner, and D. R. Offord. 1988. "Characteristics of Borderline Personality Disorder: A Canadian Study." *Canadian Journal of Psychiatry* 33:336–340.

McGlashan, T. H. 1986. "Long-Term Outcome of Borderline Personalities." The Chestnut Lodge Follow-up Study. III. *Archives of General Psychiatry* 43:20–30.

McKay, M., J. C. Wood, and J. Brantley. 2007. *The Dialectical Behavior Therapy Skills Workbook*. Oakland, CA: New Harbinger Publications.

McKay, M., P. Fanning, K. Paleg, and D. Landis. 1996. *When Anger Hurts Your Kids: A Parent's Guide*. Oakland, CA: New Harbinger Publications.

Moskovitz, R. A. 1996. *Lost in the Mirror: An Inside Look at Borderline Personality Disorder.* Dallas, TX: Taylor Publishing Company.

Nace, E.P., J. J. Saxon, and N. Shore. 1983. "A Comparison of Borderline and Nonborderline Alcoholic Patients." *Archives of General Psychiatry* 40:54–56.

Nash, M. 1997. "The Chemistry of Addiction." *Time* 149(18):69–76.

Newman, C. F. 1997. "Maintaining Professionalism in the Face of Emotional Abuse from Clients." *Cognitive and Behavioral Practice* 4:1–29.

Novak, J. 1996. *Wisconsin Father's Guide to Divorce and Custody.* Madison, WI: Prairie Oak Press.

Oldham, J. M. 1997. "Borderline Personality Disorder: The Treatment Dilemma." *The Journal of the California Alliance for the Mentally Ill* 8(1):13–17.

Oldham, J. M., A. E. Skodol, H. D. Kellman, S. E. Hyler, N. Doidge, L. Rosnick, and P. Gallaher. 1995. "Comorbidity of Axis I and Axis II Disorders." *American Journal of Psychiatry* 152:571–578.

Preston, J. 1997. *Shorter-Term Treatments for Borderline Personality Disorder.* Oakland, CA: New Harbinger Publications.

Reaves, J., and J. B. Austin. 1990. *How to Find Help for a Troubled Kid: A Parent's Guide for Programs and Services for Adolescents.* New York: Henry Holt.

Roth, K., and F. B. Friedman. 2003. *Surviving a Borderline Parent.* Oakland, CA: New Harbinger Publications.

Santoro, J., and R. Cohen. 1997. *The Angry Heart: A Self-Help Guide for Borderline and Addictive Personality Disorders.* Oakland, CA: New Harbinger Publications.

Siever, J., and W. Frucht. 1997. *The New View of Self: How Genes and Neurotransmitters Shape Your Mind, Your Personality, and Your Mental Health.* New York: Macmillan.

Silk, K. R. 1997. "Notes on the Biology of Borderline Personality Disorder." *California Alliance for the Mentally Ill Journal* 8:15–17.

Stone, M. H. 1990. *The Fate of Borderline Patients.* New York: Guilford Press.

Thornton, M. F. 1998. *Eclipses: Behind the Borderline Personality Disorder.* Madison, AL: Monte Sano Publishing.

Tong, D. 1996. *Ashes to Ashes… Families to Dust: False Accusations of Child Abuse: A Roadmap for Survivors.* Tampa, FL: FamRights Press.

Waldinger, R. J. 1993. "The Role of Psychodynamic Concepts in the Diagnosis of Borderline Personality Disorder." *Harvard Review of Psychiatry* 1:158–167.

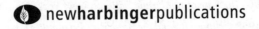

Paul T. Mason, MS, is a seasoned health care executive currently serving as vice president of Ascension Medical Group in Wisconsin. His research on borderline personality disorder (BPD) has been published in the Journal of Clinical Psychology, and his written work has appeared in national and international print media.

Randi Kreger is author of *The Stop Walking on Eggshells Workbook* and *The Essential Family Guide to Borderline Personality Disorder*. Her website, www .StopWalkingOnEggshells.com, offers material related to BPD. She also provides a free online family support group, Moving Forward, at groups.io/g /MovingForward. She gives workshops throughout the US and Japan.

MORE BOOKS from
NEW HARBINGER PUBLICATIONS

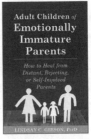